# Conducting
# Post–World War II
# National Security Research
# in Executive Branch Records

# Conducting Post–World War II National Security Research in Executive Branch Records

## A COMPREHENSIVE GUIDE
### James E. David

Published in association with the
Smithsonian National Air and Space Museum

**GREENWOOD PRESS**
**Westport, Connecticut • London**

Library of Congress Cataloging-in-Publication Data

David, James E., 1951–
    Conducting post–World War II national security research in executive branch records :
a comprehensive guide / James E. David.
        p.   cm.
    Includes index.
    ISBN 0–313–31986–3 (alk. paper)
    1. National security—United States—History—20th century—Archival resources.   2.
United States—Military policy—Archival resources.   3. Government publications—
United States.   I. Title.
UA23.D275   2001
355'.033073—dc21          2001018023

British Library Cataloguing in Publication Data is available.

Library of Congress Catalog Card Number: 2001018023
ISBN: 0–313–31986–3

First published in 2001

Greenwood Press, 88 Post Road West, Westport, CT 06881
An imprint of Greenwood Publishing Group, Inc.
www.greenwood.com

Printed in the United States of America

The paper used in this book complies with the
Permanent Paper Standard issued by the National
Information Standards Organization (Z39.48–1984).

10  9  8  7  6  5  4  3  2  1

# Contents

# Preface

When I first started doing research in U.S. government records in the early 1990s, I quickly discovered that I was working in a maze. There was no information available that described in any detail the many different repositories where records were stored and their holdings. Just trying to learn where relevant records were physically located was often a huge undertaking and sometimes an unsuccessful one. Even after records of interest were found, the vast majority were classified and thus inaccessible. Learning on occasion that important records once existed but had been destroyed increased the frustration.

During this experience I periodically thought about one question—why not put into one work all the information learned about what governs the retention and disposal of records, the classification and declassification of records, the various repositories where records are held, and what records are at each. This book attempts to accomplish this and, notwithstanding some gaps, I trust that researchers and others will find it helpful.

I have many people to thank in the writing of this book. For reading and commenting on the manuscript I would like to thank Michael Neufeld of the Department of Space History at the National Air and Space Museum and Cole Goldberg, a volunteer in the department. The chairs of the department—Gregg Herken, Robert Smith, and Allan Needell—have given me support, and for this I am appreciative. I would also like to thank Michael Kurtz, Richard Wood, Gary Stern, Jeanne Schauble, and Judy Barnes of the National Archives and Records Administration for the many courtesies extended to me over the years. Finally, I am grateful to Steven

Aftergood of the Federation of American Scientists for gathering and posting on the FAS homepage a wide range of information concerning government secrecy issues. He performs a tremendous public service and has made my job considerably easier.

In the end, however, I am solely responsible for any errors or misjudgments, and the opinions expressed in this book do not necessarily represent the views of the National Air and Space Museum or the Smithsonian Institution.

# 1

# Introduction

This work is a guide for both beginning and experienced researchers for performing post–World War II national security research in Executive Branch records. Its purpose is to assist the researcher in determining exactly what agency and White House records of possible interest exist, where they are located, and which ones are accessible by the public and which ones are not.

The quantity of postwar records of the many agencies that have been involved in national security issues is staggering. There are at least several thousands of miles of paper records and huge but unknown quantities of photographs, films, maps, charts, electronic recordings, and other types of records. Almost all such records that still exist today are at one of three repositories—a National Archives, a Federal records center, or the agencies themselves. Significant holdings of each individual agency at the National Archives and Federal records centers are described in considerable detail, as well as what portions are open to the public and what portions are not. For those desiring more information on these records or for those who wish to locate records not specifically mentioned herein, this work takes the researcher through the various steps necessary to do this. Important holdings still at the agencies are also set forth by individual agency, but unfortunately in most cases not in similar detail because so little information can be obtained on these holdings.

The quantity of postwar White House records, in comparison, is extremely small. Almost all such records that exist today are at only one repository—a presidential library. The holdings at each are described in detail, as well as what portions are open to the public and what portions are not.

Initially, however, two very critical issues must be examined. The first is the rules governing which records are kept and which records are destroyed. Each year the Executive Branch accumulates a huge quantity of records, of which only a small percentage is retained forever. Not only would it be physically impossible and inordinately expensive to store and maintain all the records permanently, but also most records are no longer needed after short periods of time. There are numerous laws governing which records fall into each category. Unfortunately, there are instances through the years where these laws have not been followed and, as a result, important records documenting our nation's history have been destroyed.

The second critical issue is the classification and declassification of records. Almost all national security records in the postwar period have been originally classified under various legal authorities and thus inaccessible to the public. At the same time, there have been various procedures under which some of these records could be declassified and made available to the public. Until 1995, however, these procedures were ineffective in reducing the mountain of classified records. During that year, President Clinton signed an executive order instituting a new procedure that initially made some headway in decreasing the massive number of classified records. The progress (or lack thereof) of each individual agency and presidential library in complying with the mandates of this order is described herein. The Fiscal Year (FY) 1999 and FY 2000 National Defense Authorization Acts and White House exemptions from automatic declassification granted in 1999, though, will reverse this trend, and undoubtedly the coming years will see a return to the days of very few records being declassified.

# 2

# Retention and Disposal of Executive Branch Records

For many decades, the Executive Branch each year has generated and received a huge quantity of textual (paper) records and nontextual records (maps, charts, photographs, films, imagery, sound recordings, and other electronic records). Recent years, of course, have seen a massive increase in the amount of electronic records, and these pose some unique problems. Historically, only about 3% of all the records are kept forever.[1] The balance is destroyed after the records are no longer needed for current business.

The issues of which records are kept and which records are destroyed are absolutely critical. As discussed in the following section, there are numerous laws and regulations designed to ensure that comprehensive records are made documenting the essential business of the federal government and that the most important of these records are preserved forever. Although compliance with these laws and regulations has generally been good, there have been some notable instances where they have not been followed and the result was the loss or destruction of records that merited permanent preservation. When this occurs, of course, the nation forever loses a part of its history.

## RECORDS MADE OR RECEIVED BY THE AGENCIES

Records made or received by the agencies are denominated *federal records*. They are defined by the Records Disposal Act as all materials, regardless of form, made or received by an agency "in connection with the transaction of public business and preserved or appropriate for preservation by that agency or its legitimate successor as evidence of the organization, functions, policies, decisions, procedures, operations, or other activities of the Government or because of the informational value of data in them."[2] This law and the Federal Records Act of 1950[3] require agencies to prepare records that adequately document their organization, functions, policies, decisions, procedures, and essential transactions; decree that the government owns all *federal records*; provide procedures for their preservation and disposition; and specify that they may not be removed or destroyed except as provided in the acts.

At the center of this mandate to preserve and dispose of records are *records retention and disposition schedules (records schedules)*. All *federal records* must be covered by a *records schedule*. The National Archives and Records Administration (NARA) has issued several *General Records Schedules* that provide disposal authority for different types of records common to all agencies. Among other things, these include records relating to civilian personnel, fiscal accounting, and procurement. Approximately one-third of all *federal records* are subject to the *General Records Schedules*.

Each agency is required to develop *records schedules* covering all of its other *federal records*. These dictate for each type or category of subject record that they be *appraised* as *permanent* (those that must be preserved and never be destroyed) or *temporary* (those that may be destroyed after a specified period of time). Additionally, they state when each type or category of *permanent* records is eligible for transfer to the National Archives. Agencies send their draft *record schedules* to NARA for review and approval. Once approved, they provide guidance to agency and NARA personnel in *appraising* records. When agencies create or receive new types or categories of records or wish to change their current *records schedules*, they are obligated to develop and submit new draft *records schedules* for approval. Records awaiting *appraisal* are denominated *unappraised* or *unscheduled*.[4]

The number of *records schedules* varies from agency to agency. For example, the Department of Energy currently has fifteen *records schedules* covering everything from nuclear weapons records to legal records. The Office of the Secretary of Defense, on the other hand, has only one. The *records schedules* of most agencies are available through their records management offices or, in a few cases, their homepages.[5] However, public access to the *records schedules* of the Central Intelligence Agency and National Security Agency is impossible because they are classified.

The critical importance of developing *records schedules* and *appraising* records cannot be overestimated. When these mandates are ignored or are performed incompletely, serious problems arise. Agencies do not know then which records they hold and, most significantly, records that document our nation's history often are destroyed. The following examples clearly show the magnitude of the problem. In late 1996 and early 1997, about 2.25 million pages of *temporary* Naval Research Laboratory correspondence from 1918–1986 and laboratory notebooks from 1942–1969 were routinely destroyed. A subsequent NARA investigation determined that many of the records should have been *appraised* as *permanent* and concluded that the main reason for this failure was ambiguity in the pertinent *records schedule*.[6] As another example, the Federal Bureau of Investigation for many years did not have a *records schedule* and destroyed a wide range of what it considered nonrecord material. In 1969, the agency developed its first *records schedule*, but NARA's predecessor was only permitted to review the document briefly and never obtained a copy. The unauthorized destruction of certain types of records continued during the 1970s, including J. Edgar Hoover's "Personal and Confidential" file shortly after his death. It did not stop until the American Friends Service Committee filed suit in 1979 and a new comprehensive *records schedule* was developed under court order. Although there is no record of exactly what was destroyed over the years, from the available evidence there is no question that a great deal of it would have been *appraised* as *permanent* under a proper *records schedule*.[7] Other examples include the Central Intelligence Agency's destruction during 1959–1963 of its Iran operations records from 1953. When NARA investigated this in the late 1990s, the agency claimed that the destruction was proper under the then pertinent *records schedules*, but NARA disagreed and concluded that it was in fact "unauthorized."[8] In 1973, the Central Intelligence Agency destroyed what it believed to be all the records on its human experimentation program in the 1950s and 1960s (the program was called MKULTRA). The Director of Central Intelligence, Richard Helms, ordered this done for the apparent purpose of preventing access to them by Congress and others.[9] The nearly-complete destruction of an entire program's records most certainly was not in accordance with any *records schedule*. Lastly, from 1947 to 1978, all meetings of the Joint Chiefs of Staff were recorded in various forms. In August 1974, the Secretary of the Joint Chiefs of Staff determined that the transcripts were not official minutes but merely working papers reflecting the reporter's version of events. The Secretary ordered all existing and future transcripts over six months old to be destroyed after screening for historical significance. From these decades of transcripts, all that survives to this day are about thirty typed pages of notes prepared by the Joint Staff History Office relating to the Cuban Missile Crisis and the October 1973 Arab-Israeli war. Significantly, all this took place before the Joint Chiefs of Staff adopted its first *records schedule* in 1980.[10]

To be fair, most agencies have performed their records management duties competently through the years. Recent years have seen the correction of some long-standing deficiencies (the adoption of *records schedules* by the National Reconnaissance Office and the Federal Bureau of Investigation being two notable examples). Nevertheless, major problems still exist. NARA admits that it cannot determine whether all agencies are in compliance with the federal laws on records management. There is also the immense challenge posed by electronic records. Not only do many existing *records schedules* not cover electronic records, but also there is the very real problem of ensuring that the records can be read in the future. As part of its strategic plan, NARA has established a number of performance targets by 2007 to address these issues.[11] These targets must be met to ensure that all agencies have implemented proper records management programs and that comprehensive records documenting the government's decisions and activities are created, maintained, and preserved as required under federal law.

## RECORDS MADE OR RECEIVED BY THE WHITE HOUSE

Throughout most of the nation's history, the records of the President, Vice-President, and their White House advisors were not considered property of the federal government, but the personal property of the individuals concerned. Nevertheless, as a matter of practice, most of the records of the Presidents, Vice-Presidents, and their White House advisors from the Hoover administration through the Carter administration were placed in the appropriate presidential library. The one exception to this was the Nixon White House tapes and records. Passage of the Presidential Recordings and Materials Preservation Act of 1974[12] provided, among other things, that NARA was to obtain and retain complete possession and control over all Nixon White House tapes and records and develop regulations governing access thereto.

The Presidential Records Act of 1978[13] established that, beginning with the new administration in January 1981, the records of the President, Vice-President, and their White House advisors relating to the performance of official duties were the property of the federal government. This law requires the President, Vice-President, and their White House advisors to create records (denominated *Presidential records*) adequate to document "the activities, deliberations, decisions, and policies that reflect the performance of his constitutional, statutory, or other official or ceremonial duties." While still in office, the President may dispose of *Presidential records* that no longer have "administrative, historical, informational, or evidentiary value" if the Archivist of the United States (the head of NARA) is first contacted. If the Archivist does not concur, the disposal can take place only after specified Congressional committees are notified. After a President leaves office, the Archivist assumes custody and control of all *Presidential records* and they must be placed eventually in a presidential library. They can be destroyed only if *appraised* as *temporary* and prior notice is given in the *Federal Register*.

## NOTES

1. Author's conversation with National Archives and Records Administration personnel, December 1998.

2. 44 United States Code (U.S.C.) 3301.

3. 44 U.S.C., chs. 29 and 31.

4. 36 Code of Federal Regulations (C.F.R.), Part 1228.

5. The records schedules of the Department of Energy are available on its homepage (www-it.hr.doe.gov/records), and those of the Department of State on its home page (foia.state.gov/records.htm). A list of the records officers of most agencies is available on NARA's homepage at ardor.nara.gov.

6. The report, *Inquiry into the Disposal of Records of the Naval Research Laboratory*, can be found on NARA's home page at www.nara.gov/records/nrlrpt.

7. *Appraisal of the Records of the Federal Bureau of Investigation, A Report to Hon. Harold H. Greene, United States District Court of the District of Columbia* (Washington, D.C.: National Archives and Records Administration and Federal Bureau of Investigation, November 9, 1981), pp. 2–7 through 2–9. This report is available in hard copy at the National Archives.

8. *Records Management in the Central Intelligence Agency—A NARA Evaluation* (Washington, D.C.: National Archives and Records Administration), p. 22. This report is available on the Federation of American Scientists (FAS) homepage at www.fas.org and in hard copy at the National Archives.

9. U.S. Congress, Senate Committee on Intelligence and Senate Committee on Human Resources, *Project MKULTRA, the CIA's Program of Research in Behavioral Modification* (Washington, D.C.: U.S. Government Printing Office, 1977), pp. 3–5.

10. Edmund F. McBride, Chief, Documents Division, Joint Secretariat to James Hastings, Director, Records Appraisal and Disposition Division, National Archives, January 25, 1993; Box no. 86; Entry no. 4; Records of the JFK Assassination Records Review Board, RG 541; National Archives, College Park, Maryland.

11. *Ready Access to Essential Evidence—The Strategic Plan of the National Archives and Records Administration, 1997–2007* (Washington, D.C.: National Archives and Records Administration, 1997). This publication is available on NARA's home page at www.nara.gov/nara/vision/naraplan.

12. 44 U.S.C. 2111 note.

13. 44 U.S.C., ch. 22.

# 3

# Classification and Declassification of Executive Branch Records

Practically all Executive Branch national security records created in the postwar period originally have contained classified information.[1] This means that, at the time of their creation, some or all of the information in them merited protection against public disclosure under the relevant legal guidelines, and the records were marked accordingly (or, in a few cases, were not marked but should have been). The type of information requiring protection under these legal authorities has always been extremely broad.

At the same time, there has been a varying series of legal authorities under which information that no longer deserves protection could be declassified and the records made accessible to the public for the first time. Unfortunately, these processes have usually been slow, cumbersome, and have received few resources. As a result, an ever-growing mountain of classified records has accumulated since World War II. Because of a radical change in the legal guidelines in 1995, however, for the first time ever the Executive Branch overall started declassifying more records each year than it was creating, and the massive amount of classified records was reduced slightly. This promising trend was not to continue for long though; legislation in 1998 and 1999 and White House actions in 1999 have and will continue to slow down greatly the declassification effort.

## CLASSIFICATION OF EXECUTIVE BRANCH RECORDS

Through the years, there have been three distinct and separate categories of information that have been classified. The first is National Security Information (NSI). The current system of classification and declassification of NSI is set forth in Executive Order 12958 (E.O. 12958) signed by President Clinton on April 17, 1995. This is the latest in a series of executive orders on NSI, which date back to World War II. In general conformity with its predecessors, E.O. 12958 preserves the classification of information classified under predecessor orders and mandates that newly created information in seven broad categories be classified. These categories are (1) military plans, weapons systems or operations; (2) foreign government information; (3) intelligence activities, sources, methods, or cryptology; (4) foreign relations or foreign activities of the United States, including confidential sources; (5) scientific, technological, or economic matters relating to national security; (6) U.S. government programs for safeguarding nuclear materials or facilities; and (7) vulnerabilities or capabilities of systems, installations, projects, or plans relating to national security.[2] Information falling in one or more of these categories is to be classified Top Secret, Secret, or Confidential, depending on the damage to national security reasonably expected to occur from its unauthorized disclosure.[3] For the first time in decades, it requires classification authorities "attempt to establish a specific date or event for declassification based upon the duration of the national security sensitivity of the information." This date shall not exceed ten years from the date of original classification, unless the information falls within one or more of eight enumerated categories, in which case no specific date needs to be set.[4]

The second category of classified information is that generally relating to atomic energy and nuclear weapons. The original authority in this area was the Atomic Energy Act of 1946, which was superseded by the Atomic Energy Act of 1954.[5] Among other things, this legislation mandates information be classified as Restricted Data (RD) if it concerns (1) the design, manufacture or utilization of atomic weapons; (2) the production of special nuclear material; or (3) the use of special nuclear material in the production of energy, but not data declassified or removed from the RD category. It also requires information be classified as Formerly Restricted Data (FRD) if it primarily concerns the military utilization of atomic weapons and Unclassified Controlled Nuclear Information if it concerns certain safeguards and security measures or details of facilities involved in producing special nuclear weapons materials or nuclear weapons. Any information that is classified as RD or FRD is also classified as NSI, but not vice versa.

The third category of classified information is Sensitive Compartmented Information (SCI). SCI is information concerning or derived from intelligence sources, methods, or analytical processes, which is required to be handled within formal access control systems established by the Director of Central Intelligence. It is designated by codewords representing information in a broad area and additional codewords representing more specific types of information (or compartments) under each broad area. These codewords are themselves classified, and only in recent years have a few been declassified. For example, TALENT-KEYHOLE designates the product of certain overhead collection systems, and compartments under it include RUFF (imagery from satellites) and CHESS (imagery from U-2s). The authorities for SCI are National Security Decision Directives, National Security Council Intelligence Directives, Director of Central Intelligence Directives, and Department of Defense Directives.[6] Just as with RD and FRD, any information classified as SCI is also classified as NSI, but not vice versa.

There are, in addition, several statutes that require narrow and specific types of information to be classified. For example, one statute prohibits the disclosure or publication of the "organization, functions, names, official titles, salaries, or numbers of personnel" employed by the Central Intelligence Agency.[7]

## DECLASSIFICATION OF RD AND FRD UNDER THE ATOMIC ENERGY ACT OF 1954

The 1946 legislation initially establishing the Atomic Energy Commission and the follow-on Atomic Energy Act of 1954 mandate that there be a continuous review of RD and FRD to determine which information may be declassified (the review of FRD is done jointly with the Department of Defense).[8] It is important to note that all the law requires is that a review be conducted to determine which, if any, types of information should be declassified; the law does not require that any types of information actually be declassified and, significantly, does not require that when information is declassified there be any review and declassification of the records containing such information.

In recent years, the Department of Energy has issued a series of publications containing the RD and FRD declassified from 1946 to the present. The latest version, *Restricted Data Declassification Decisions 1946 to the Present (RDD-7)*, was issued in January 2001 and is available on the Federation of American Scientists (FAS) home page at www.fas.org.

## DECLASSIFICATION OF NSI AND SCI UNDER EXECUTIVE ORDERS AND SPECIAL LEGISLATION

For many years after World War II, there was no requirement that the Executive Branch conduct a declassification review of its records containing NSI and both NSI and SCI. Although some of the early executive orders on classification and declassification of NSI mandated that a specific date be established for the automatic downgrading of certain types of classified information, these procedures were unevenly implemented and proved ineffective in releasing many records to the public.

Executive Order 11652, signed by President Nixon in 1972, required for the first time that all agencies conduct systematic declassification review of their *permanent* classified records thirty years old and older (fifty years old and older with respect to intelligence records). This provision was basically continued intact in President Carter's E.O. 12065 from 1978. Neither order of course applied to RD or FRD (because an executive order cannot supersede a statute), and thus many classified records did not even fall within their purview. Nevertheless, due to the systematic declassification review requirements, for the first time a relatively large volume of records was declassified. At long last, the growing gap between the number of declassified records and the number of classified records was narrowed slightly.

President Reagan's E.O. 12356 of 1982, however, eliminated the requirement that the agencies conduct systematic declassification review (except for the National Archives). A few agencies continued performing systematic declassification review on a voluntary basis, but the effect of the new order was to reduce greatly the number of classified records being opened up. For example, in FY 1981, more than 30 million pages were reviewed for declassification, while in FY 1983, only 12.5 million were reviewed.[9] The paltry numbers of classified records being opened up continued through the thirteen years the order was in effect, and at the end of this period the gap between the number of declassified records and the number of classified records had increased dramatically.

Executive Order 12958, signed by President Clinton in April 1995, provides in part that all *permanent* pre-1975 classified agency records would be automatically declassified in April 2000 "whether or not the records have been reviewed" unless they had been exempted from automatic declassification. All such post-1975 records are to be automatically declassified twenty-five years after their creation regardless of whether they have been reviewed unless they have been exempted from automatic declassification (for example, *permanent* 1976 classified records would be automatically declassified in 2001 unless exempted). Before October 1995, agencies were to submit the proposed exemptions of specific file series from automatic declassification to the President through the Assistant to the President for National Security Affairs. They were to be submitted on the basis that the release of information in the records should be expected to "(1) reveal the identity of a confidential human source, or reveal information about the application of an intelligence source or method, or reveal the identity of a human intelligence source when the unauthorized disclosure of that source would clearly and demonstrably damage the national security interests of the United States, (2) reveal information that would assist in the development or use of weapons of mass destruction, (3) reveal information that would impair U.S. cryptologic systems or activities, (4) reveal information that would impair the application of state of the art technology within a U.S. weapons system, (5) reveal actual U.S. military war plans that remain in effect, (6) reveal information that would seriously and demonstrably impair relations between the United States and a foreign government, or seriously and demonstrably undermine ongoing diplomatic activities of the United States, (7) reveal information that would clearly and demonstrably impair the current ability of United States Government officials to protect the President, Vice President, and other officials for whom protection services, in the interest of national security, are authorized, (8) reveal information that would seriously and demonstrably impair current national security emergency preparedness plans, or (9) violate a statute, treaty, or international agreement."[10] Exemptions of individual records could of course occur after the agency reviewed the record and determined that they still merited classification under one or more of the above.

Executive Order 12958 also requires once again that all agencies and the National Archives conduct systematic declassification review of their *permanent* classified records twenty-five years old and older and presidential libraries (in consultation with the relevant agencies because the libraries themselves have no declassification authority) of their classified records twenty-five years old and older, regardless of whether the records have been exempted from automatic declassification. Agencies and presidential libraries were to prioritize their review based on the recommendations of a newly created Information Security Advisory Council (which has never met) or the degree of researcher interest and the likelihood of declassification upon review.

It is important to note that both the automatic declassification and systematic declassification review provisions apply only to agency records that have been *appraised* as *permanent*. They do not apply to *unappraised* records or *temporary* records. As has been mentioned, some agencies have huge backlogs of *unappraised* records. Not all *unappraised* classified records will ultimately be *appraised* as *permanent*, but those that should be will not fall under the purview of E.O. 12958 until such time as they are actually so *appraised*.[11] Furthermore, the order of course only applies to NSI and SCI and not RD and FRD.

By October 1995, every agency was to have submitted a plan to the Information Security Oversight Office (ISOO) setting forth its procedures for complying with the automatic declassification and systematic declassification review provisions of the order, and each plan was to have included the requirement that the agency declassify at least 15% of their nonexempt records each year.[12]

Although the details of the implementation of E.O. 12958 by each agency will be discussed in the following chapter, a brief overview will be given here. Initially, few agencies were able to provide reliable figures on the total number of *permanent* pre-1975 classified records subject to E.O. 12958. This was largely due to the fact that many agencies have records for which there are no finding aids or inventories, or the finding aids and inventories that do exist are incomplete. As a result, these agencies did not know the quantity, nature, date range, classification status, or *appraisal* status of records in their custody.

Nevertheless, the initial estimates that were furnished disclosed a staggering number. (As a yardstick, there are about 13.2 million pages in one mile of records.) Some holdings were relatively small, such as those of the U.S. Information Agency (13 million pages), the State Department (35 million pages), and the Arms Control and Disarmament Agency (3.2 million pages). Others were huge, including the Department of Defense (1.5 billion pages) and the Central Intelligence Agency (166 million pages). Some agencies (such as the Federal Bureau of Investigation) never came up with any estimate. It should be noted, however, that the use by some agencies and others of only "pages" in quantifying their subject holdings was somewhat erroneous. The fact is that some agencies have *permanent* pre-1975 classified maps, charts, photographs, films, sound recordings, and other nontextual records. Only the Defense Intelligence Agency, though, provided any estimate of *permanent* pre-1975 classified nontextual records.

It is not known whether the presidential libraries provided estimates of their pre-1975 classified records subject to E.O. 12958.

The implementation by the agencies and presidential libraries, unfortunately, has been mixed. Virtually every agency submitted to the ISOO in late 1995 or early 1996 the required proposed implementation plan.[13] Sixteen agencies at the same time submitted initial lists of file series they proposed for exemption from automatic declassification. Six agencies subsequently withdrew their requests, and in early 1999 without any publicity the White House approved in whole or part the remaining ten agency lists of file series proposed for exemption. The approved exemptions are as follows:

1. Army (27 million pages or 10% of its subject records)
2. Central Intelligence Agency (94.5 million pages or 60% of its subject records)
3. Defense Intelligence Agency (26 million pages or 38% of its subject records)
4. Office of the Secretary of Defense (7.3 million pages or 30% of its subject records)
5. Joint Chiefs of Staff (1.5 million or 17% of its subject records)
6. National Security Agency (27.6 million pages or 38% of its subject records)
7. National Security Council (65,000 pages or 15% of its subject records)
8. National Reconnaissance Office (720,000 pages or 63% of its subject records)

9. President's Foreign Intelligence Advisory Board (77,500 pages or 48% of its subject records)
10. State Department (1.6 million pages or 3.8% of its subject records).[14]

Once again, the use of only "pages" in describing the quantity of exempted records is somewhat erroneous. Undoubtedly, some of the exempted records are nontextual records. The most comprehensive exemption, however, was not granted in 1999 but four years earlier. In October 1995, again without any publicity, the directors of the Federal Bureau of Investigation and the ISOO signed an agreement that exempted *all* that agency's records from automatic declassification on the basis that their automatic release would "almost invariably violate the Privacy Act of 1974."[15]

With respect to the declassification review of subject records, some agencies have committed sufficient resources and done an outstanding job while others have not. From the beginning, many, but not all, agencies conducted the type of review they have always done through the years—page by page. Page-by-page review naturally results in far fewer records being reviewed than if some sort of sampling method is used. At the same time, however, almost every agency is reviewing on a "pass-fail" basis. This means that if there is any information in a document that still merits classification, that information is not *redacted* but the entire document remains classified.[16] The fact that there is no *reduction* permits much greater numbers of records to be reviewed, but also results in a higher number of records remaining classified. Only the Central Intelligence Agency and the National Security Agency are *redacting* in their systematic declassification review programs.

The only publicly available source of information on the progress of the agencies in completing their review of *permanent* pre-1975 classified records and presidential libraries in completing their review of pre-1975 classified records is the annual report the ISOO compiles and sends to the President. Since 1995, these reports have simply set forth the total number of pages declassified for each individual agency and the NARA (the latter presumably covering both the National Archives and presidential libraries, but this has never been made clear). Many ISOO reports prior to this listed both the number of pages reviewed for declassification and the number of pages actually declassified (which is much more useful), but for unknown reasons the ISOO discontinued this practice. The ISOO reports disclosed that in FY 1996, the Executive Branch declassified 196 million pages, 204 million pages in FY 1997, 193 million pages in FY 1998, and 127 million pages in FY 1999.[17] However, for several reasons, the numbers that some individual agencies are credited with in the reports, and thus the totals, do not appear to be entirely accurate. First, it is likely that some agencies are reporting to the ISOO the total number of pages reviewed for declassification and not just the number of pages actually declassified. Second, there is some indication of at least partial duplication between the figures NARA and the individual agencies are credited with. Third, the use of "pages" as the only standard of measurement is erroneous since some agencies are reviewing and declassifying nontextual records. Even with these qualifications, though, there is no question that the Executive Branch has declassified far more records in the short period E.O. 12958 has been in effect than in the previous fifteen years combined.

Much more important to the public than the raw numbers, however, is information on exactly what records are being reviewed. Quite simply, the records of greatest interest to the greatest number of people are high-level records. For example, records of the Army Chief of Staff and Assistant or Deputy Chiefs of Staff are relevant to far more researchers than records of the Quartermaster Corps and Office of Surgeon General. Have the former been reviewed or are they currently undergoing review? Executive Order 12958 requires the NARA, ISOO, and the agencies to establish a "Governmentwide database of information that has been declassified" and mandates that the public have access thereto. However, absolutely nothing has been done since 1995 to create this central database.[18] The fact that the public does not have this resource available to learn about which records the agencies and presidential libraries have declassified qualifies as a major failure in the implementation of the new order. What the public has to do now is spend many hours trying to gain some sort of access to the internal databases most agencies maintain that list the records reviewed for declassification. Not surprisingly, the public is often denied access to them.[19]

There was no automatic declassification, however, of any unreviewed nonexempt records in April 2000 nor will there be on any subsequent date due to legislation passed in 1998 and 1999. Section 3161 of the FY 1999 National Defense Authorization Act (Public Law 105–261) mandates that every collection of records must undergo a page-by-page review by a specially trained reviewer unless the agency certifies that the collection is "highly unlikely" to contain RD or FRD. With the exception of the Federal Emergency Management Agency, no agency has certified any collection as "highly unlikely" to contain RD or FRD.[20] Section 3149 of the FY 2000 National Defense Authorization Act (Public Law 106–65) provides in part that "No records of the Department of Defense that have not been reviewed for declassification shall be subject to automatic declassification unless the Secretary of Defense certifies to Congress that such declassification would not harm the national security" and "No records of the Department of Energy that have not as of the date of the enactment of this Act been reviewed for declassification shall be subject to automatic declassification unless the Secretary of Energy certifies to Congress that such declassification would not harm the national security" (the latter provision is especially redundant because most classified records of the Department of Energy contain both NSI and RD or FRD). Not surprisingly, neither the Secretary of Defense nor the Secretary of Energy has made any such certifications.

The legislation, though, affects the declassification effort beyond effectively prohibiting automatic declassification. As will be explained in more detail in the following chapter, both the FY 1999 National Defense Authorization Act and FY 2000 National Defense Authorization Act impose far-reaching requirements on the Department of Energy to re-review records reviewed by other agencies to ensure that there has been no "inadvertent releases" of RD or FRD (the plan adopted to implement these provisions is commonly known as the Kyl Plan and will be referred to as such herein). This greatly increases the time between when records undergo declassification review and when they are actually made available to the public. The latter law additionally imposed a cap of $51 million dollars on Department of Defense FY 2000 expenditures to comply with E.O. 12958. A provision in the FY 2001 National Defense Authorization Act places an even smaller cap of $30 million dollars on Department of Defense FY 2001 expenditures to comply with E.O. 12958 and other declassification reviews mandated by statute. These budgetary limitations have a major impact on the department's declassification efforts.

The last in the recent series of actions greatly altering E.O. 12958 is E.O. 13142, signed by President Clinton on November 19, 1999. Among other things, this order: (1) postpones the original automatic declassification date of April 2000 to April 2003 of nonexempt *permanent* pre-1975 classified records that have the *equities* of more than one agency or contain information "that almost invariably pertains to intelligence sources or methods," (2) postpones the original automatic declassification date of April 2000 to October 2001 for all other nonexempt *permanent* pre-1975 classified records, (3) extends the time in which agencies can submit lists of file series proposed for exemption from automatic declassification to 180 days prior to the newly established deadlines. Ironically, E.O. 13142 is largely irrelevant because the FY 1999 and FY 2000 National Defense Authorization Acts by themselves effectively prohibited any automatic declassification in April 2000 or on any subsequent date.

In short, these actions in recent years have greatly altered the operation of E.O. 12958, and the promising trends of recent years will be reversed. The possibility of automatic declassification no longer exists. For all practical purposes, every classified record falling under the purview of E.O. 12958 will have to be reviewed page by page regardless of the nature, date, or level of classification. Budget cuts will further dramatically reduce the declassification efforts of some agencies.

It should be noted that in the 1990s, there have also been several executive orders and laws that have mandated the declassification of narrow categories of classified records. Executive Order 12937 of November 1994 declassified several tens of millions of pages of World War II and prewar records in twenty-one *record groups* at the National Archives. Executive Order 12951 of February 1995 declassified the satellite imagery from the CORONA, LANYARD, and ARGON missions. This order also mandates the Director of Central Intelligence periodically to review imagery from subsequent space-based national intelligence reconnaissance systems "with the objective of making available to the public as much imagery as possible consistent with the interests of national defense and foreign policy." The review with respect to "imagery from obsolete broad-area film-return systems other than CORONA, ARGON, and LANYARD" was to have been completed by February 2000 (as of this writing, studies and associated actions to make some post-CORONA imagery available are ongoing). The President John F. Kennedy Assassination Records Collection Act of 1992 mandated the gathering and declassification (with some exceptions) of all records concerned with the death of the President. The Nazi War Crimes Disclosure Act requires a similar effort with respect to records on war criminals.

## DECLASSIFICATION OF NSI, SCI, RD, AND FRD UNDER THE FREEDOM OF INFORMATION ACT (FOIA) AND MANDATORY DECLASSIFICATION REVIEW (MDR)

With the two other methods of declassification review, the FOIA and MDR, a member of the public initiates the request for review. Although a comprehensive discussion of either procedure is outside the scope of this work, some basic information concerning both will be given.

It is significant to note that, with two exceptions, both the the FOIA and MDR procedures can be used for any agency's records, regardless of their dates, *appraisal* status, or the type of classified information contained therein. The first exception is that the Central Intelligence Agency Information Act of 1984[21] authorizes the Director of Central Intelligence to exempt operational files of the Directorate of Operations, Directorate of Science and Technology, and Office of Security within the Directorate of Administration from the provisions of the FOIA (E.O. 12958 exempts these files from the provisions of MDR). There is no information publicly available on the number or percentage of operational files that have been exempted.[22] The second exception is that the FY 2000 Intelligence Authorization Act authorizes the Director of the National Imagery and Mapping Agency (in coordination with the Director of Central Intelligence) to exempt from the provisions of the FOIA operational files of that agency and the former National Photographic Interpretation Center "that document the means by which foreign intelligence and counterintelligence is collected through scientific and technical systems." It is not known whether these exemptions have been finalized yet.

With respect to presidential library records, however, only MDR can be used for review of pre-1981 donated historical materials or presidential historical materials in presidential libraries. Both the FOIA and MDR can be used for *Presidential records* of President Reagan and his successors after certain periods of time have elapsed.

The FOIA, originally passed by Congress in 1966 and amended several times since, is a much better known and more widely used procedure than MDR. A FOIA request should be labeled as such; identify with as much specificity as possible the records in question; and have the signature, address, and telephone number of the requestor. Additionally, if the documents sought are for the purposes of scholarly research, there should be a request for a waiver of any fees involved. Under the FOIA, an agency is required to determine within twenty days whether to comply with the request and promptly thereafter disclose the documents it is releasing and the reasons it is withholding any documents.[23] However, virtually no agency is able to comply with these time limits on account of such factors as the size and number of pending requests, and it is not unusual for a final determination to take many years. The FOIA authorizes an agency to withhold information if it falls under one or more of the nine exemptions enumerated in the statute. The most significant of these exemptions for purposes of discussion here is the first one, which permits the withholding of documents properly classified under an executive order. There are, however, four other exemptions that are often invoked regarding national security-related records. These are the third exemption for "information exempt under other laws" (among other things, this is used to withhold RD and FRD that still merit being classified), the fifth exemption for "internal government communications," the sixth exemption for "personal privacy," and the seventh exemption for "law enforcement."[24] In the event of a partial or total denial, there are administrative appeal rights and, ultimately, the right to challenge the denial in federal district court.[25]

The MDR procedure, originally established under E.O. 12065 signed by President Carter, was designed to be a speedier and less adversarial declassification procedure than the FOIA. A MDR request should be labeled as such; identify with as much specificity as possible the records in question; and have the signature, address, and telephone number of the requestor. Section 3.6 of E.O. 12958 requires agencies to declassify information pursuant to a MDR "that no longer meets the standards for classification under this order." There are, however, certain types of information exempt from the MDR provisions, including information reviewed by the agency for declassification within the previous two years and information generated by the incumbent President and his White House advisors. In the event of a partial or total denial, the requestor has only the right of appeal to the Interagency Security Classification Appeals Panel and not the right to go to federal court as under the FOIA.[26] In the past, documents often took as long to be reviewed under MDR as they were under the FOIA. However, under E.O. 12958 and its enabling regulations, a requestor can apparently appeal to the Interagency Security Classification Appeals Board if the agency in question has not acted on the initial request within one year of its submittal.[27]

## NOTES

1. The term "unclassified" as used throughout means both individual records and collections that were determined when originally generated not to contain any classified information under the relevant guidelines and thus should be available for public review. "Classified" means (1) in the case of individual records that they were determined to contain classified information when originally created and continue to do so, or (2) in the case of a collection of records, that at least one record therein still contains classified information. Such individual records and collections can only be examined by those with the proper security clearances. "Declassified" means (1) in the case of an individual record that it was determined to contain classified information when originally generated, but that it has been deemed to no longer contain such information or the portions that still do have been *redacted*, or (2) in the case of a collection of records, that at least one record therein used to contain classified information, but that any and all such records have been deemed no longer to contain such information or that the portions that still do have been *redacted*. Such individual records and collections should be available for public examination after certain further steps are taken.

2. Section 1.5, E.O. 12958.

3. Section 1.3, E.O. 12958.

4. Section 1.6, E.O. 12958.

5. 42 U.S.C. 2011, et seq.

6. For an excellent discussion of SCI and its various components, see Jeffrey Richelson, *The U.S. Intelligence Community* (Boulder: Westview Press, 1999). A 1987 Director of Central Intelligence Directive on SCI is posted on the FAS home page at www.fas.org.

7. 50 U.S.C. 403g.

8. 42 U.S.C. 2162.

9. *Annual Report to the President, FY 1984* (Washington, D.C.: Information Security Oversight Office, 1985), p. 16.

10. Section 3.4, E.O. 12958.

11. Any confusion on this point of exactly which records are covered by E.O. 12958 is cleared up by its implementing directive found at 32 C.F.R. 2001. In relevant part it states that "Classified information in records that have not been scheduled for disposal or retention by NARA is not subject to section 3.4 of the Order. Classified information in records that are scheduled as permanently valuable when that information is already more than 20 years old shall be subject to the automatic declassification provisions of section 3.4 of the Order five years from the date the records are scheduled." In short, there is no provision whatsoever requiring any systematic declassification review or providing for the automatic declassification of any *unappraised* or *temporary* records.

12. Sections 3.4 and 3.5, E.O. 12958.

13. Unfortunately, access to these plans is difficult. The ISOO, which has copies of all of them, requires prior approval of an agency before releasing its plan to the public. Many agencies have given such approval, but a few have refused. For example, the Central Intelligence Agency's plan is marked "For Official Use Only," and it will not permit the public to see it. Moreover, the proposed implementation plan of the National Security Agency is itself classified.

14. *1998 Report to the President* (Washington, D.C.: Information Security Oversight Office, 1999), p. 5. The same problem exists with respect to public access to these lists of exempted files as it does with the proposed implementation plans—prior approval of the agency is required. Moreover, the lists of the Central Intelligence Agency and the National Security Agency are themselves classified.

15. The agreement is on file at the ISOO.

16. An agency's jurisdiction over the classified information in a record is called *equities*. An individual record has either the *equities* of a single agency or multiple agencies. No agency has the training or legal authority to declassify the *equities* of another agency. Under systematic declassification review, in contrast to declassification review under the FOIA and MDR, there is no requirement for an agency to *redact* still-sensitive information in its *equities*. The agency simply does not declassify it, and the entire record remains classified. Any member of the public who wants to see the record has to file a FOIA or MDR request. Furthermore, under systematic declassification review, also in contrast to declassification review under the FOIA and MDR, there is no requirement that any agency refer a record containing the *equities* of another agency to that agency for review. All that is required is that the agency reviewing the record notify the other agency that the record contains its *equities*. The following example illustrates this. Only the Navy can declassify information regarding modern U.S. submarines. If the Air Force in its systematic declassification review program encounters a record having such information, it does not have to refer it to the Navy but can simply notify the Navy. The record remains classified, and any member of the public who wishes to see that record has to file a FOIA or MDR request. *See*, 32 C.F.R. 2001.51(k) and 2001.55.

17. *1996 Report to the President* (Washington, D.C.: Information Security Oversight Office, 1997), pp. 25–26; *1997 Report to the President* (Washington, D.C.: Information Security Oversight Office, 1998), pp. 27–28; *1998 Report to the President* (Washington, D.C.: Information Security Oversight Office, 1999), pp. 16–17; *1999 Report to the President* (Washington, D.C.: Information Security Oversight Office, 2000), pp. 20–22. These reports are available on the FAS home page at www.fas.org.

18. Section 3.8, E.O. 12958. Along these lines, in September 1997, the author proposed to the interagency Classification Management Committee that each agency be required to submit annually to the National Archives a publicly accessible report containing the following information for each collection reviewed: a brief description; the approximate size (in cubic feet or pages), and the approximate percentage declassified; the location and, if not already at the National Archives, the plans for transferring it there. The committee neither discussed the proposal nor adopted it.

19. The author has contacted numerous agencies requesting information on which records they are reviewing under the order. Only six agencies—the Air Force, Arms Control and Disarmament Agency, Army, National Imagery and Mapping

Agency, National Security Agency, and Navy—have provided the author with such information.

20. Presentation by Department of Energy representatives at an October 1999 meeting of the DOE/NARA panel on declassification held at the College Park National Archives.

21. 50 U.S.C. 431.

22. The author has attempted unsuccessfully to get from the Central Intelligence Agency the number or percentage of subject operational files that have been exempted.

23. The FOIA is set forth at 5 U.S.C. 552. An excellent and easy-to-use guide to the law is *A Citizen's Guide on Using the Freedom of Information Act and the Privacy Act of 1974 to Request Government Records* (Washington D.C.: Government Printing Office, 1989). This publication includes sample request letters and is also available on the Government Printing Office's homepage at www.access.gpo.gov. Sample request letters are also available on a number of other homepages.

24. 5 U.S.C. 552(b).

25. 5 U.S.C. 552(a) (4B).

26. Section 3.6, E.O. 12958. The Interagency Security Classification Appeals Board reports detailing its actions on MDR appeals can be examined on the FAS homepage at www.fas.org.

27. 32 C.F.R., Appendix A to Part 2001.

# 4

# Where Agency Records Are Located

## THE THREE CATEGORIES OF AGENCY RECORDS

There are three general categories of agency records and each is subject to
a distinct record-keeping practice. The first general category is the unclassified periodic and nonperiodic publications of the agencies. These
publications can take many forms, including annual reports to Congress
by individual agencies or a report by an agency on a particular program
or policy. Copies of these publications are placed at numerous private and
public libraries around the nation. They are listed in the *Guide to U.S.
Government Publications*, a standard reference work available in most libraries. One is of particular importance here—the annual *United States
Organization Manual* (formerly *United States Government Organization
Manual*) that is also available in many libraries. Among other things, this
work lists the personnel holding high-level positions at each agency and
gives a brief description of the major offices, bureaus, and divisions at each
agency. Its utility to the researcher is that it can give the names of both the
individuals and offices whose records may be of interest. For example, a
researcher may be interested in locating records of the Office of the Secretary of Defense from the 1950s concerning intelligence, counterintelligence, special operations, and related topics. What office or offices had
those responsibilities? A quick review of the *United States Government
Organization Manual* from this period will show that from 1954–1961,
these responsibilities were given the Assistant to the Secretary of Defense
(Special Operations). After learning this, the researcher can then attempt
to locate the records of this office.

A second general category is the research and development reports and studies done in-house or by outside contractors for the Department of Defense and other agencies since the 1940s. Copies of these can often be found in the vast collections of agency records; however, there are two central repositories for them. As will be explained in more detail, such reports and studies prepared by or for the department are placed in the Defense Technical Information Center (DTIC). Unclassified and declassified reports and studies from the Defense Technical Information Center, as well as those from other agencies, are placed in the Department of Commerce's National Technical Information Service.

The third category of records consists of all the many other types of records created by agencies, including but not limited to letters, memoranda, transcripts of communications or meetings, periodic and nonperiodic official histories, logs, studies, reports, publications, estimates, maps, charts, films, photographs, and electronic records. This category of records is, without question, the largest and most difficult to use.

All records in this third category have met one of six fates: (1) they have been transferred to the National Archives, (2) they have been transferred to a Federal records center, (3) they are still with the agency or a successor, (4) they have been destroyed, (5) they have been lost, or (6) they have been removed by an official, and either been destroyed or lost, kept by the official, or placed in some repository.[1]

## REPOSITORIES FOR AGENCY RECORDS

This section will discuss the general workings of the various repositories where agency records are located: the National Archives, Federal records centers, the agencies themselves, Library of Congress, Defense Technical Information Center/National Technical Information Service; it will also discuss means of locating relevant documents at these repositories and how to request the declassification review of records.

### Records at the National Archives

The National Archives is one component of NARA and is broadly charged under federal law with effecting the transfer to it of *permanent federal records* and thereafter assuming their custody, care, and control. It is the one federal repository that is expressly charged with making available to the public those records that can be made available. Federal law provides that records are to be transferred to the National Archives when they have been determined to be of sufficient historical or other value to warrant preservation (for example, *permanent* records) and they are thirty years old or, regardless of age, when the originating agency no longer needs to use the records in its regular current business and the agency's needs will be satisfied by access to the records at the National Archives.[2] *Permanent* records more than thirty years old may be retained by an agency only when its head certifies to the Archivist of the United States "that the records must be retained in agency custody for use in the conduct of the regular current business of the agency," unless the agency's *records schedule* permits their retention by the agency for more than thirty years. In such cases, the agency head only has to submit the required certification if the agency retains the *permanent* records longer than the period called for in the *records schedule*.[3]

As a practical matter, virtually no agency involved in national security issues in the postwar period has transferred all of its *permanent* records thirty years old and older to the National Archives, and some have not transferred any. There are several reasons for this. First, all *permanent* records still held by the agencies and at Federal records centers are grouped in collections, and what triggers the eligibility date for transfer of a collection to the National Archives is the date of the most recent document therein. For example, one collection of records of the Office of the Secretary of Defense's Vietnam Task Force (in existence from 1967–1969) at the Federal records center in Suitland, Maryland, contains the following: (1) War Department, Navy Department, State Department, and Department of Defense cables on Southeast Asia from 1940–1968; (2) War Department, Navy Department, White House, State Department, Department of Defense, and Central Intelligence Agency memos and reports on Southeast Asia from 1945–1968; (3) working files on the 1954 Geneva Conference, U.S. aid programs and related topics from the 1950s and 1960s. Under the Office of the Secretary of Defense *records schedule*, they are not eligible for transfer to the National Archives until they are forty years old, and thus this collection is not eligible until 2008—sixty-eight years after the date of the earliest document therein. As another example, there is a collection of State Department Office of Legal Adviser records from 1922–1983 primarily concerning chemical and biological warfare at the Federal records center in Suitland, Maryland. Under the State Department *records schedule*, they are not eligible for transfer to the National Archives until they are thirty years old, and thus this collection is not eligible until 2014—ninety-two years after the date of the earliest document therein. Second, there are some *records schedules* that provide that certain *permanent* records are not even eligible for transfer to the National Archives until more than thirty years after their creation. For example, the Office of the Secretary of Defense *records schedule* states that the records of the Secretary, Deputy Secretary, Special Assistants, Assistant Secretaries, and selected other high-level officials and groups are to be transferred to the National Archives when they are forty years old (the Vietnam Task Force records mentioned above fall into this category). The Federal Bureau of Investigation *records schedule* provides that most of its records are to be transferred to the National Archives when they are fifty years old. The Central Intelligence Agency *records schedules* also provide for a fifty-year retention period.[4] It is not known why such *records schedules* have been approved, because it is difficult to understand the need for any agency to retain records older than thirty years. What also should not be forgotten in this discussion is the fact that some agencies have large numbers of *unappraised records*, some of which should be *permanent* and be at the National Archives. Third, agencies must give their permission for the transfer of eligible *permanent* records from a Federal records center or the agency itself to the National Archives. For any number of reasons some agencies refuse to grant permission, and there is little if anything the National Archives can do about it.

There are two National Archives facilities in the Washington, D.C., area. The downtown National Archives at 7th and Pennsylvania Avenues in Washington, D.C., has Executive Branch records from the 1700s and 1800s and all Legislative Branch records. The College Park National Archives in College Park, Maryland, has Executive Branch records from the 1900s. There are also thirteen regional National Archives around the nation: Waltham, Massachusetts; New York, New York; Philadelphia, Pennsylvania; East Point, Georgia; Chicago, Illinois; Kansas City, Missouri; Lee's Summit, Missouri; Fort Worth, Texas; Denver, Colorado; Laguna Niguel, California; San Bruno, California; Seattle, Washington; and Anchorage, Alaska. Information on the research room hours, addresses, e-mail contacts, and phone and fax numbers of each of the fifteen National Archives is on NARA's home page at www.nara.gov.

Records of agency offices in the Washington, D.C., area are to be transferred to the College Park National Archives, while records of agency offices elsewhere are to be transferred to the appropriate National Archives regional facility.[5] However, the regional National Archives can hold only relatively small numbers of records and most do not have the capability to hold any classified records. Consequently, if the records (both unclassified and classified) of overseas diplomatic posts and military commands from around country and world are at any National Archives, they are almost invariably at College Park.

Although the National Archives assume legal custody and control over the records, there are definite limitations in their ability to declassify many of them. Under its declassification review program mandated by E.O. 12958, the National Archives can declassify information in its holdings only when given authority to do so by the agencies whose *equities* are involved.[6] When it receives a FOIA or MDR request for classified information in its holdings, the National Archives can declassify such information only when it is twenty-five years old or older and the agencies whose *equities* are involved have given it authority to do so.[7] Many agencies have given the National Archives at least some limited authority to review their classified information, but some, such as the Central Intelligence Agency and Department of Energy, have not given any.

All records of a particular agency, and in cases of very large agencies such as the military services the records of various offices within the agency, are put in a separate collection by the National Archives. These collections are called *record groups*, and each receives its own descriptive title and number (the latter carries no significance other than being a shorthand method of referring to the collection). At the present time, there are more than 525 *record groups*. Of the ones containing postwar national security-related records, some do not contain any records while others contain many millions of pages. Most *record groups* are organized into a series of *entries*. An individual *entry* often contains records from a single office or individual of the same classification status (unclassified, Confidential, Secret or Top Secret) from one year or other period of time. Large *record groups* usually have hundreds of *entries*, each of which can contain anywhere from a few pages to many tens of thousands of pages.

The first step in utilizing records at the National Archives is to determine the *record group(s)* that might have relevant material. In the sections discussing the records of individual agencies and departments, there is extended discussion on their records at the National Archives and the *record group(s)* they are in. For information in this regard, a researcher can also review the three-volume *Guide to Federal Records in the National Archives of the United States* (Washington, D.C.: National Archives and Records Administration, 1995). This publication is available in hard copy at the National Archives or on the NARA homepage at www.nara.gov. For each *record group*, this work provides a short organizational history of the department, agency, or office in question; a summary of the quantity, types, and dates of records; what other *record group(s)* at the National Archives have related records; and what presidential libraries have records of the department, agency, or office. It should be noted, however, that there are some limitations in using this work. First, it does not cover the large numbers of records that have or will be added to some *record groups* since its publication in 1995. Second, the work does not give the specific classification level of the records. Third, it does not state in many cases whether the records are available to the public. Another means of finding out the relevant *record group(s)* is to contact an archivist in the branch of the National Archives who has cognizance over records in the particular area of research. These branches are Modern Military and Civil. Archivists are generally well acquainted with the organizational structure of the agency in question and have considerable experience in working with at least a portion of the agency's records.

The next step after determining the *record group(s)* of interest is to identify as narrowly as possible the specific records therein to be reviewed. A few *record groups* are small enough so that this does not pose a problem;

however, this is the exception rather than the rule. The first step researchers should take in this regard is to review any *finding aids*. Some *finding aids* are prepared by agencies when they transfer their records to the National Archives, while others are prepared by National Archives staff. At a minimum, *finding aids* give a brief description of the contents, dates covered, and size of the *entries* within the *record group*. The really useful *finding aids* will list each folder title by box. It should be noted, however, that some *finding aids* are obsolete by reason of the *entries* being rearranged or the addition of significant quantities of records since their preparation. At times, the descriptions of the contents or dates covered are erroneous. Although archivists often know in great detail at least parts of the *record groups* with which they work, it is not reasonable to expect that they have this level of knowledge with all portions. This is simply because most *record groups* are so large and the archivists have to work with so many of them.

Researchers also should always attempt to identify the particular filing system used in the collection to be reviewed. Is it a simple chronological file or reading file? Or is it a more complicated numerical or subject file? Some filing systems are well known. For example, many individuals and offices within the Office of the Secretary of Defense (including the Secretary of Defense and Deputy Secretary of Defense), Army, Air Force, and other Department of Defense components have used a modified War Department Decimal System since the 1940s. In this system, each number represents a specific topic or subject (for example, "360.2" represents research and development; "381," war plans; "385," chemical, biological, and radiological warfare; and "452," airplane development). As another example, the State Department Central Files through the years have used a series of numerical filing systems. Some filing systems are described in publications (for example, the Modern Military Branch has publications describing the War Department Decimal System and the Civil Branch has publications describing the State Department Central Files numerical systems), while information on others must be obtained from the archivists or other sources. By no means are all the filing systems used over the years by the various offices, agencies, departments, and others known or understood, but when they are, it can save the researcher countless hours of examining irrelevant materials.

Once pertinent records in a *record group* have been identified, there is no assurance the researcher will be able to review them because they could be in a classified collection that has never been reviewed for declassification or in a collection that has been reviewed for declassification but not re-reviewed by the Department of Energy under the Kyl Plan (if needed) or not *processed*. In December 1997, the College Park National Archives estimated it had more than 500 million pages of military and civil records not accessible by the public. The figure as of this writing may be higher because the P-2000 Project will transfer about 80,000 cubic feet (c.f.) of *permanent* classified records from the Federal records center in Suitland, Maryland, to the College Park National Archives by the end of 2001 (the records to be transferred under the P-2000 Project are discussed in detail in the following sections on the location of records of individual agencies). *Processing*, a task performed only by the National Archives, is the procedure under which a collection of records that has been reviewed for declassification is made ready for public access. It involves removing documents that were not declassified, inserting "pull cards" in the files for them, and labeling the box to permit the public to review its contents. It is a time-consuming procedure but must be done before the public can examine any collection. Moreover, the normal *processing* procedure of the National Archives has been complicated by reason of the above-mentioned provision in the FY 1999 and FY 2000 National Defense Authorization Acts, which, among other things, authorize the Department of Energy to re-review all the declassified but *unprocessed* records at the National Archives to ensure that there has been no inadvertent release of Restricted Data or Formerly Restricted Data.[8] In short, there are currently a huge number of records at the National Archives that are inaccessible by the public, and this situation will not likely change for some years.

Researchers encountering "pull cards" in an open collection can submit either a FOIA or MDR request for a declassification review of the classified record or records in question. As mentioned above, when the record is twenty-five years old or older and the National Archives has received authority from the agencies to review the information, it will go ahead and review the record in-house. If the National Archives has not received this authority or the record is less than twenty-five years old, the National Archives will forward the record to the agency or agencies with *equities* in it.

Researchers who want an entire classified collection reviewed should first check with the archivists to see if the collection has been systematically reviewed for declassification under E.O. 12958 or will be shortly and, if so, when it will be re-reviewed by the Department of Energy under the Kyl Plan (if needed) and then finally *processed* by the National Archives. If the collection is not scheduled for systematic review for some time or has been declared "exempt" from the automatic declassification provisions of E.O. 12958, the researcher should go ahead and file either a FOIA or MDR request.

### Records at the Federal Records Centers

Federal records centers are also part of NARA, but as will be seen, their procedures and rules governing access to records are very different from those of the National Archives. In contrast to the National Archives, there is no requirement that any agency send records to a Federal records center. Federal records centers are established solely to assist agencies in the storage, servicing, and processing of their records.[9] Records that are transferred to a Federal records center are still in the legal custody and control of the originating agency and, absent the permission of this agency, the records can be examined only by it.[10] For researchers, this means that even for collections of completely unclassified records, permission must first be obtained from the agency before examining them.

Records transferred by an agency are to be placed in the same *record group* as that agency's records are at the National Archives (however, this is not always the case). Every *record group* at a Federal records centers is organized by *accessions*—there are no *entries* in *record groups* at Federal records centers as there are in *record groups* at the National Archives. Each individual transfer of records by an agency is called an *accession* and receives its own number. All such numbers have three parts, for example, "330–60–2400." The first set of numbers represents the *record group*, the second set of numbers is the last two digits of the year in which the records were transferred, and the third set of numbers represents the shipment number during that year.

The largest and most important Federal records center for national security-related records is the Washington National Records Center in Suitland, Maryland. It currently holds about 3.5 million c.f. of *unappraised*, *temporary*, and *permanent* records, of which the vast majority are textual records. As mentioned above, under the P-2000 Project about 300,000 c.f. of *permanent* records from the Washington National Records Center will be transferred to the College Park National Archives by the end of 2001, of which approximately 80,000 c.f. are in classified *accessions*. The key factor in determining what *accessions* are to be transferred is of course whether they are past their due date for transfer to the National Archives under the pertinent *records schedule*. It should be noted that, in a few instances, the agencies have refused to give permission for the transfer of eligible *permanent* records, and there is virtually nothing the National Archives can do about this. There are also ten regional Federal records centers: Waltham, Massachusetts; Philadelphia, Pennsylvania; East Point, Georgia; Dayton, Ohio; Chicago, Illinois; St. Louis, Missouri; Kansas City, Missouri; Fort Worth, Texas; Denver, Colorado; and San Bruno, California.

Records of an agency in the Washington, D.C., area that are transferred to a Federal records center must go to the Washington National Records Center, while records from agencies in other parts of the country or the world are to be transferred to the appropriate regional Federal records center.[11] However, the regional Federal records centers can hold only relatively small numbers of records, and most do not have the capability to hold any classified records. Consequently, most records (both unclassified and classified) of overseas diplomatic posts and military commands from around the country and world that are at a Federal records center are at the Washington National Records Center.

In contrast to the National Archives, there are no archivists to consult or *finding aids* to review to determine what records are at a Federal records center. Determining what is in a *record group* at a Federal records center is a multistep process. The first step is examining the *Standard Form-135s* (*SF-135s*), the transmittal form Federal regulations require to be prepared by an agency when it ships an *accession* to a Federal records center.[12] For many years it has been required that a *SF-135* list all the folder titles in an *accession* of *permanent* records (unfortunately, compliance with this has varied).[13] The *SF-135s* for each *record group* are filed together in a series of manila folders. Individual *SF-135s* can run into many hundreds of pages (depending on the size of the *accession* and detail given on the records) and for large *record groups*, the *SF-135s* often total many tens of thousands of pages. Although reviewing *SF-135s* is a tedious process, only by examining them can one determine exactly what is in a *record group*.

There is, however, no guarantee that just because a *SF-135* is in the file drawer, the *accession* is still at the Federal records center. This is because in many instances, the *SF-135s* for *accessions* that have been sent to the National Archives, withdrawn by the agency, or destroyed are still in the file drawers. When researchers review a *SF-135* that describes records of interest, they should always then examine the *O-1 list* for the *record group* to determine whether the *accession* is still at the Federal records center. The *O-1 list* is generated by the Federal records center every three months, and for each *accession* it gives the size (in cubic feet), a three- or four-word description of the records, the date range of the records, the *appraisal* status, the eligibility date for transfer to the National Archives (for *permanent* records), and the eligibility date for destruction (for *temporary* records). The *O-1 lists* are in three-ring binders that are kept in the same area as the *SF-135s*. If the *accession* is not set forth in the *O-1 list*, the researcher should then review the *O-1 history list* for the *record group* in question. The *O-1 history lists*, also created periodically by the Federal records center, set forth every *accession* that used to be at the Federal records center and whether it was transferred to a National Archives, withdrawn by the agency or destroyed. The *O-1 history lists* are also in three-ring binders that are kept in the same area as the *SF-135s* and *O-1 lists*.

After the researcher has located records of interest, the problem of actually examining them arises. As mentioned earlier, even for *accessions* containing completely unclassified records, the researcher must first obtain permission from the originating agency before examining them. The Federal records center can provide the names and addresses of the individuals at the agencies who need to be contacted in this regard. These requests are usually granted quickly, but in a few cases agencies have been known to take months to act on them.[14]

The public also cannot examine *accessions* that have been reviewed for declassification by the agencies. Such records have not been re-reviewed by the Department of Energy under the Kyl Plan (if needed) nor *processed* and will not be until they are transferred to the National Archives. Of course, in the meantime, a researcher can submit either a FOIA or MDR request for any such records to the appropriate agency.

There is generally a much higher percentage of classified material in a *record group* at a Federal records center than in the same *record group* at the National Archives. There are several reasons for this. First, in contrast to the National Archives, Federal records centers do not declassify any records at all because they do not have legal custody and control of them and have been given no authority to review and declassify them. Second, only a few agencies have conducted any declassification review of their records at the Federal records centers.

### Records at Agencies

Compared with records at the National Archives and Federal records centers, records still at an agency are usually much more difficult to identify and access. Many agencies have central records storage facilities that hold large numbers of records (for example, the Central Intelligence Agency has the Agency Records Center and the Department of State has the Records Service Center). However, often it is impossible to obtain any information on the holdings at these facilities or on those at individual offices, branches, divisions, or directorates. Consequently, in the vast majority of cases, researchers need to submit a FOIA or MDR request to learn in the first place whether an agency even holds relevant records and, if so, to attempt to gain access to them.

The one exception is that some agencies have history offices or FOIA offices that have unclassified or declassified holdings that are available to the public. These sources of information should always be investigated.

### Records at the Defense Technical Information Center (DTIC) / National Technical Information Service (NTIS)

The DTIC is the repository for a huge quantity of material relating to research and development performed by or for the Department of Defense. The most significant part of the DTIC is the Technical Report collection, which has about two million unclassified, declassified, and classified print and nonprint documents. Each document receives its own DTIC identification number. The Technical Report collection includes technical reports and studies done by the various laboratories and development centers of the services (for example, the Navy's Office of Naval Research) or by defense contractors (for example, RAND Corporation and Mitre Corporation), pertinent directives and instructions, patent applications, and foreign open source literature. The material in the Technical Report collection covers a wide range of subjects, including but not limited to aeronautics, missile technology, space technology, navigation, nuclear science, electronics, explosives, biology, chemistry, oceanography, mechanical engineering, computer sciences, and sociology.

The public, however, does not have direct access to the DTIC as it only serves the Department of Defense and its contractors. To obtain unclassified and declassified documents from the DTIC's holdings, the public must utilize the NTIS. The NTIS, part of the Department of Commerce, receives copies of most unclassified and declassified DTIC documents as well as unclassified and declassified research and development reports and studies from other agencies. Copies of all the NTIS holdings are placed in selected repositories around the nation, including the Library of Congress. The key to using the NTIS is obtaining the DTIC identification number, and there are various methods of doing so. Unclassified DTIC documents from 1987 on are listed on the Public STINET portion of the DTIC's homepage (http://www.dtic.mil/stinet/). A CD-ROM available at the Library of Congress and through commercial vendors[15] lists all the NTIS holdings from 1964 to the present. For pre-1964 materials, researchers must review the semi-annual and annual *U.S. Government Research Reports* and *Government Reports, Announcements, and Index*, available at the Library of Congress and many libraries around the country.

### Records at the Library of Congress (LOC)

The most significant executive branch primary source materials are in the Manuscript Division and the Science and Technology Division. The Manuscript Division contains the personal papers of many military officers and civilian officials, as well as those of numerous other individuals from a wide range of professions. A complete listing in a single work of all the personal paper collections is not available outside the library. The papers acquired since 1959 will be briefly described in the *National Union Catalog of Manuscript Collections*, which is published by the library and available in many libraries across the country. Since 1979, the library has also published *Library of Congress, Acquisitions, Manuscript Division* annually, which discusses in considerable detail the papers acquired by the Manuscript Division in the year in question. Of course, the Division can be contacted directly to determine whether a particular individual's papers are there. In the Manuscript Division's reading room, there are comprehensive *finding aids* for each collection, which, among other things, list all the folder titles. In some instances, there are restrictions on access to the papers. All the collections have been given to the library by the individuals themselves or their families after their deaths, and as part of this process the individuals and families can impose any number of limitations on access.

These limitations often take the form of denying all access for a given number of years or requiring written permission from the individual or his family before being permitted to review the papers. Additionally, some collections contain classified records. Being a part of the Legislative Branch, the LOC is exempt from the FOIA and MDR. Notwithstanding this, however, the Manuscript Division accepts declassification requests and treats them as if they were submitted under the MDR procedure.

The Science and Technology Division also contains a number of primary source Executive Branch documents, chiefly in its NTIS collection. All can be called up and reviewed in the Science and Technology Division's reading room. The previous section on DTIC and NTIS records describe the various indexes that must be used to identify specific documents of interest.

### Records at Private Repositories

The private repository that has the largest and most significant number of declassified government records on U.S. foreign policy, nuclear weapons, and intelligence available for public examination is the National Security Archive in Washington, D.C. This independent nonprofit institution is a frequent requestor for the declassification of records and is an archive of declassified records and also a publisher of them. It can be contacted by writing to it at The Gelman Library, George Washington University, Suite 701, 2130 H Street, N.W., Washington, D.C. 20037; by phoning 202–994–7400; by faxing 202–994–7005; or by e-mailing nsarchiv@gwu.edu.

A number of important records are available on the homepage (www.gwu.edu/nsarchiv), either in "electronic briefing books" or in the sections describing the various projects of the staff. The homepage also lists the microfiche sets and hardcover publications on various topics, as well as the unpublished collections available for examination at the offices at the George Washington University.

## THE LOCATION OF RECORDS OF INDIVIDUAL AGENCIES

Set forth in the following sections in alphabetical order are the agencies involved since World War II in various national security issues. The quantity, nature, and classification status of the records of each agency at the various repositories is given, as well as the agency's progress (or lack thereof) in its declassification review program under E.O. 12958. Additionally, records scheduled for transfer from the Washington National Records Center to the College Park National Archives under the P-2000 Project are identified. Lastly, the addresses of the offices to which FOIA and MDR requests should be submitted are set forth.

### Agency for International Development (AID) / Economic Cooperation Administration (ECA) / Mutual Security Agency (MSA) / Foreign Operations Administration (FOA) / Institute of Inter-American Affairs (IIAA) / Technical Cooperation Administration (TCA) / International Cooperation Administration (ICA) Records at the National Archives and Federal Records Centers

A huge number of records of the AID (1961–present) and its predecessors, the ECA (1948–1951), MSA (1951–1953), FOA (1953–1955), IIAA (1942–1950), TCA (1950–1953), and ICA (1955–1961), are in two *record groups* at the College Park National Archives and the Washington National Records Center. No other National Archives or Federal records center has any records of these agencies.

The AID's progress in its declassification review under E.O. 12958 has been very good, as it reviewed virtually all of its *permanent* pre-1975 classified records by 2000. The FY 1996, FY 1997, FY 1998, and FY 1999 ISOO annual reports list the agency as having declassified more than 22 million pages.

Record Group (RG) 469 has the records of the predecessors to the AID, and at the College Park National Archives RG 469 has more than 21 million pages of records.[16] The *finding aids* are very good. Almost all the records have been reviewed for declassification and *processed* and they include:

1. Secret and below files of the Office of the Administrator and other headquarters offices of the ECA, as well as those of several country missions, from 1948–1951;

2. Secret and below files of the Office of the Administrator and other headquarters offices of the MSA from 1951–1953;

3. Top Secret and below subject files, general files, geographic files, country files, and other records of the Special Representative and the Office of the United States Special Representative in Europe from 1948–1953;

4. Secret and below subject files, geographic files, and country files of the Office of the Administrator and other headquarters offices of the TCA from 1950–1953;

5. Secret and below minutes of IIAA Executive Board meetings from 1943–1950 and assorted other records of the IIAA from 1942–1950;

6. Top Secret and below subject files, geographic files, and decimal files from 1953–1959 of the various divisions of the U.S. Mission to the North Atlantic Treaty Organization and European Regional Organization, including those of the Executive Secretary, Office of Political Affairs, and Office of European Operations;

7. Top Secret and below Director of the ICA subject files, regional files, country files, and chronological files from 1955–1961;

8. Top Secret and below country files, subject files, program files, and other records of ICA headquarters offices, including the Deputy Director for Operations, Deputy Director for Program and Planning, and the geographic bureaus;

9. Secret and below files of the overseas ICA missions.

There are no records in RG 469 at the Washington National Records Center.

Record Group 286 contains the records of the AID, as well as a limited number of its predecessor agencies. At the College Park National Archives, RG 286 has about 2 million pages of records. Virtually all the records have been reviewed for declassification and most have been *processed* and they include:

1. Top Secret and below mail briefs, regional files, country files, subject files, and chronological files of the Administrator and Deputy Administrator from the 1960s into the early 1980s;

2. Top Secret and below development plans of the Office of Program and Policy Coordination from 1961–1966;

3. Secret and below files of the National Bi-Partisan Committee on Central America from 1986–1988;

4. Secret and below subject files, contract files, country files, program files, and loan files from the 1960s and 1970s of the Bureau for Africa, Bureau for Far East, Bureau for Latin America, Bureau for Near East and South Asia, and Bureau for Vietnam;

5. Secret and below subject files and other files of individual AID missions from the 1960s and 1970s;

6. Secret and below Director, Office of Public Safety numerical files from 1956–1974, program surveys and evaluations from 1959–1974, regional planning and fact books from 1965–1973, and general records from 1957–1964;

7. Secret and below Training Division, Office of Public Safety subject files from 1963–1972, Latin American Branch country files from 1955 into the 1970s, East Asia Branch country files from the 1950s into the 1970s, and Vietnam Division subject files from 1955 into the 1970s;

8. Secret and below Technical Services Division, Office of Public Safety correspondence files from 1966–1968 and country files from 1961–1970;

9. Secret and below Office of International Training third country training records from 1956–1964.

Record Group 286 at the Washington National Records Center has more than 62 million pages of classified and unclassified records of the AID and its predecessors as of 2000 (75% *permanent*, 15% *temporary*, and 10% *unappraised*).[17] As part of the P-2000 Project, about 13.3 million pages of unclassified *permanent* records and 14.6 million pages of classified *permanent* records will be transferred to RG 286 at the College Park National Archives by the end of 2001. Although all the *permanent* pre-1975 classified records will have been reviewed for declassification by the time of their transfer, they will not be available to the public until they are possibly re-reviewed by the Department of Energy (DOE) under the Kyl Plan and then *processed* by the National Archives. Records to be transferred include:

1. Secret and below reports from the 1970s prepared by AID employees for the Administrator on conditions, specific problems, and accomplishments;
2. Confidential and below reports from the 1970s prepared for the Administrator on international conferences;
3. Confidential and below headquarters regular and special staff meeting records from the 1970s;
4. unclassified speeches, media interviews, and transcripts of meetings and briefings from the 1960s and 1970s;
5. Secret and below records of the President's General Advisory Committee on Foreign Assistance Programs from 1966–1970;
6. Secret and below records from the 1950s into the 1980s regarding AID and predecessor participation in or interest in foreign assistance programs of international agencies, private organizations, and other countries;
7. unclassified agendas and minutes of AID and predecessor/nongovernmental organization meetings and studies and reports on nongovernmental organizations from the 1940s into the 1980s;
8. Secret and below Office of Congressional Affairs files from the 1960s into the 1980s;
9. unclassified Office of Public Affairs press releases from 1955–1975;
10. Secret and below official project/official loan files from the 1950s into the 1980s containing complete documentation on economic, technical, and capital assistance projects;
11. Secret and below program subject files from the 1960s into the 1980s containing correspondence, meeting minutes, studies, and position pa-

pers regarding development and administration of AID programs in lesser developed countries;

12. Secret and below project case files from the 1960s and 1970s with complete documentation of social and institutional development projects;

13. unclassified correspondence, reports, and other records from the 1960s into the 1980s relating to disaster relief.

Among the records that are not eligible for transfer to RG 286 at the College Park National Archives by 2001 are:

1. Top Secret and below subject files, country files, and program files of the Administrator and Deputy Administrator from the 1980s and 1990s;

2. Top Secret and below Executive Secretariat reports of international conferences from the 1970s into the 1990s, master telegram and airgram files from the 1970s and 1980s, and agendas and minutes to staff meetings from the 1980s and 1990s;

3. unclassified administration and management records from 1956 into the 1990s;

4. Secret and below Office of Program Coordination subject files from the 1970s into the 1990s;

5. Secret and below subject files, country files, and program files of the Office of International Training from the 1970s into the 1990s;

6. Secret and below Office of Congressional Affairs files from the 1980s and 1990s;

7. Secret and below subject files and other files of individual AID missions from the late 1970s into the 1990s;

8. Secret and below office project/official loan files, program subject files, and project case files from the 1980s and 1990s;

9. unclassified correspondence, reports, and other records from the 1980s and 1990s regarding disaster relief.

### AID and Predecessor Agency Records at the AID and Presidential Libraries

The Center for Development Information and Evaluation at the main AID building in Washington, D.C., is a library open to the public (202–712–0579). In addition to a considerable amount of secondary literature, the library contains many unclassified and declassified records on past and current programs including: (1) congressional presentations on the AID's

budget, (2) Program Objective Documents, (3) Action Plans, (4) Technical
Services and Grant Reports (the "Yellow Book"), (5) U.S. Overseas Loans
and Grants Reports (the "Green Book"), (6) project and technical documents (field studies, manuals, and research reports, as well as project design, implementation, and evaluation reports). Complete information of the
holdings is on a database at the library. This database is also available for
purchase on a CD-ROM disk. The library provides lists of AID records in
a specific area or field upon written request, and both written and oral
requests are accepted for the document identification numbers of specific
documents. From outside the Washington, D.C., area, documents can be
ordered in paper or microfiche format using the document identification
number.

The quantity, nature, and *appraisal* status of other records at the AID
are not known.

The Kennedy Library has microfilm copies of the Administrator's files
and other headquarters files from 1961–1963 in RG 286.

Requests under the FOIA or MDR for records at the Washington National Records Center or at the AID should be submitted to the Chief,
Information & Records Division, Office of Administrative Services, United
States Agency for International Development, Room 2.07C, Ronald Reagan Building, Washington, D.C. 20523–2701.

### Department of the Air Force Records at the National Archives and Federal Records Centers

A large number of Air Force records are in four *record groups* at the
National Archives and Federal records centers (records of the predecessor
Army Air Forces are discussed separately in a following section).

The Air Force originally estimated in 1995 that it had more than 176
million pages of records subject to E.O. 12958, but in 1999 it revised this
figure dramatically downward to 74 million pages.[18] Progress in its declassification review under the order has been very good, with the Air Force
reporting that as of March 1999, it had reviewed 55 million pages and
declassified about 35 million pages. The Air Force did not propose any
records for exemption from automatic declassification, but it is declaring a
limited number of collections exempt from automatic declassification after
their review because they are replete with nuclear weapons information or
information on intelligence sources and methods.[19]

Record Group 340 contains the records of the Office of the Secretary of
the Air Force (OSAF), and at the College Park National Archives RG 340
has more than 6 million pages of records. No other National Archives has
any RG 340 records. The *finding aids* are good. Among the records that
have been reviewed for declassification and *processed* are:

1. Top Secret/Restricted Data and below files of the Secretary from 1947–1954;
2. a limited number of Top Secret and below Assistant Secretary of the Air Force (Management) files from 1947–1952;
3. a limited number of Top Secret and below Assistant Secretary of the Air Force (Material) files from 1951–1952;
4. Top Secret and below files from 1943–1955 of the Office of Legislation and Liaison and its predecessor offices;
5. Top Secret and below records from the early 1950s of interservice boards such as the Joint Air Defense Board;
6. Top Secret and below records from 1950–1955 of various Special Assistants to the Secretary.

As of this writing there are a limited number of records that are still classified or that have been reviewed for declassification but are awaiting possible re-review by the DOE under the Kyl Plan and *processing* by the National Archives before being made available to the public, and these include:

1. Top Secret/Restricted Data and below files of the Secretary from 1955–1965 and the Under Secretary from 1947–1951;
2. Top Secret and below Office of General Counsel files from 1949–1954;
3. Top Secret and below Special Assistant for Research and Development files from 1948–1951.

Record Group 340 at the Washington National Records Center contains more than 17 million pages of mostly classified records as of 2000 (40% *permanent* and 60% *temporary*). No other Federal records center has any RG 340 records. As part of the P-2000 Project, about 1.4 million pages of unclassified *permanent* records and 1.1 million pages of classified *permanent* records will be transferred to RG 340 at the College Park National Archives by the end of 2001. Although most if not all of the classified *permanent* records will have been reviewed for declassification by the time of their transfer, they will not be available to the public until they are possibly re-reviewed by the DOE under the Kyl Plan and then *processed* by the National Archives. Records to be transferred include:

1. Top Secret/Restricted Data and Top Secret files of the Secretary and Chief of Staff from 1970–1972;
2. Secret/Restricted and below files of the Secretary and several Assistant Secretaries from 1966–1975.

Among the records not eligible for transfer to RG 340 at the College Park National Archives by 2001 are:

1. Secret/Restricted Data and below files of the Chief of Staff from 1973 into the early 1990s;
2. Secret/Restricted Data and below files on the Chief of Staff Worldwide Commanders' Conferences from 1971 into the early 1990s;
3. Secret/Restricted Data and below files of the Secretary and several Assistant Secretaries from 1976 into the early 1990s;
4. Top Secret/Restricted Data and below files of the Assistant Secretary (Research & Development)/Assistant Secretary for Research, Development & Logistics from the mid-1970s into the early 1980s;
5. Secret/Restricted Data and below agendas and recommendations of the Air Force Council, as well as the Chief of Staff decisions thereon, from the mid-1970s into the 1990s (it is not known where the minutes are);
6. Secret/Restricted Data and below agendas, minutes, and reports from the same time period of the boards that advised the Air Force Council, including the Systems Review Board, Air Staff Board, Reconnaissance & Intelligence Panel, Mobility Panel, Space Panel, Force Structure Committee, Strategic Panel, Tactical Panel, and Air Defense Panel;
7. Secret and below files on the Senior Statesman Symposium Conferences from the 1970s;
8. Confidential and below Office of Security Review files from the late 1960s and early 1970s;
9. Secret and below Office of the General Counsel subject files from 1957–1977 and files on individual nations from 1954–1966.

Record Group 341 contains the records of Air Force headquarters, and at the College Park National Archives RG 341 contains more than 20 million pages of records. No other National Archives has any RG 341 records. The *finding aids* to RG 341 are useful in generally describing the contents, size, and date range of all the *entries*, but they do not cover some *entries* in any detail. In these cases, the only means of determining exactly what records are in an *entry* is to examine the *SF-135s* that are available through the Modern Military Branch archivists if the records were transferred from the Washington National Records Center. Records that have been reviewed for declassification and *processed* include the following:

1. Secret and below files of the Chief of Staff and Vice Chief of Staff from 1947–1952, and the Secret and below files of their equivalents with the Army Air Forces from 1942–1947;

2. a very limited number of Top Secret/Restricted Data and below Vice Chief of Staff files from 1956–1960;

3. Top Secret/Restricted Data and below incoming and outgoing messages of the Air Staff from 1948–1957;

4. Secret/Restricted Data and below *Daily Staff Digests* of Air Force activities from 1949–1955, and the Top Secret/Restricted Data and Top Secret supplements thereto from 1950–1955;

5. Top Secret and below files of the Deputy Chief of Staff/Comptroller and its many subordinate offices from 1947–1953;

6. a limited number of Top Secret/Restricted Data and below files of the Deputy Chief of Staff/Development and its subordinate offices from the early 1950s, as well as the Top Secret and below records from as early as World War II of its many predecessor offices;

7. a limited number of Top Secret and below files of the Air Force Office of Atomic Energy from 1951–1953 concerning biological and chemical warfare;

8. Top Secret/Restricted Data and Top Secret Director of Intelligence decimal correspondence files from 1947–1955 and Secret/Restricted Data and below subject files from 1955;

9. Top Secret/Restricted Data and below decimal files, estimates, studies, war plans, and reports from 1942–1954 of the Directorate of Plans and its predecessor offices;

10. Top Secret/Restricted Data and below files from 1948–1952 of the Deputy Chief of Staff/Material and the Top Secret and below files of its many subordinate and predecessor offices from World War II to the mid-1950s;

11. a limited number of Top Secret/Restricted Data and below files, studies, and reports from 1949–1961 of the Operations Analysis Office;

12. Top Secret and below agendas and minutes of the Chief of Staff Worldwide Commanders' Conferences from 1954–1956;

13. Top Secret and below agendas, minutes, and reports of the Aircraft and Weapons Board from 1947–1949, as well as those of its successor, the Board of Senior Officers from 1949–1950;

14. Secret/Restricted Data and below agendas and recommendations of the Air Force Council, as well as the Chief of Staff decisions thereon, from 1951–1964 (it is not known where the minutes are);

15. a limited number of Secret/Restricted Data and below agendas, minutes, and reports of the four boards (Aircraft & Weapons Board, Force Estimates Board, Budget Advisory Board, and Major Construction Board), which advised the Air Force Council from 1950–1958;

16. Secret/Restricted Data and below agendas, minutes, and reports of the two boards (Weapons Board and Systems Review Board), which advised the Air Force Council from 1958–1962;

17. Secret/Restricted Data and below agendas, minutes, and reports of the panels and committees of the Scientific Advisory Board from 1948 to the late 1950s;

18. a limited number of Secret/Restricted Data and below records of the Chief Scientist of the Air Force from 1951–1953 and 1956–1957;

19. Secret/Restricted Data and below correspondence files and reports of the Director of the Directorate of Operational Requirements from 1958–1961;

20. Secret/Restricted Data and below Directorate of Operational Requirements control and warning systems files from 1951–1961; air defense weapons files from 1950–1960; communications systems and equipment files from 1951–1963; F-108 files from 1958–1961; and guided missiles files from 1955–1958.

Records that have been reviewed for declassification but still require possible re-review by the DOE under the Kyl Plan and *processing* before they will be available to the public include:

1. a very limited number of Vice Chief of Staff Top Secret/Restricted Data and Top Secret general files from 1961 and Top Secret/Restricted Data and below files on the Minuteman from 1963;

2. Top Secret and below Reconnaissance Group files on Project 119-L from 1953–1956;

3. Secret/Restricted Data and below Directorate of Operational Requirements and predecessor executive office general correspondence files from 1952–1958, individual weapons systems R&D requirements files from 1946–1955, and tactical aircraft weapons systems R&D files from 1959–1961;

4. Secret/Restricted Data and below Deputy Chief of Staff/Development and predecessor executive office general correspondence files from 1953–1957; long-range R&D files from 1952–1956; individual weapons systems files from 1949–1959; high energy fuel program files from 1947–1958; and R&D Coordinating Committee on Piloted Aircraft files from 1954–1960;

5. Secret/Restricted Data and below Assistant Chief of Staff for Guided Missiles files from 1950–1958;

6. Secret and below Air Force Letters, Manuals, Regulations, Orders, Notices, and Directives from 1952–1963;

7. Directorate of Procurement Policy and predecessor general files from 1953–1965.

There are some records that are still classified as of this writing, and they include:

1. a limited number of Top Secret/Restricted Data and below decimal files of the Air Force Office of Atomic Energy and its predecessor offices from 1945–1954;

2. Director of Intelligence and Assistant Chief of Staff/Intelligence Top Secret/Restricted Data and Top Secret briefing files and background materials from 1958–1963; Top Secret and below histories from 1955–1961 (copies of these should also be at the U.S. Air Force Historical Research Agency and the Air Force History Office discussed in the following section); Top Secret and below intelligence report files from 1954–1961; Secret/Restricted Data and below decimal correspondence files from 1947–1958; and Secret/Restricted Data and below intelligence policy directives from 1948–1965;

3. a number of records of subordinate offices under the Director of Intelligence and the Assistant Chief of Staff/Intelligence and predecessor offices, including but not limited to Top Secret/Restricted Data and below reports, decimal files, and related records from World War II to the early 1960s of the Directorate for Collection and Dissemination and its predecessor offices; Top Secret/Restricted Data and below reports, decimal files, and related records from World War II to the late 1950s of the Directorate for Estimates and its predecessor offices; Top Secret/Restricted Data and below technical reports and estimates from 1942–1957 and 1962 of the Directorate for Targets and its predecessor offices; Top Secret/Restricted Data and below target jackets from 1938–1955 of the Directorate for Targets and its predecessor offices (this collection was reviewed for declassification, but the Air Force concluded little information could be declassified and declared it exempt from automatic declassification—researchers must file a FOIA or MDR request to try to see any of the records); Top Secret/Restricted Data and below reports of the Physical Vulnerability Branch from 1949–1955; Top Secret/Restricted Data and below reports of the Directorate of Warning and Threat Assessment from 1957–1960 and briefings given by this office to the Chief of Staff and others from 1952–1957; a limited number of Top Secret/Restricted Data and below reports, decimal files, and related records from 1946 to the early 1960s of the Air Technical Intelligence Center and Foreign Technology Division; and Top Secret/Restricted Data and below intelligence reports prepared by civilian contractors from 1952–1964;

4. a small number of files of various subordinate offices under the Directorate of Operations, including but not limited to Top Secret/Restricted Data and below war plan implementation booklets and special weapons capabilities booklets of the Priorities & Programs Branch from 1954–1959 (this collection was reviewed for declassification, but the Air Force concluded little information could be declassified and declared it exempt from automatic declassification—researchers must file a FOIA or MDR request to try to see any of the records); Secret/Restricted Data and below case files of the Strategic Division from 1956–1959; and Secret/Restricted Data and below case files of the Strategic Air Division from 1948–1962;

5. Top Secret/Restricted Data and Top Secret Directorate of Plans decimal files, estimates, studies, war plans, and reports from 1955–1966 (these records were reviewed for declassification, but the Air Force concluded little information could be declassified and declared them exempt from automatic declassification—researchers must file a FOIA or MDR request to try to see any of the records);

6. Secret/Restricted Data and below Directorate of Plans decimal files, estimates, studies, war plans, and reports from 1955–1966 and Library Branch case files from 1947–1962.

Record Group 341 at the Washington National Records Center has more than 42 million pages of largely classified records as of 2000 (20% *permanent*, 20% *temporary*, and 60% *unappraised*). No other Federal records center has any RG 341 holdings. As part of the P-2000 Project, about 1.6 million pages of unclassified *permanent* records and 1.2 million pages of classified *permanent* records will be transferred to RG 341 at the College Park National Archives by the end of 2001. Although most if not all of the classified *permanent* records will have been reviewed for declassification by the time of their transfer, they will not be available to the public until they are possibly re-reviewed by the DOE under the Kyl Plan and then *processed* by the National Archives. The records to be transferred include:

1. Top Secret/Restricted Data and below agendas and recommendations of the Air Force Council, as well as the Chief of Staff decisions thereon, from 1965–1973 (it is not known where the minutes are);

2. Top Secret/Restricted Data and below reports from 1963–1973 of the various groups that advised the Air Force Council, including the Air Staff Board, Force Structure Committee, Program Review Committee, Air Defense Panel, C3 Panel, Reconnaissance/Intelligence Panel, Space Panel, Strategic Panel, and Tactical Panel;

3. Secret/Restricted Data and below *Daily Staff Digests* from 1968–1972;

4. Secret/Restricted Data and below files on the 1964–1970 Chief of Staff Worldwide Commanders' Conferences;

5. Secret and below Air Force Letters, Manuals, Orders, Notices, Regulations, and Directives from 1951–1971;

6. Top Secret/Restricted Data and below Directorate of Plans decimal files, estimates, war plans, and reports from 1967 into the early 1970s;

7. Top Secret/Restricted Data and below Directorate of Plans Joint Chiefs of Staff tasking files from 1969;

8. Top Secret/Restricted Data and below Directorate of Plans Joint Chiefs of Staff briefing packages from 1970–1973;

9. Secret Reconnaissance Division subject files from the 1960s on the Peacetime Airborne Reconnaissance Program;

10. a limited number of Secret/Restricted Data and below Special Advisory Group, Assistant Chief of Staff/Intelligence studies, reports, and files on Cuba, counterinsurgency, weapons systems, and other topics from 1961–1970; and Secret and below files on RAND's work in the intelligence field from 1967–1970;

11. a limited number of Secret/Restricted Data and below Director of Intelligence and Assistant Chief of Staff/Intelligence *Air Intelligence Studies*, *PV Interim Memos*, *Collection Briefs*, *Air Intelligence Notes*, and *Photo Intelligence Reports* from 1950–1967;

12. Assistant Chief of Staff/Studies and Analysis records, including but not limited to the Top Secret/Restricted Data *Tactical Air Warfare Study II* from 1965–1967; Secret/Restricted Data and below reports and files on force structure, weapons systems, reconnaissance systems, Vietnam, and other topics from 1965–1971; and Secret/Restricted Data and below studies on airlift, aerospace rescue and recovery, fighter interceptors and surface-to-air missiles, tactical aircraft basing, bomber penetration, comparison of worldwide tactical air forces, and other topics from 1966–1967;

13. a limited number of Secret/Restricted Data and below Office of Operations Analysis memos, files, and reports from 1950–1970;

14. Top Secret/Restricted Data and below agendas, minutes, reports, subject files, and other records of the Scientific Advisory Board from the early 1960s to 1974;

15. Top Secret/Restricted Data and below Joint Continental Defense Systems Integration Plan Staff records from 1968–1972;

16. Secret and below Directorate of Command, Communications & Control subject files from 1970–1974;

17. Top Secret/Restricted Data and below Directorate of Aerospace Programs master copies of programming documents from 1956–1966;

18. Top Secret/Restricted Data and below Directorate of Programs Peacetime Program files from 1968–1975;

19. Secret and below Inspector General files from 1952–1966;

20. a wide range of Secret/Restricted Data and below historical documents collected by the Office of Air Force History in 1968–1971 from the Air Staff and major commands;

21. Top Secret/Restricted Data and below Air Force Office of Atomic Energy-1/Air Force Technical Applications Center R&D planning and program files, budget files, politico-military files, analyses, studies, reports, and other records from the 1950s and 1960s;

22. Top Secret/Restricted Data and below Tactical Air Command war plans from 1965–1969;

23. Secret and below Directorate of Operational Requirements files on the F-105 from 1951–1966;

24. Secret and below Assistant for Foreign Development Mutual Weapons Development files from 1959–1967.

Other records that are not eligible for transfer to RG 341 at the College Park National Archives by 2001 include:

1. a limited number of Top Secret/Restricted Data and below Department of Defense reports and correspondence from the Chief of Staffs' files from 1947–1984;

2. Secret and below Chief of Staff and Secretary of the Air Force general correspondence files from 1995–1999;

3. Top Secret/Restricted Data and below agendas and recommendations of the Air Force Council, as well as the Chief of Staff decisions thereon, from 1974 into the mid-1980s (it is not known where the minutes are);

4. Top Secret/Restricted Data and below reports from 1974–1975 of the groups that advised the Air Force Council, including the Air Staff Board, Force Structure Committee, Program Review Committee, Air Defense Panel, C3 Panel, Reconnaissance/Intelligence Panel, Space Panel, Strategic Panel, and Tactical Panel;

5. Top Secret/Restricted Data and below Directorate of Plans USAF War and Mobilization Plans from 1970–1988;

6. Secret/Restricted Data and below planning records of the Strategic Planning Division from 1979–1985;

7. Secret/Restricted Data and below Arms Control and International Negotiations Division geographic and subjective wartime planning records and operations analyses and reports from 1979–1987;

8. Secret/Restricted Data and below Deputy Chief of Staff/Plans & Operations Follow on Forces Attack and Joint Theater Air Issues records from 1984–1988;

9. Secret/Restricted Data and below agendas, minutes, reports, subject files, and other records of the Scientific Advisory Board from the late 1970s;

10. Top Secret/Restricted Data and below Directorate of Programs Peacetime Program files from the late 1970s;

11. Secret and below Directorate of Aerospace Program program documents from 1967–1968;

12. Secret/Restricted Data and below minutes of the 1972–1984 meetings of the Requirements Review Group under the Requirements Division;

13. Secret/Restricted Data and below Secretary of Defense Decision Guidance and USAF Program Change Decisions on weapons, bases, and other topics from 1965–1966;

14. Secret and below Air Force Regulations, Notices, and Directives from the early 1970s into the 1980s;

Record Group 342 contains the records of non-headquarters commands, activities, and organizations (for example, the Air Force Systems Command, Military Airlift Command, and Tactical Air Command). At the College Park National Archives, RG 342 has more than 17.5 million pages of textual records and a large number of nontextual records. Four regional National Archives have RG 342 holdings, which together total less than 125,000 pages. Records at the College Park National Archives include:

1. microfilm copies of periodic and programmatic histories of Army Air Forces and Air Force headquarters offices and other commands, activities, and organizations from the 1920s into the early 1970s. (Many of the postwar histories are still classified. The problem is compounded by the fact that they are on microfilm. While the paper copy of a history may have been reviewed and released at least in part by the U.S. Air Force Historical Research Agency, *redaction* is of course impossible with microfilm and thus the entire microfilm copy of the history remains classified.);

2. Assistant Chief of Staff/Intelligence, Strategic Air Command, Military Airlift Command, Pacific Air Forces, 8th Air Force, and 7th Air Force records from the 1960s and early 1970s pertaining to air operations in

Southeast Asia (these records have been reviewed for declassification and *processed*);

3. 5th Air Force operations analysis reports and mission and unit reports from 1950–1953 on air operations in the Korean War (these records have been reviewed for declassification and *processed*);

4. research and development project files of the Engineering Division, Air Material Command from 1938 to 1951. (All these records have been reviewed for declassification and *processed*. There is no printed *finding aid*, however, and the only index is contained on 100 microfiche cards. Apart from the sheer size of the index, it is difficult to use because the records are only listed by project or contract number.);

5. a limited number of Top Secret/Restricted Data/Single Integrated Operational Plan and below Strategic Air Command operations planning files from 1947–1964 and operations plans and orders from 1949–1965; Pacific Air Forces operations plans from 1953–1966; Air Defense Command operations plans from 1946–1948; Air Force Logistics Command and predecessor operations plans from 1953–1960; Air Force Systems Command and predecessor operations orders from 1952–1959; Continental Air Defense Command emergency war plans and operational histories from 1949–1965 and operations plans and orders from 1952–1961; and Tactical Air Command operations plans and orders from 1951–1964. (These records were reviewed for declassification, but the Air Force concluded little information could be declassified and declared them exempt from automatic declassification—researchers must file a FOIA or MDR request to try to see any of the records.);

6. a small quantity of Top Secret/Restricted Data/Single Integrated Operational Plan and below operations plans and orders and related records of many numbered air forces, air divisions, wings, groups, and squadrons from the 1940s into the 1960s. (These records were reviewed for declassification, but the Air Force concluded little information could be declassified and declared most exempt from automatic declassification—researchers must file a FOIA or MDR request to try see any of the records.);

7. a limited number of Top Secret/Restricted Data and below Air Force Special Weapons Center correspondence files on various weapons systems from 1946–1954. (These records were reviewed for declassification, but the Air Force concluded little information could be declassified and declared them exempt from automatic declassification—researchers must file a FOIA or MDR request to try to see any of the records.).

Record Group 342 at the Washington National Records Center has more than 165 million pages of largely classified records as of 2000 (35% *per-*

*manent*, 25% *temporary*, and 40% *unappraised*). As part of the P-2000 Project, about 4.1 million pages of unclassified *permanent* records and 2.6 million pages of classified *permanent* records will be transferred to RG 342 at the College Park National Archives by the end of 2001. Although most if not all of the classified *permanent* records will have been reviewed for declassification by the time of their transfer, they will not be available to the public until they are possibly re-reviewed by the DOE under the Kyl Plan and then *processed* by the National Archives. The records to be transferred include:

1. a large number of Secret and below Air Technical Intelligence Center/ Foreign Technology Division studies, reports, foreign development files, translations, contract files, and related records from 1947 into the early 1970s;

2. Secret and below indexes to the 1951–1965 Air Technical Intelligence Center/Foreign Technology Division reports and studies;

3. Secret and below Wright Air Development Center/Aeronautical Systems Division R&D project reports, R&D planning files, R&D development files, contract files, and related records from the early 1950s into the 1970s;

4. Secret/Restricted Data and below Air Defense Command/Aerospace Defense Command, Continental Air Command, and North American Air Defense Command headquarters general correspondence files, publications, regulations, manuals, OPLANS, and OPORDS from 1966–1975 (as mentioned in the section on records of interservice agencies, RG 334 at the Washington National Records Center also has records of some these commands);

5. Secret and below North American Air Defense Command/Air Force Space Command Space & Warning System Center space object detection & tracking system element data from 1986–1990 and observation data from 1973–1990;

6. Secret and below Air Force Communications Service/Air Force Communications Command headquarters general correspondence files, Instructions, Directives, publications, and related records from the 1960s;

7. a limited number of Air Force Special Weapons Center staff studies, analyses, and summaries; and R&D project and program files from the early 1960s;

8. Secret and below Arnold Engineering Development Center finished foreign intelligence reports and R&D files from the 1960s;

9. Secret/Restricted Data and below Air Force Systems Command headquarters publications, RDT&E program documents, general corre-

spondence files, R&D project case files, AFSC meeting reports, AFSC Commanders' Conference reports, and AFSC/AFLAC/AMC Commanders' Conference reports from 1961–1968; and Secret/Restricted Data and below R&D development plans from 1965 into the early 1970s;

10. Secret and below intelligence reports from the Air Force Eastern Test Range on Soviet and United States satellites, missile ranges, and ground-based tracking systems from 1962–1965; and plans, logs, and related records from 1966–1967;

11. Secret/Restricted Data and below Air Force Office of Atomic Energy-1/Air Force Technical Applications Center R&D test analysis and evaluation reports and R&D project case files from 1946–1975; scientific and technical reference files from the 1950s to 1975; data collection records from the 1960s into the 1970s; and headquarters correspondence files from 1973–1974;

12. Top Secret/Restricted Data and below USAF Intelligence Service History Office records, including files from 1941–1967 on counterinsurgency, the Defense Intelligence Plan, space surveillance, and Soviet partisan operations in World War II; files from 1949–1962 on the Soviet military structure and weapons systems; Special Study Group background documents from 1950–1958; and Major General George Keegan's personal papers from 1948–1958;

13. Top Secret/Restricted Data and below Commander in Chief, Pacific Air Forces wartime planning records, regulations, and publications from 1966–1972 (as discussed in the section on records of interservice agencies, RG 334 at the Washington National Records Center also has Pacific Air Forces records);

14. a limited number of Ballistic Missiles Division/Space and Missiles Systems Organization files from the early 1960s;

15. Strategic Air Command headquarters records, including Top Secret/Restricted Data/Single Integrated Operational Plan/Extremely Sensitive Information OPLANS and EWOS from 1968–1972; Top Secret/Restricted Data and below Director of Future Force Structure & Evaluation analyses and studies from 1966–1975; Top Secret/Restricted Data and below Aircraft Test Division analyses from 1963–1975; and Secret/Restricted Data and below regulations, publications, and manuals from the early 1970s;

16. Top Secret/Restricted Data and Top Secret Tactical Air Command OPLANS and OPORDS from 1962–1975;

17. Top Secret/Restricted Data and Top Secret U.S. Air Force Europe headquarters OPLANS from 1964–1973 and Secret/Restricted Data and

below general correspondence files from the late 1960s and early 1970s.

Records that are not eligible for transfer to RG 342 at the College Park National Archives by 2001 include the following:

1. a large number of Secret and below Foreign Technology Division studies, reports, foreign development files, translations, correspondence files, contract files, and related records from the early 1970s into the 1980s;

2. Secret and below Aeronautical Systems Division R&D project reports, R&D planning files, R&D development files, contract files, and related records from the early 1970s into the 1990s;

3. Secret/Restricted Data and below Air Force Systems Command headquarters publications, RDT&E program documents, general correspondence files, and R&D project case files from 1969 into the 1980s; Secret/Restricted Data and below R&D development plans from the 1970s; Secret/Restricted Data and below Committee for Joint Services Activities meeting and conference records from 1975–1979; and Secret/Restricted Data and below War & Contingency Support Plans and War & Mobilization Plans from the 1970s and 1980s;

4. Top Secret/Restricted Data and below Air Research and Development Command/Air Force Systems Command historical records (studies, appraisals, and program reviews) from 1954–1969 on a wide range of subjects;

5. Secret and below Armament Development Test Center R&D project case files from the 1960s;

6. Secret/Restricted Data and below Air Force Special Weapons Center staff studies, analyses, and summaries; R&D project and program files; and related records from the mid-1960s into the 1980s;

7. Secret and below Rome Air Development Center R&D project and program files, contract files, and related records from the 1960s into the 1990s;

8. Secret and below Air Force Flight Test Center project and program files and related records from the 1960s;

9. Secret and below Arnold Engineering Development Center R&D project and program files and related records from the 1970s and 1980s;

10. Secret and below Office of Aerospace Research R&D project and program files, contract files, and related records from the 1960s;

11. Secret and below Air Force Weapons Laboratory reports, program files, general correspondence files, and related records from the 1970s;

12. Secret and below Ballistic Missiles Division/Space and Missiles Systems Organization finished intelligence reports from the early 1960s to 1975;

13. Secret/Restricted Data and below Ballistic Missiles Division and predecessor organization reports, R&D case files, program files, general correspondence files, and related records from 1951–1967;

14. Secret and below Space and Missile Systems Organization reports, R&D case files, program files, general correspondence files, and related records from 1967 into the 1970s;

15. Secret and below Special Air Warfare Center/Special Operations Force headquarters general correspondence files, Orders, Directives, and publications from 1967;

16. Secret and below Alaskan Command reports from 1966–1970 (as mentioned in the section on records of interservice agencies, RG 334 at the Washington National Records Center also has Alaskan Command records);

17. Top Secret/Restricted Data and Top Secret U.S. Air Force Europe headquarters OPLANS from 1974–1975; and Secret/Restricted Data and below general correspondence files, Regulations, studies, and manuals from the early 1970s;

18. a wide range of Strategic Air Command headquarters records, including but not limited to Top Secret/Restricted Data and below Commander in Chief general correspondence files from the late 1960s to the late 1980s; Top Secret/Restricted Data and below Deputy Chief of Staff/Plans and Deputy Chief of Staff/Operations general correspondence files from 1973–1989; Top Secret/Restricted Data/Single Integrated Operational Plan/Extremely Sensitive Information wartime plans from 1973–1987 (OPLANS, EWOS, COPSACS, CINCSAC OPLANS, and CINCSAC CONPLANS); Top Secret/Restricted Data and below Operational Analysis reports from the 1970s and 1980s; Secret/Restricted Data and below Ballistic Missile Evaluation Administration Division files from the 1970s and 1980s; and Secret/Restricted Data and below minutes to meetings of the SAC Council and other groups from the 1970s and 1980s;

19. a limited number of Secret and below 7th Air Force headquarters files from the 1960s;

20. Secret and below Air Force Communications Service/Air Force Communications Command headquarters general correspondence files, In-

structions, Directives, publications, and related records from the 1970s into the 1990s;

21. Secret/Restricted Data and below Air Force Technical Applications Center R&D case files, R&D project case files, data collection records, intelligence reference records, technical reports, test and evaluation reports, and general correspondence files from the 1970s and 1980s; politico-military matter files from the 1970s and 1980s; planning records from the 1960s and 1970s; and AFTAC Council records from the 1980s;

22. mostly unclassified Air Force Astronautics Laboratory and Air Force Rocket Propulsion Laboratory R&D project case files from the 1960s into the 1990s;

23. unclassified Office of Scientific Research reports, R&D files, contract files, and related records from the 1960s and 1970s;

24. unclassified Cambridge Research Laboratory reports, R&D files, contract files, and related records from 1952 into the 1990s.

Record Group 342 at the San Bruno Federal Records Center has about 11.5 million pages of records as of 2000 (5% *permanent* and 95% *temporary*). The vast majority are unclassified administrative records, but there are also the following classified *permanent* records of interest:

1. Secret/Restricted Data and below general correspondence files from 1960–1963 of the Commander, Ballistic Missiles Division, Air Force Systems Command;

2. Secret/Restricted Data and below Ballistic Missiles Division Atlas R&D project case files from 1957–1965;

3. Secret/Restricted Data and below Ballistic Missiles Division Atlas, Titan, Thor, and Minuteman management reports, program schedules, and data documents from 1955–1962;

4. Secret and below Air Force Advisory Group (South Vietnam) files from 1973.

It is not known whether any of these have been reviewed for declassification. Even if they have been, they will not be available to the public until they are transferred to the San Bruno National Archives, possibly reviewed by the DOE under the Kyl Plan, and then *processed* by the National Archives.

Record Group 342 at the St. Louis Federal Records Center has about 355 million pages of records as of 2000 (77% *temporary* and 23% *unappraised*). The vast majority are civilian personnel records and military personnel and medical records. There are some relevant records, however, and these include:

1. Secret/Restricted Data and below Strategic Air Command headquarters publications, general correspondence files, organization planning files, studies, and other records from 1947 into the early 1960s;

2. Secret and below Pacific Air Forces headquarters general correspondence files and publications from the mid-1950s;

3. Secret below U.S. Air Force Europe headquarters general correspondence files, studies, development documents, and other records from the late 1940s into the early 1960s;

4. Secret and below Air Defense Command headquarters general correspondence files, studies, and publications from the 1950s and early 1960s;

5. Secret/Restricted Data and below Missile Development Center (Holloman AFB) headquarters studies, analyses, publications and other records from the 1950s and 1960s.[20]

It is doubtful that any of these have been reviewed for declassification because they are not *permanent* records at this point. Even assuming that they are eventually appraised as *permanent* and reviewed for declassification, they will not be available to the public until they are transferred to a National Archives, possibly re-reviewed by the DOE under the Kyl Plan, and then *processed* by the National Archives.

Record Group 342 at the Boston Federal Records Center has about 15 million pages of records as of 2000, but they are almost exclusively unclassified *temporary* records from Hanscom Air Force Base and other Air Force facilities in the region.[21]

Record Group 18 (records of the Army Air Forces) at the College Park National Archives also has some Air Force records from the late 1940s, principally in the *entries* containing the Secret and below files of the Commanding General and the ones containing R&D files. All the records have been reviewed for declassification and *processed*, and the *finding aids* to them are good. There are no records in RG 18 at the Washington National Records Center.

### Air Force Records at Air Force Commands, Presidential Libraries, and the Library of Congress

There are numerous Air Force commands around the world, and some have significant record holdings with which researchers should be familiar. It should be noted, however, that the following list is not comprehensive as there is no information available on the holdings at some commands.

The U.S. Air Force Historical Research Agency (AFHRA) at Maxwell Air Force Base, Alabama, has a large number of significant collections. The AFHRA can be contacted at 600 Chennault Circle, Maxwell AFB, AL 36112–6424; 334–953–2395; or www.au.af.mil/au/afhra. Most of its holdings are duplicated either in paper form or on microfilm at the Air Force History Office (AFHO) at Bolling Air Force Base in Washington, D.C. The AFHO can be contacted at Building 5681, Bolling AFB, Washington, D.C. 20332–6089; 202–404–2167; or www.airforcehistory.hq.af.mil.

In addition to a great amount of secondary literature, the AFHRA and AFHO have the following broad categories of records. First, they have all the periodic and programmatic histories of Air Force headquarters offices and other Air Force commands, activities, and organizations from 1947 to the present. The majority of these remain classified, with the exception of a number of histories of the Air Research and Development Command/Air Force Systems Command and their subordinate organizations, which have been the subject of ongoing declassification review under E.O. 12958. Second, the AFHRA and AFHO have almost 400 personal paper collections of various military and civilian personnel of the Air Force and the Army Air Forces. A complete listing of the collections, along with a brief description of the contents of each, is available on the AFHRA's homepage. The usefulness of the collections varies widely. Some collections are quite small and contain few official records, while others are large and have a considerable number of official records. Third, they have a huge collection of oral history interviews of military and civilian personnel of the Air Force and the Army Air Forces. For example, there are interviews (in some cases, multiple interviews) with Generals White, Weyland, Vandenberg, Twining, McKee, and LeMay. The usefulness of the interviews varies widely, depending on their length and the subjects discussed. Only a small number are classified. Interviews conducted through 1988 are listed in *Catalog of the United States Air Force Oral History Collection* (U.S. Air Force Historical Research Center, 1989). Fourth, the AFHRA and AFHO have the numbered USAF historical studies, which are studies done over the years by USAF historians on a wide range of topics and which primarily are for internal USAF use. Only a small number are classified. A partial listing of the numbered studies is available on the AFHRA's homepage. Fifth, the two repositories have the reports of Project CHECO (Contemporary Historical Examination of Current Operations). This project began in 1962 and, among other things, produced a number of reports on the air war in Vietnam. Most have been reviewed for declassification under E.O. 12958. Sixth, the AFHRA and AFHO have the Gulf War Air Power Survey collection, which includes unit histories, material used in writing the survey, and imagery. Detailed information on this collection is available on the AFHRA's homepage. Lastly, they have supporting documentation used in writing some of the periodic and programmatic histories, a limited number of research and development reports, small collections of office correspondence files, Air War College theses and lectures, and other diverse holdings. Many of these records are classified.

The Pacific Air Forces History Office holds about 100,000 classified and declassified documents relating to that command dating from World War II to the present. These include monographs, official correspondence and studies, oral history interviews, end-of-tour reports, and periodic and programmatic histories (copies of the histories should also be at the AFHRA and AFHO). Most of the *finding aids* are available to the public.[22] The History Office can be contacted regarding access to available records at HQ PACAF/HO, 25 E Street, Suite C-119, Hickam AFB, HI 96853-5410 or 808–449–3924. The quantity, nature, and *appraisal* status of holdings outside the History Office are unknown.

The Space and Missiles Command History Office has roughly 2.5 million pages of records and a small quantity of photographs and films. They date from 1947 to the present and include records of the current command and its predecessors, the Western Development Division, Ballistic Missiles Division, Space and Missile Systems Organization, and Space Systems Division. The majority of the records are classified, as are the *finding aids*.[23] The History Office can be contacted concerning access to available records at SMC/HO, Suite 1467, 2420 Vela Way, Los Angeles AFB, Los Angeles, CA 90245–4659 or at smc.ho@losangeles.af.mil. The quantity, nature, and *appraisal* status of holdings outside the History Office are unknown.

The Air Force Space Command History Office has about 3.75 million pages of mostly classified records and a small quantity of mostly classified records stored on microfilm, microfiche, aperture cards, and magneto-optical disks. The date range is from the end of World War II to the present, and the records are from the current command and a number of predecessor organizations. There are materials concerning air defense radars and weapons systems, missile warning radars, space surveillance, guided missiles, military satellite systems, satellite command and control, launch vehicles, military space policy, and other related topics. The *finding aids* are classified. The History Office can be contacted about access to available records at 719–554–3081.[24] The quantity, nature, and *appraisal* status of holdings outside the History Office are unknown.

The Alaskan Command History Office has an archives that consists mostly of the periodic and programmatic histories of the command from 1947 to the present (copies of these should also be at the AFHRA and AFHO). The majority of the records have been reviewed for declassification and are available to the public.[25] The History Office can be contacted at 907–552–5217. The quantity, nature, and *appraisal* status of holdings outside the History Office are unknown.

The Special Collections section of the Air Force Academy library has four collections of interest: (1) background materials used by Lt. Col. Harry

Borowski, USAF (Ret.) in writing *A Hollow Threat: The Strategic Air Command and Containment Before Korea*, (2) background materials collected by Dr. Murray Green on General Arnold, (3) personal papers of Lieutenant General Kuter, (4) personal papers of General Twining. All have been reviewed for declassification and are available to the public. The Special Collections section can be contacted at 719-333-4674.

The Air Force Material Command History Office has a small archives, but most of the holdings are classified and there is no public access.[26] Commands that do not have any archives or central records storage facility include the Air Combat Command and the Air Force Technical Applications Center.[27] The quantity, nature, and *appraisal* status of the holdings at these commands are unknown.

The Truman Library has the personal papers of Thomas Finletter (Secretary of the Air Force from 1950–1953) and the personal papers of Stuart Symington (Secretary of the Air Force from 1947–1950). The personal papers of General Norstad are at the Eisenhower Library. All three of these collections are open to the public.

There are also several relevant personal paper collections in the Manuscript Division of the Library of Congress, including those of Generals Arnold, White, LeMay, Spaatz, Fairchild, Twining, and Vandenberg. The usefulness of these collections varies widely, depending primarily on the type and amount of official records contained therein. General Arnold's papers have few postwar materials, and what there are consist almost exclusively of speeches, writings, and related items. General White's collection is much more significant, containing a large number of official records from his tenure as Chief of Staff (1957–1961). Approximately half the materials remain classified. Similarly, General LeMay's papers have a considerable amount of official records from his tenure as head of the Strategic Air Command (1948–1957), Vice Chief of Staff (1958–1961), and Chief of Staff (1961–1965). Although many of the items are declassified, some significant portions remain classified. The papers of General Spaatz have a limited amount of official records from his service as Chief of Staff (1946–1948), all of which are declassified. General Fairchild's collection has only a few official records from his tenure as Vice Chief of Staff from 1948–1950. General Twining's papers have a large amount of official records from his service as Vice Chief of Staff (1950–1953) and Chief of Staff (1953–1957). Although the majority of the collection is declassified, some important parts remain classified. The collection of General Vandenberg has only a limited number of official records from his tenure as Chief of Staff (1948–1953), all of which are declassified.

Requests under the FOIA or MDR for records at Federal records centers or at Air Force commands can be submitted to the commanding officer of the command holding the records, or if there is doubt as to which command holds the records, the requests should be sent to the Secretary of the Air

Force, ATTN: SAF/AAIS (FOIA), Pentagon, Room 4A1088C, Washington, D.C. 20330–1000.

### Arms Control and Disarmament Agency (ACDA) / U.S. Disarmament Administration (USDA) and Predecessor Agency Records at the National Archives and Federal Record Centers

A large number of records of the ACDA (1961–1999),[28] USDA (1960–1961), and various Department of State and White House offices involved in disarmament prior to 1960 are in RG 383 at the College Park National Archives and Washington National Records Center. No other National Archives or Federal records center has any RG 383 holdings.

The ACDA estimated in 1995 that it had about 3.2 million pages of *permanent* pre-1975 classified records subject to E.O. 12958.[29] By 1999, it had reviewed all of its subject records and thus qualified as one of the few agencies that had accomplished this by the original deadline of April 2000.[30]

At the College Park National Archives, RG 383 contains about 2 million pages of records. Records that are either unclassified or that have been reviewed for declassification and *processed* include:

1. speeches of the ACDA Director, William Foster, from 1960–1968;
2. speeches of the ACDA Director, Paul Warnke, from 1977–1978;
3. minutes of the 1962–1978 meetings of the United Nations Conference of the Committee on Disarmament and the 1979–1982 meetings of the United Nations Committee on Disarmament;
4. unofficial transcriptions of informal meetings from 1979–1982 of the United Nations Committee on Disarmament and its Ad Hoc Working Groups;
5. numbered documents from 1962–1978 of the U.S. delegation to the United Nations Conference of the Committee on Disarmament;
6. Secret and below 1961–1962 ACDA subject files and budget files;
7. Secret and below Office of the Director briefing books from 1961–1962;
8. Secret and below reports on U.S. government studies on arms control and disarmament from 1962–1966;
9. Secret and below ACDA reports and position papers from 1962–1966;
10. Secret and below minutes, background papers, and related materials concerning the Conference on Discontinuing of Nuclear Weapons Tests held from 1958–1961;

11. Secret and below Office of Public Affairs reading files and records re-
    garding conferences from 1978–1980 and a report from 1980 on the
    settlement of the *U.S. v. The Progressive Inc.* lawsuit;

12. Secret and below Office of General Counsel files on arms control trea-
    ties and related issues from the 1970s.

The one set of records that is still classified is the Top Secret/Restricted
Data and below agendas, minutes, and reports of the General Advisory
Committee on Arms Control and Disarmament from 1969–1972.

At the Washington National Records Center, RG 383 has more than 4.5
million pages of records of the ACDA and its predecessors as of 2000
(almost all of which are *permanent*). As part of the P-2000 Project, about
600,000 pages of classified *permanent* records, as well as a small number
of classified nontextual records, will be transferred to RG 383 at the College Park National Archives by the end of 2001. Although all have been
reviewed for declassification, they will not be available to the public until
they are possibly re-reviewed by the DOE under the Kyl Plan and then
*processed* by the National Archives. The records to be transferred include:

1. Secret/Restricted Data and below Office of the Director subject files
   from 1961–1966; staff meeting files from 1963–1967; correspondence
   with the White House, Department of State, and Department of Defense from 1958–1968; disarmament policy subject files from 1961–
   1968; Test Ban Treaty violation and verification subject files from
   1962–1966; and SALT contingency and negotiating papers from 1969;

2. Secret/Restricted Data and below Office of the Executive Director subject files from 1961–1969 and NPT and nuclear safeguards subject files
   from 1960–1968;

3. Secret/Restricted Data and below ACDA subject files from 1963;

4. Secret/Restricted Data and below records of Special Assistant to the
   Director, Clement Conger, including working files from 1961–1969;
   general files from 1962–1968; files on the 1967 deputies meetings,
   1964 Committee of Principals meetings, and 1964 General Advisory
   Committee meetings; files on criteria for militarily acceptable comprehensive arms control and disarmament proposals; files on draft treaties
   from 1963–1965; and files on the Intelligence Committee from 1961;

5. Secret/Restricted Data and below Deputy Director Adrian Fisher
   chronological and working files from 1958–1969 and subject files from
   1961–1968;

6. Secret and below distribution and no-distribution telegrams from
   1961–1965;

7. Secret/Restricted Data and below General Advisory Committee on Arms Control and Disarmament subject files from 1961–1969;

8. Secret/Restricted Data and below Chief Science Advisor subject files from 1962–1966;

9. Secret/Restricted Data and below Office of General Counsel general subject files from 1961–1968 and subject files on ACDA authorizing legislation and appropriations from 1961–1968;

10. Secret/Restricted Data and below Office of Public Affairs historical documents on the NPT and the Johnson Historical Project from 1961–1969, and Secret and below chronological files from 1983–1984;

11. Secret/Restricted Data and below Bureau of Intelligence, Verification, and Information Management and predecessor office files of U.S. delegation papers at the Eighteen Nation Disarmament Conference from 1945–1969; files on Committee of Principals actions from 1965–1968; and Secret and below subject files on the United Nations General Assembly from 1961–1968;

12. Secret/Restricted Data and below subject files from 1960–1969 of the Economic Office under the Bureau of Intelligence, Verification, and Information Management;

13. Secret/Restricted Data and below Bureau of Nonproliferation & Regional Arms Control subject files on Project CLOUD GAP field test programs from 1963–1976 and Project CLOUD GAP field test films from 1964–1966.

Other records that are not eligible for transfer to RG 383 at the College Park National Archives by 2001 include:

1. Top Secret/Restricted Data and below Office of the Director historical files on the Atomic Energy Commission, USDA, and ACDA from 1945–1978;

2. Top Secret/Restricted Data and below Office of the Director files and SALT Ambassador files from 1969–1979 on cruise missiles, SALT, Comprehensive Test Ban Treaty, and memcons with France and the United Kingdom;

3. Top Secret/Restricted Data and below Office of the Director briefing books from 1963–1980 on disarmament and arms control; files from 1963–1980 on National Security Study Memorandums, National Security Decision Memorandums, National Security Decisions, Presidential Review Memoranda, and White House correspondence; and memcons with foreign officials from 1963–1980;

4. Secret and below Office of the Director speech files and congressional correspondence files from 1964–1975;

5. Secret/Restricted Data and below Office of the Director files from 1963–1989 on anti-ballistic missiles, INF, and cruise missiles;

6. Secret/Restricted Data and below Office of the Director subject files on SALT and INF from 1979–1982;

7. Top Secret/Restricted Data and below Office of the Director Standing Consultative Commission files from 1968–1985 on anti-satellite weapons, and Standing Consultative Commission files from 1963–1989 on anti-submarine warfare;

8. Secret/Restricted Data and below Office of the Director general subject files, chronological files, and tasker files from the late 1960s into the early 1990s;

9. Secret/Restricted Data and below subject files from 1975–1986 of Assistant Director Lewis Dunn, head of the Bureau of Nuclear & Weapons Control;

10. Secret/Restricted Data and below general files and meeting files from 1981–1986 of the Special Advisor for Arms Control Talks, Ambassador Rowny;

11. Top Secret/Restricted Data and below subject and other files from the late 1960s to 1980 of Special Assistant to the Director, Clement Clonger;

12. Secret/Restricted Data and below files from 1960–1979 of Ambassador Gerard Smith;

13. Top Secret/Restricted Data and below chronological files of Paul Warnke from 1966–1972;

14. Secret and below files of Ambassador Stephen Ledogar from 1981–1997 on the Conference on Disarmament, Conference on Security and Cooperation in Europe, and chemical warfare negotiations;

15. Secret/Restricted Data and below Arms Transfer Division, Bureau of Nuclear & Weapons Control Arms Transfer Case Memos from the 1970s on;

16. Secret/Restricted Data and below Defense Programs & Analysis Division, Bureau of Weapons Evaluation & Control/Bureau of Nuclear & Weapons Control chronological files and background material for Arms Control Impact Statements from 1969–1992;

17. Secret/Restricted Data and below Bureau of Nonproliferation & Regional Arms Control files from 1961–1979 on peaceful nuclear explosions and the production, cut-off, and transfer of nuclear weapons material;

18. Secret/Restricted Data and below Bureau of Nonproliferation & Regional Arms Control and predecessor office subject files from 1957–1974 on military safeguards;

19. Secret/Restricted Data and below Bureau of Weapons Evaluation & Control files from 1972–1983 on comprehensive test bans;

20. Secret/Restricted Data and below Bureau of Intelligence, Verification & Information Management subject files from the 1970s and 1980s; files on the ABM, chemical weapons, and the NPT from 1973–1987; and files on Antisatellite Backup, START, and the Standing Consultative Commission from 1974–1985;

21. Secret and below International Security Policy Division, Bureau of Multilateral Affairs files on the Conference on Security and Cooperation in Europe and the Conference on Disarmament from 1977–1986; and briefing memos, tasking sheets, and activity reports from the mid-1980s;

22. Secret and below Bureau of Multilateral Affairs files from the Hague on the Conference on Disarmament, chemical warfare negotiations, Working Groups, and U.S./U.S.S.R. bilaterals from 1974–1993; and files from Vienna on the Mutual Balanced Forces Reduction negotiations and the Conference on Disarmament implementation from 1973–1987;

23. Secret/Restricted Data and below Science & Technology Division, Bureau of Multilateral Affairs files from 1964–1985 on International Atomic Energy Agency Ad Hoc Advisory Group meetings, Lucerne and Lugano Conferences, Conference of the Committee on Disarmament meetings on chemical warfare, and the Qattara Depression Project;

24. Top Secret/Restricted Data and below Science & Technology Division, Bureau of Multilateral Affairs and predecessor office files from 1958–1988 on the Threshold Test Ban Treaty, negotiations regarding peaceful nuclear explosions, and Comprehensive Test Ban Treaty negotiations;

25. Secret and below Science & Technology Division, Bureau of Multilateral Affairs files on outer space arms control from 1966–1987;

26. Secret and below Chemical & Biological Policy Division, Bureau of Multilateral Affairs files from the Hague from 1974–1993 on the Chemical Warfare Convention, Conference on Disarmament, Western Group meetings, and the U.S. delegation to the Organization for Prohibition of Chemical Warfare;

27. Top Secret/Restricted Data and below Chemical & Biological Policy Division, Bureau of Multilateral Affairs files on chemical warfare and radiological warfare from 1976–1987;

28. Secret and below European Security Policy Division, Bureau of Multilateral Affairs files on the Mutual Balanced Forces Reduction negotiations from 1963–1989; and files on the Conference on Security and Cooperation in Europe meetings from 1972–1988;

29. Top Secret/Restricted Data and below International Security & Nuclear Policy Division, Bureau of Multilateral Affairs and predecessor office files on the Comprehensive Test Ban Treaty negotiations and trilaterals from 1958–1985;

30. Top Secret/Restricted Data and below International Relations Division, Bureau of Multilateral Affairs files from 1965–1984 on chemical warfare and biological warfare arms control, nuclear testing verification and compliance, missile technology, missile countermeasures, missile survivability, and missile technology transfer;

31. Top Secret/Restricted Data and below Strategic Negotiations & Implementation Division, Bureau of Strategic & Eurasian Affairs files on SALT from 1962–1985;

32. Secret and below Strategic Negotiations & Implementation Division, Bureau of Strategic & Eurasian Affairs files on PRD-34 and START from 1991–1996;

33. Secret and below Office of General Counsel files on Soviet statements at the Nuclear and Space Arms Talks from 1985–1995; files on Conventional Armed Forces in Europe talks from 1989–1995; and files on the Chemical Warfare Convention Treaty and bilateral destruction;

34. Secret/Restricted Data and below Office of General Counsel subject files from 1963–1987 on SALT, START, INF, and the Threshold Test Ban Treaty; files from 1959–1989 on SALT I accident agreements, the Backfire bomber, SALT I ratification, and the NPT; files on congressional hearings and legislation from the late 1960s on; and general subject files from the late 1960s into the 1990s;

35. Top Secret/Restricted Data and below Office of General Counsel files from 1971–1987 on ratification of the SALT and ABM Treaty;

36. Secret and below Office of Public Affairs files from 1982–1985 on the Conference of the Committee on Disarmament; and files from 1932–1987 on the Conference on Non-Nuclear States, United Nations Disarmament Commission, League of Nations Conference for Reduction of Armaments, Conference on Surprise Attack, Ten Power Disarmament Commission, and Sea Bed Treaty negotiations;

37. Secret/Restricted Data and below library files on ACDA publications, ACDA external research reports, and State Department publications on arms control from 1945–1985;

38. Top Secret/Restricted Data and below General Advisory Committee on Arms Control and Disarmament agendas, minutes, and reports from 1961–1968 and from 1973 into the 1980s; and policy and briefing papers, subject files, and related records from 1961 into the 1980s;

39. Secret and below files from the 1950s of the USDA and Harold Stassen, Special Advisor to the President on Disarmament Matters, relating to Geneva conferences and disarmament issues.

## ACDA and USDA Records at the Department of State

There is a small library in the main Department of State building in Washington, D.C., containing many ACDA and some USDA records that is open to the public by appointment (202–647–5969). The diverse holdings of the library are completely unclassified or declassified. Among the holdings are: (1) transcripts of the Geneva disarmament conferences from 1962 to the present, (2) research reports done for the agency by defense contractors, universities, and others (there is an index for these through 1980), (3) the annual *Documents on Disarmament* prepared by the Historians Office, (4) speeches and related materials of all the ACDA directors. In addition, the library has the lengthy index of all ACDA Historical Research Studies done through 1985 by the Historians Offices of the ACDA and the USDA. Some of these are still classified, but those that are not can be made available for review at the library.

The quantity, nature, and *appraisal* status of other ACDA records still at the Department of State are not known.

Requests under the FOIA or MDR for records at the Washington National Records Center or at the Department of State should be submitted to Director, Office of Freedom of Information, Privacy, and Classification Review, Department of State, 2201 C Street, N.W., Washington, D.C. 20520.

## Department of the Army Records at the National Archives and Federal Record Centers

There are a large number of Army records in several *record groups* at the College Park National Archives and Washington National Records Center.

The Army estimated in 1995 that it had 270 million pages of *permanent* pre-1975 classified records subject to E.O. 12958.[31] As of March 1999, the Army reported that about 42 million pages had been reviewed and approximately 30 million pages declassified.[32] In early 1999, the White House granted the Army an exemption from automatic declassification for approximately 27 million pages.

The Office of the Secretary of the Army (OSA) records are in RG 335 and at the College Park National Archives, RG 335 has almost 10 million pages of records. No other National Archives has any RG 335 records. The *finding aids* are good. Records that have been reviewed for declassification and *processed* include:

1. unclassified decimal files of the Secretary from 1947–1964;
2. Secret and below State-Army-Navy Coordinating Committee and State-Army-Navy-Air Force Coordinating Committee records from 1944–1949;
3. Secret/Restricted Data and below decimal files of the Under Secretary from 1947–1954 and 1965–1972;
4. Secret and below decimal files of the Assistant Secretary of the Army (Installations & Logistics) from 1955–1964;
5. Top Secret and below files of the Assistant Secretary of the Army (General Management) from 1950–1953;
6. Secret and below Office of General Counsel files on Congressional investigations from 1954 and files on domestic civil disturbances from 1963–1968;
7. Secret and below Chief of Legislative Liaison files from 1955–1964.

Records that are still classified or that have been reviewed for declassification but await possible re-review by the DOE under the Kyl Plan and then *processing* by the National Archives before they will be available to the public include:

1. Confidential through Top Secret/Restricted Data decimal files of the Secretary from 1947–1964;
2. Top Secret and below Cuban Crisis files of the Secretary from 1962–1964;
3. Top Secret and below daily and weekly *Summaries of Significant Actions* for the Secretary from 1960–1969;
4. Top Secret and below Chief of Staff *Summaries of Action* from 1951–1952;
5. Top Secret/Restricted Data and below National Security Council agendas and records of action from 1960–1963, numbered documents from 1947–1961, memorandums from 1961–1962, and progress reports from 1950–1961;

6. Top Secret/Restricted Data and Top Secret decimal files of the Under Secretary from 1947–1952;

7. Top Secret/Restricted Data and Top Secret Assistant Secretary of the Army (Installation & Logistics) decimal files from 1955–1962.

Record Group 335 at the Washington National Records Center contains almost 22.5 million pages of records as of 2000 (20% *permanent* and 80% *temporary*). No other Federal records center has any RG 335 holdings. As part of the P-2000 Project, about 1 million pages of unclassified *permanent* records and 230,000 pages of classified *permanent* records will be transferred to RG 335 at the College Park National Archives by the end of 2001. Even if the classified *permanent* records have been reviewed for declassifi cation by the time of their transfer, they will not be available to the public until they are possibly re-reviewed by the DOE under the Kyl Plan and then *processed* by the National Archives. The records to be transferred include:

1. Top Secret/Restricted Data and below decimal files of the Secretary from 1973–1976 and Secret/Restricted Data and below chronological files from 1977–1980;

2. Top Secret/Restricted Data and below *Summaries of Significant Actions* for the Secretary from 1970–1974;

3. Top Secret/Restricted Data and below minutes of the 1966–1973 Army Policy Council meetings.

Among the records that are not eligible for transfer to RG 335 at the College Park National Archives by 2001 are:

1. Top Secret/Restricted Data and below decimal files of the Secretary from the 1980s, with a few small miscellaneous files dating from the 1950s and early 1960s;

2. Top Secret/Restricted Data and below daily and weekly *Summaries of Significant Actions* for the Secretary from 1975 into the 1980s;

3. Top Secret/Restricted Data and below decimal files of the Under Secretary from 1974 into the 1980s;

4. Top Secret/Restricted Data and below files of the Office of General Counsel, Chief of Legislative Liaison, Assistant Secretary of the Army (Financial Management), Assistant Secretary of the Army (Manpower and Reserve Affairs), Assistant Secretary of the Army (Installations and Logistics), Assistant Secretary of the Army (Research and Development), and their successors from the 1960s into the 1980s;

5. Secret/Restricted Data and below decimal files of the Chief of Staff from the 1980s.

Record Group 319 contains records of the Army Staff, and at the College Park National Archives, RG 319 contains more than 87.5 million pages of records. No other National Archives has any RG 319 records. The *finding aids* are generally good. Among the records that have been reviewed for declassification and *processed* are:

1. Top Secret/Restricted Data and Top Secret decimal files of the Chief of Staff from 1948–1952;

2. Secret/Restricted Data and below decimal files of the Chief of Staff from 1948–1955;

3. Top Secret and below indexes to the Chief of Staff Top Secret/Restricted Data and below decimal files from 1948–1962;

4. Top Secret and below General Council meeting minutes from 1942–1954 and General Staff Council meeting minutes from 1955–1958;

5. Top Secret and below incoming and outgoing messages of the Department of the Army headquarters message center from 1942–1962;

6. Secret and below Chief of Staff Regulations from 1954–1972;

7. Top Secret and below Assistant Chief of Staff/Intelligence executive office records, including project decimal files from 1941–1952; decimal files from 1941–1952; incoming and outgoing messages from 1942–1951; incoming and outgoing cables from 1942–1952; and transcripts of 1941–1946 teletype conferences between the Army and foreign military and diplomatic representatives;

8. a number of Top Secret and below records of the Collection and Dissemination Division under the Assistant Chief of Staff/Intelligence, including files from 1942–1948 relating to the escape, evasion, or capture of military personnel and to interrogations of prisoners of war; reports and messages from 1918–1951; publications ("P") files from 1946–1951; and geographical indexes to the 1944–1951 numerical series of intelligence documents;

9. a limited number of Top Secret and below intelligence and investigative dossiers on individuals and organizations from 1939–1976 of the Investigative Records Repository under the Assistant Chief of Staff/Intelligence;

10. Top Secret and below records of the Counter Intelligence Corps under the Assistant Chief of Staff/Intelligence, including official histories from 1917–1953 and background files used in writing these histories; Soviet publications on their armed forces from 1935–1959; and files from 1945–1946 on German and Austrian scientists brought to the United States under the PAPERCLIP program;

11. Top Secret/Restricted Data and below records of the executive office of the Assistant Chief of Staff/Operations and Deputy Chief of Staff

for Military Operations, including but not limited to project decimal files from 1948–1949; general decimal files from 1944–1955; general correspondence files from 1956–1960; subject indexes to the 1950–1955 classified correspondence; summary sheets from 1962; memorandums for record from 1952–1953 and 1957; minutes of division directors' meetings from 1957–1960; summaries of action from 1957; joint situation reports relating to Korea from 1951–1953; situation reports/summary of operations messages concerning Laos from 1960; correspondence files of Major General Paul Harkins from 1956; speeches of Lieutenant General C.D. Eddleman from 1957; history of the Army section of the Military Assistance Advisory Group Taiwan from 1953–1957; general correspondence files of the Strategy and Tactics Analysis Group from 1960–1962; domestic disturbance files (OPERATIONS STEEP HILL in Washington D.C., OAK TREE-PALM TREE, Arkansas, and Oxford, Mississippi) from the late 1950s and early 1960s; and records relating to electronic intelligence activities from 1955–1956;

12. a limited number of Top Secret and below records of various divisions and branches under the Assistant Chief of Staff/Operations and Deputy Chief of Staff for Military Operations, including Far East and Pacific Branch Korean armistice negotiation files and message files from 1950–1954; Foreign Military Training Division files from the 1950s and early 1960s; and Chief of Civil Affairs & Military Government executive office decimal files from 1948–1954 and general correspondence files from 1955–1962;

13. Assistant Chief of Staff/Personnel records, including but not limited to Top Secret and below executive office decimal files from 1949–1954;

14. Assistant Chief of Staff/Logistics records, including but not limited to Top Secret/Restricted Data and below executive office decimal files from 1947–1954 and General Magruder's files from 1951–1958;

15. Comptroller of the Army records, including but not limited to Top Secret and below executive office decimal files from 1947–1954, numbered memorandums from 1951–1956, and weekly activity reports from 1955–1962;

16. Chief of Legislative Liaison records, including but not limited to Top Secret and below Congressional Investigations Division decimal files and numerical-subject files from 1948–1952 and Legislative Division correspondence relating to pending and enacted legislation from 1943–1954;

17. Chief of Research and Development and predecessor executive office records, including Secret/Restricted Data and below decimal files from 1948–1952; correspondence files of Lieutenant General Trudeau from

1958–1962; general correspondence files from 1958–1959; records relating to the organization of Army R&D activities from 1943–1960; and records concerning the R&D Policy Council from 1953–1957;

18. records of various divisions and branches under the Chief of Research and Development and predecessor offices, including but not limited to Secret/Restricted Data and below Review and Analysis Branch general correspondence files from 1960–1962; Policy Branch general correspondence files from 1960–1962; Programs Branch general records from 1960–1962; Geophysical Sciences Branch general correspondence files from 1954–1962, project control files from 1955–1958, and International Geophysical Year files from 1955–1960; Physical Sciences Division general correspondence files from 1960–1962; Environmental Sciences Division general correspondence files from 1958–1962; Foreign Research Branch general correspondence files from 1960–1962; Research Program Division general correspondence files from 1962; International Division general correspondence files from 1960–1962; and Aircraft Research and Development Branch R&D project control files from 1961–1962;

19. Chief of Information records, including but not limited to Top Secret and below executive office decimal files from 1950–1954, correspondence files from 1960–1964, and weekly summaries from 1952–1953;

20. Chief of Special Warfare Confidential and below correspondence files from 1951–1954, Secret and below correspondence relating to special warfare area handbooks from 1954–1958, and Secret and below intelligence studies of communist nations from 1951–1958;

21. selected records of the United Nations Command delegation in Korea from 1951–1958, including some records of the Military Armistice Commission and the Neutral Nations Supervisory Commission (as mentioned in the section on records of international commands and organizations in which the U.S. military has participated, RG 331 and RG 333 at the College Park National Archives also have records of the United Nations Command);

22. a large number of Secret/Restricted Data and below office files, background files, publications, and unpublished manuscripts of the Chief of Military History/Center for Military History, from the 1940s through the 1970s.

Records that are still classified or that have been reviewed for declassification but await possible re-review by the DOE under the Kyl Plan and then *processing* by the National Archives before they will be available to the public include:

1. Top Secret/Restricted Data and Top Secret decimal files of the Chief of Staff from 1953–1969;

2. Secret/Restricted Data and below decimal files of the Chief of Staff from 1956–1973;

3. Top Secret/Restricted Data and below Chief of Staff memos, reports, studies, and related records from 1967–1972 collected by the Center for Military History (it is not known whether these records duplicate what is in the Chief of Staff decimal files from this period);

4. Secret/Restricted Data and below chronological files of General Johnson from 1964–1966;

5. Top Secret/Restricted Data and below cables and cable coversheets from 1961–1978 of Fritz Kraemer, Special Advisor on Politico-Military Affairs to the Chief of Staff (the cables, among other things, concern arms control, European security, terrorists, domestic dissidents, and the United Nations);

6. Top Secret/Restricted Data and below congressional testimony of the Chief of Staff and other headquarters personnel from 1958–1970;

7. Top Secret and below annual histories of headquarters offices from 1957–1975 (copies of these should also be at the Center for Military History and the Military History Institute discussed in the following section);

8. a large number of records of the executive office of the Assistant Chief of Staff/Intelligence and its predecessors, including but not limited to Top Secret/Restricted Data and below project decimal files and decimal files from 1953–1964; Top Secret and below cross reference sheets to the 1941–1952 decimal files; Top Secret and below subject indexes to the 1953–1956 decimal files; Top Secret and below subject indexes to the 1953–1956 project decimal files; Secret and below general correspondence files from 1965; Top Secret and below incoming and outgoing messages from 1953–1964; Top Secret and below numerical indexes and subject indexes to the 1957–1964 incoming and outgoing messages; Top Secret and below incoming and outgoing cables from 1953–1965; Top Secret and below subject indexes and individual and organizational name indexes to the 1943–1946 cables; Top Secret and below index cards to the 1950–1965 incoming and outgoing cables; Top Secret and below "S-Series" dispatches and cables from 1941–1965; telecom records from 1951–1956; Secret and below records regarding individuals ("Personal Name File") from 1941–1956; Secret and below records regarding miscellaneous organizations, associations, subjects, and titles from 1941–1957; Secret and below Consolidated Intelligence Program records from 1966–1973; Secret and below intelligence management files from 1960–1969; Secret and below intel-

ligence inventory books from 1960; Top Secret and below Army Intelligence Plans, master plans, and reorganization plans from the 1960s; and Secret and below attaché country files, alphabetical files, and "C" letter files from 1961–1964;

9. a huge number of Top Secret and below records of the Collection and Dissemination Division under the Assistant Chief of Staff/Intelligence, including but not limited to intelligence document ("ID") files from 1944–1955; intelligence document files publications from 1947–1962; numerical series of intelligence documents from 1946–1961; registers to the numerical series of intelligence documents; 930200 files from 1956–1960; printed reports from foreign sources from 1950–1958; list of Special Dispatch ("SD") intelligence documents from 1944–1951; subject, title, and source indexes to the "P," "ID," and "SD" files; and lists of Joint Intelligence Committee documents;

10. Top Secret and below records from 1945–1948 of the Captured Documents Branch under the Assistant Chief of Staff/Intelligence concerning German documents;

11. Top Secret and below records from 1948–1954 of the Eurasian Division under the Assistant Chief of Staff/Intelligence concerning military installations in East Germany and Poland;

12. Top Secret and below records of the Operations Branch under the Assistant Chief of Staff/Intelligence and its predecessors, including decimal files from 1941–1962, clandestine intelligence operations controlled files from 1946–1963, and Central Intelligence Agency correspondence and reports from 1958–1960;

13. Top Secret and below records of the Counter Intelligence Corps under the Assistant Chief of Staff/Intelligence, including but not limited to the Thomas M. Johnson memorial files; organizational history files; historian source files concerning the U.S. Army Intelligence Command; command reporting files; domestic intelligence reports from 1941–1956; permanent retention files from 1918–1963; historical records of G-2 components from 1918–1959; records relating to intelligence operations in Latin America from 1941–1947; and records concerning special studies of the Army intelligence system from 1944–1953;

14. numerous Top Secret and below records of other divisions and branches under the Assistant Chief of Staff/Intelligence and its predecessors, including but not limited to the majority of Investigative Records Repository intelligence and investigative dossiers on individuals and organizations from 1939–1976 and the personal name file for these dossiers; Strategic Intelligence School files from 1945–1954; and Army attaché station files from 1943–1956 and organization files from 1950–1965;

15. a large number of records of the executive offices of the Assistant Chief of Staff/Operations, Deputy Chief of Staff for Military Operations, and Assistant Chief of Staff for Force Development, including but not limited to Top Secret/Restricted Data and below general correspondence files from 1960 into the early 1970s; Secret/Restricted Data and below alphabetical, numerical, and name indexes to the 1950–1955 classified correspondence; Secret and below administrative memorandums from 1956–1964; Secret/Restricted Data and below summary sheets from 1963; Top Secret/Restricted Data and below National Security Council actions from 1947–1961; Top Secret and below reports on counter-insurgency programs from 1962–1963; Top Secret and below Joint Planning Comment files from 1972; and Secret and below field experiment final evaluation files regarding the Vietnam and European build-ups from 1961–1963;

16. numerous records of various divisions and branches under the Assistant Chief of Staff/Operations, Deputy Chief of Staff for Military Operations, and Assistant Chief of Staff for Force Development, including but not limited to Top Secret and below Command and Control Division correspondence files from 1963–1964; Secret and below Vietnam psychological operations records from 1964–1974; Secret and below Western Hemisphere Division records relating to special operations from 1964–1965; Top Secret and below Chief of Civil Affairs & Military Government/Director of the International & Civil Affairs Directorate subject files from 1949–1967, special warfare and regular country books from 1956–1969, and files regarding civil affairs in the Ryuku Islands from 1950–1968; Secret and below Foreign Training Division correspondence files from 1955–1967; and Secret and below Director for Civil Disturbance Planning & Operations domestic disturbance files from 1967–1974;

17. Assistant Chief of Staff for Logistics/Deputy Chief of Staff for Logistics executive office records, including Top Secret/Restricted Data and below decimal files and correspondence files from 1955–1963 and various Top Secret/Restricted Data and below records from the 1950s and early 1960s of their many subordinate divisions;

18. Chief of Research and Development and predecessor executive office records, including Top Secret/Restricted Data and below decimal files from 1952–1954 and general correspondence files from 1955–1963; Secret/Restricted Data and below general correspondence files from 1964–1970; annual historical summaries and background files from 1959–1973; and records relating to the Army Scientific Advisory Panel from 1952–1968;

19. various records of the many divisions, directorates, and branches under the Chief of Research and Development and predecessor offices, in-

cluding but not limited to Secret/Restricted Data and below International Division cooperative R&D files, organizational history files, international standardization files, standardization committee files, Mutual Weapons Development project files, international treaty files, foreign scientific information files, and project manager control files from the 1950s and 1960s; Secret and below Chemical-Biological Division general correspondence files from 1959–1962; Secret/Restricted Data and below Atomic Office general correspondence files from 1960–1962; Secret/Restricted Data and below Nuclear Weapons Branch project control files from 1959–1962; Secret/Restricted Data and below Nuclear Energy & Effects Branch R&D project control files from 1960–1962; Secret/Restricted Data and below Tactical Missiles Branch/Missiles & Space Directorate/Nike X & Space Division R&D project control files and other records on numerous missile systems from 1956 to the late 1960s, including the Corporal, Hawk, Honest John, Jupiter, Lacrosse, Lance, Little John, Nike Hercules, Nike Zeus, Pershing, and Sergeant; Secret/Restricted Data and below Air Defense & Missiles Division R&D project control files from 1956 into the early 1960s; Secret and below Air Mobility Division R&D project control files, R&D supervisory files, and other records from the 1960s; Secret and below Communications-Electronics Division R&D project control files from the 1960s; Secret and below Southeast Asia Division R&D project control files from the 1960s; and Secret and below Special Warfare Division R&D project control files from the early 1960s;

20. Chief of Special Warfare Top Secret and Secret correspondence files from 1950–1958, Confidential correspondence files from 1955–1958, and Top Secret and below special operations planning files from 1956–1958;

21. Assistant Chief of Staff for Communications-Electronics and predecessor Secret and below publications from 1961–1965; and Confidential and below communications instructions files from 1953–1964, facility project files and R&D project control files from 1958–1965, and communications planning files from 1963–1965;

22. Secret and below Comptroller reviews of Army programs from 1957–1968 and command analyses from 1963–1967;

23. Secret and below Adjutant General Consolidated Intelligence Program documents from 1966–1967.

Record Group 319 at the Washington National Records Center contains more than 12.5 million pages of mostly classified records as of 2000 (60% *permanent*, 30% *temporary*, and 10% *unappraised*). No other Federal records center has any RG 319 holdings. As part of the P-2000 Project, about 1.4 million pages of unclassified *permanent* records and 1.8 million pages of classified *permanent* records will be transferred to RG 319 at the College Park National Archives by the end of 2001. Even if the classified *permanent* records have been reviewed for declassification by the time of their transfer, they will not be available to the public until they are possibly re-reviewed by the DOE under the Kyl Plan and then *processed* by the National Archives. The records to be transferred include:

1. Secret and below Assistant Chief of Staff/Intelligence publications and Regulations from 1960–1977;
2. Secret and below files on strategic studies conducted by all the military services from 1957–1966;
3. Secret/Restricted Data and below Deputy Chief of Staff for Military Operations/Deputy Chief of Staff for Operations & Plans exercise and test files from 1968–1977;
4. Secret/Restricted Data and below Chief of Research & Development and predecessor historical policy files from 1949–1961 and a limited number of other types of files from the 1960s.

Other records that are not eligible for transfer to RG 319 at the College Park National Archives by 2001 include:

1. Top Secret/Restricted Data and Top Secret Chief of Staff decimal files from 1970–1972 and Secret/Restricted Data and below decimal files from 1973 into the 1990s;
2. Assistant Chief of Staff/Intelligence Top Secret and below attaché reports from 1952–1963; Secret and below attaché reports from 1963–1969, reports of the HUMINT Branch of the Collection Division from 1966–1968, and publications and regulations from the late 1970s into the 1980s;
3. Secret and below Chief of Military History/Center for Military History periodic and programmatic histories from the 1970s and 1980s and background files used in writing published and unpublished works from this period (as discussed in the following section, copies of the histories should also be at these two repositories);
4. Secret/Restricted Data and below Deputy Chief of Staff for Military Operations/Assistant Chief of Staff for Force Development/Deputy Chief of Staff for Operations and Plans records, including strategic, capabilities, and mobilization files from 1973–1977; emergency planning files, nuclear/biological/chemical files, security assistance planning files, and security assistance programming files from the 1970s; and joint planning comment files, international conference files, international treaty files,

operation planning files, and operation procedures files from the 1970s and 1980s;

5. Secret/Restricted Data and below Chief of Research and Development and Deputy Chief of Staff/Research, Development, and Acquisition R&D project control files, R&D supervisory files, R&D administrative files, and other files from the early 1970s into the 1980s;

6. Secret and below journals, logs, command reports, special reports, evaluations, recommendations, maps, photos, and other records of the Gulf War Declassification Project.

Record Group 337 has the records of the Army Ground Forces (1942–1948), Army Field Forces (1948–1955), and Continental Army Command (1956–1973). At the College Park National Archives there are about 7.5 million pages of records in RG 337. No other National Archives has any RG 337 records. The *finding aids* are very good, listing in most cases all the folder titles by box. Most of the records have been reviewed for declassification and *processed*, and they include:

1. Top Secret files of the Commanding General from 1942–1950;

2. Secret and below files of the Commanding General from 1942–1954;

3. Top Secret and below records of the headquarters staff sections from 1942–1949.

Record Group 337 at the Washington National Records Center has almost 1.5 million pages of mostly classified records as of 2000 (all of which are *permanent*). No other Federal records center has any RG 337 holdings. As part of the P-2000 Project, virtually all the records will be transferred to the College Park National Archives by the end of 2001. Even if they have been reviewed for declassification by the time of their transfer, they will not be available to the public until they are possibly re-reviewed by the DOE under the Kyl Plan and then *processed* by the National Archives. The records to be transferred include selected Secret and below files of the Commanding General, Continental Army Command from 1957 into the early 1960s. It should be noted that RG 338 at the Washington National Records Center has a number of important records of both the Army Field Forces and Continental Army Command.

Record Group 472 contains records of the Army in Vietnam, and at the College Park National Archives, RG 472 has more than 37.5 million pages of records. No other National Archives has any RG 472 records. The *finding aids* are excellent. Almost all the records have been reviewed for declassification and *processed*, and they include:

1. various records of the Military Assistance Advisory Group Vietnam from 1950–1964 and the Military Assistance Advisory Group Cambodia from 1955–1964;

2. subject files, correspondence files, logs, messages, and other records from 1962–1973 of the Military Assistance Command Vietnam, including those of the Secretary of the Joint Staff, Assistant Chiefs of Staff, and subordinate commands;

3. subject files, correspondence files, logs, operations reports, messages, and other records from 1962–1973 of the U.S. Army Vietnam, including those of the Secretary of the General Staff and Deputy Chiefs of Staff, and of its many subordinate commands and components;

4. various records of the U.S. Military Assistance Thailand and Joint U.S. Military Advisory Group Thailand from 1950 1976; Defense Attache Office, Saigon from 1973–1975; Military Equipment Delivery Team, Cambodia from 1971–1975; and the U.S. Delegation to the Four Party Joint Military Commission from early 1973.

There are no records in RG 472 at the Washington National Records Center or any regional Federal records center.

Record Group 338 contains the records of commands, armies, corps, divisions, bases, and arsenals from 1942 to the present. At the College Park National Archives, RG 338 has more than 80 million pages of records. A few regional National Archives have very small RG 338 holdings. The *finding aids* are good. Among the postwar records that have been reviewed for declassification and *processed* are:

1. a large number of Top Secret and below records of the General Headquarters, Supreme Commander Allied Powers (1947–1952) and General Headquarters, Far East Command (1947–1957), including but not limited to Commander in Chief subject files from 1945–1952, chronological files from 1952, and incoming and outgoing messages from 1950–1952; Assistant Chief of Staff, G-1 general decimal files from 1948–1951 and other records; Assistant Chief of Staff, G-2 general decimal files, intelligence reports, publications, and other records from 1946–1952; Assistant Chief of Staff, G-3 general decimal files from 1946–1952, daily journals from 1950–1952, staff studies and intelligence estimates from 1948–1951, and other records from the late 1940s and early 1950s; Assistant Chief of Staff, G-4 general decimal files from 1949–1952 and other records from the late 1940s and early 1950s; Assistant Chief of Staff, G-5 general decimal files from 1951–1953, civil assistance and economic aid files from 1950–1952, and command reporting files from 1952; and Military History Division general decimal files from 1951, command and staff section reports

from 1947–1952, and publications and translations from 1942–1952. (As mentioned in the section on interservice agency records, RG 334 at the Washington National Records Center has other General Headquarters, Far East Command records. Also, as set forth in the section on records of joint, specified, and unified commands, RG 349 at the College Park National Archives has other General Headquarters, Far East Command records.);

2. numerous Top Secret and below records of the many commands under General Headquarters, Supreme Commander Allied Powers and General Headquarters, Far East Command, including but not limited to general decimal files of the Military Governor of the Ryukyus Command from 1947–1950 and records of the general and special staff sections of this command from 1947–1957; U.S. Army Forces, Far East central decimal files and general orders from 1952–1957 and records of the general and special staff sections from this period; Korea Communications Zone records from 1952–1953; and Korea Military Advisory Group records from 1948–1954. (As mentioned in the section on interservice agency records, RG 334 at the Washington National Records Center has records of subordinate commands under General Headquarters, Far East Command. Also, as set forth in the section on records of joint, specified, and unified commands, RG 349 at the College Park National Archives has records of subordinate commands under General Headquarters, Far East Command.);

3. Top Secret and below U.S. Army, European Command records, including but not limited to incoming and outgoing messages from 1948–1951; central decimal correspondence files from 1947–1952; Assistant Chief of Staff, G-2 intelligence summaries, reports, and decimal files from 1947–1948; Assistant Chief of Staff, G-3 correspondence files and other records from 1946–1952; and Historical Division correspondence files, historical program files, and other records from 1946 into the early 1950s;

4. Top Secret and below U.S. Army, Europe records, including but not limited to central decimal correspondence files from the mid-1950s; Chief of Staff operations planning files from 1960–1962; Commanders' Conference notes from 1958–1961; incoming and outgoing messages from 1945–1958; Assistant Chief of Staff, G-2 reports from 1952–1956, publications from 1950–1964, weekly sitreps from 1957–1958, and cables and other records on Hungary from 1956; Assistant Chief of Staff, G-3 general correspondence files, operations planning files, and organizational planning files from 1953–1959; Historical Division files, publications, and other records from 1945–1958; and records of the War Crimes Branch, Judge Advocate General Section from World War II to the late 1950s;

5. Top Secret and below U.S. Forces, Austria central decimal correspondence files and other records of the general and special staff sections from 1944–1950;

6. Top Secret and below Berlin Command/Brigade central decimal correspondence files and other records from 1946–1948;

7. Top Secret and below Trieste, United States Troops central decimal files, incoming and outgoing messages, command reports, and other records from 1946–1954;

8. Top Secret and below U.S. Army, Caribbean central decimal correspondence files and defense plans from 1947–1951, missions summaries and command reports from 1960–1962, operations planning files from 1959–1963, operating program progress reports from 1957–1960, military assistance planning files from 1949–1963, and other records from the late 1940s into the early 1960s;

9. Top Secret and below U.S. Army, Pacific central decimal correspondence files from 1947–1949 and other records of the general and special staff sections from 1947–1963; Secret and below command reporting files from 1963–1973; and Secret and below historian's organizational history files, quarterly historical summaries, and other records from World War II to the early 1970s;

10. Secret and below U.S. Army, Japan central decimal correspondence files and other records of the general and special staff sections from 1957–1963;

11. Secret and below U.S. Army, Hawaii central decimal correspondence files and other records of the general and special staff sections from 1957–1963;

12. Secret and below U.S. Army, Ryukyus central decimal correspondence files and other records of the general and special staff sections from 1957–1961;

13. Secret and below U.S. Army, Alaska central decimal correspondence files and other records of the general and special staff sections from 1947–1961;

14. a wide range of Secret and below records of the First, Second, Third, Fourth, Fifth, Sixth, Seventh, Eighth, and Fifteenth Armies from World War II into the 1950s;

15. a wide range of Secret and below records of many of the corps from World War II into the 1950s;

16. Secret and below Executive Headquarters, Pieping central decimal correspondence files and other records of headquarters offices and field teams from 1946–1947.

Postwar records that are still classified or that have been reviewed for de-classification but await possible re-review by the DOE under the Kyl Plan and *processing* by the National Archives before being made available to the public include the following:

1. Top Secret and below Assistant Chief of Staff/Intelligence military in-telligence report files from 1947–1966;
2. Secret and below Chief of Military History/Center for Military History foreign military studies from the 1940s and 1950s;
3. Top Secret and below records relating to POWs and MIAs in Southeast Asia from 1961–1992.

Record Group 338 at the Washington National Records Center contains more than 200 million pages of largely classified records as of 2000 (35% *permanent,* 60% *temporary,* and 5% *unappraised*). Some of the records should be in other *record groups,* and this will occur with the *permanent* records in this category when they are transferred to the College Park National Archives. As part of the P-2000 Project, an unknown number of *permanent* records will be transferred to RG 338 and other *record groups* at the College Park National Archives by the end of 2001. Even if the classified *permanent* records have been reviewed for declassification by the time of their transfer, they will not be available to the public until they are possibly re-reviewed by the DOE under the Kyl Plan and then *processed* by the National Archives. Records that are both eligible and not eligible for transfer by 2001 include:

1. Secret and below Army Security Affairs Command/Army Security As-sistance Command and predecessor files on foreign military assistance from the 1960s into the 1980s;
2. Confidential and below U.S. Army Strategic Communications Com-mand publication record sets from the 1960s;
3. Secret and below U.S. Army Mapping Service/U.S. Army Topographic Command maps, charts, engineer intelligence studies, research reports, mapping and geodetic studies, and other records from the 1930s into the early 1970s;
4. Confidential and below Counter-Intelligence Corps/Intelligence Corps world-wide historical counterintelligence statistical reports from World War II to 1965;
5. a small number of Secret and below U.S. Army Intelligence Command and predecessor intelligence administrative files, publication record sets, daily journals, and emergency planning files from the late 1960s and early 1970s;

6. Secret and below U.S. Army Communications-Electronics Command and predecessor headquarters contract files, R&D files, technical reports, and other records from the 1950s into the 1990s;

7. Secret and below Chemical Corps Research and Engineering Command/Chemical Corps Research and Development Command project files, R&D files, and other records from the 1950s to 1962 (the year the Chemical Corps was disestablished);

8. Secret and below R&D files, test files, contract files, exercise files, intelligence files, and other records of the Ft. Detrick headquarters of the U.S. Army Biological Warfare Laboratories/U.S. Army Biological Center/U.S. Army Biological Defense Research Center from the 1950s into the 1970s;

9. Secret and below Chief Signal Officer Technical Committee and Board files from the 1930s to 1962 (the year the Signal Corps was disestablished), R&D files relating to satellites and other space projects from 1958–1961, and Mutual Weapons Development project files from 1959–1962;

10. Secret and below Chief of Transportation and The Quartermaster General administrative files, correspondence files, project files, reports, and other records from the 1950s to 1962 (the year the Transportation Corps and Quartermaster Corps were disestablished);

11. Secret and below Chief of Research and Development Mutual Weapons Development files from the 1950s;

12. Secret/Restricted Data and below Army Combat Developments Command administrative files, correspondence files, project files, R&D files, reports, and other records from the 1960s;

13. Secret and below U.S. Army Foreign Science & Technology Center and predecessor publications, reports, translations, and other records from 1953 into the 1970s;

14. Secret/Restricted Data and below administrative files, correspondence files, R&D files, test files, program files, and other records of the Redstone Arsenal headquarters of the Ordnance Guided Missile Center/Army Ballistic Missile Agency/Army Rocket & Guided Missile Agency/Missile Command from the 1950s into the 1980s;

15. Secret/Restricted Data and below White Sands Missile Range/White Sands Proving Ground administrative files, test files, R&D files, technical reports, and other records from the 1950s into the 1980s;

16. Secret/Restricted Data and below Army Sentinel System Command/Army Safeguard System Command administrative files, subject files, test files, technical reports, program files, R&D files, and other records from the late 1960s and early 1970s;

17. Secret and below Ballistic Research Laboratory/Army Research Laboratory notebooks, technical reports, and other records from the 1950s into the 1990s;

18. Secret and below U.S. Army Aviation Systems Command and predecessor headquarters technical reports, project files, program files, test files, specifications, and other records from the 1950s into the 1980s;

19. Secret and below U.S. Army Tank-Automotive Command and predecessor headquarters technical reports, project files, program files, test files, specifications, and other records from the 1950s into the 1980s;

20. a huge number of Secret/Restricted Data and below Army Material Command headquarters records from 1962–1976, including but not limited to administrative files; budget files; R&D files; technical reports; contract files; intelligence files; meeting and conference files; Technical Committee agendas, minutes, and reports; Mutual Weapons Development files; technological forecast files; and Military Assistance Program files;

21. Secret/Restricted Data and below Aberdeen Proving Ground headquarters technical reports, R&D files, administrative files, and other records from the 1950s into the 1980s;

22. Secret and below Dugway Proving Ground test reports, technical reports, and other records from the 1950s into the 1980s;

23. Top Secret periodic histories of the U.S. Continental Army Command from the 1960s (copies of these should also be at the Military History Institute and Center for Military History discussed in the following section), and Top Secret correspondence from 1963 to this command from Commander in Chief, Atlantic Command regarding the review of Cuban operations;

24. Secret/Restricted Data and below Commanding General, Army Field Forces/ U.S. Continental Army Command general officer correspondence files, speeches, and trip reports from 1949–1957; headquarters studies, reports, staff memos, publications, and project files from 1950–1965; headquarters budget files and training operations files from 1946–1966; and headquarters correspondence files from the 1960s;

25. Secret and below studies, reports, and files of various Army commands and units in Vietnam;

26. Secret and below U.S. Forces Dominican Republic headquarters files from 1965–1966;

27. Top Secret/Restricted Data/Single Integrated Operational Plan/Extremely Sensitive Information U.S. European Command headquarters training operation files from 1964–1965; and Top Secret/Restricted Data mobilization, operations, and planning files from 1962–1966;

28. a wide range of U.S. Army, Pacific headquarters records, including but not limited to Top Secret/Restricted Data and below Commanders' Conference files from 1966, annual historical summary files from 1963 into the early 1970s, and operation planning files from 1963–1974; Secret/Restricted Data and below intelligence collection files from 1968–1972, command reporting files from the late 1950s to 1974, publication record sets from the late 1950s to 1974, special weapons files from the late 1960s to 1974, organizational files from the 1950s to 1974, and annual historical summary files from 1959–1962; and Secret and below special warfare instruction files from 1967–1968, daily journals from the 1950s to 1974, and Vietnam reports, analyses, and studies from the 1960s and early 1970s;

29. Secret and below U.S. Forces, Austria/U.S. Army Southern European Task Force command reporting files from 1951–1961 and other records from the 1950s and 1960s;

30. a wide range of largely classified records from the 1950s and 1960s of the headquarters of U.S. Army, Alaska; U.S. Army, Caribbean; U.S. Army, Europe; U.S. Army Forces, Far East; U.S. Army, Hawaii; U.S. Army, Korea; U.S. Army, Japan; U.S. Army, Ryukyu Islands; and U.S. Army Forces Southern Command;

31. Secret and below command reporting files, historian background material files, and other records from the 1950s and 1960s of the headquarters of the First U.S. Army, Second U.S. Army, Third U.S. Army, Fourth U.S. Army, Fifth U.S. Army, Sixth U.S. Army, Seventh U.S. Army, and Eighth U.S. Army;

32. Top Secret/Restricted Data/Single Integrated Operational Plan/Special Category and below U.S. Army Intelligence and Security Command (USAISC) Pentagon telecommunication center message files from the 1960s into the 1990s;

33. unclassified On-Site Inspection Agency inspection reports, handbooks, site books, and other materials from 1985–1993.

Record Group 338 at the St. Louis Federal Records Center has about 422 million pages of records as of 2000 (89% *temporary* and 11% *unappraised*). The vast majority are civilian personnel records and military personnel and medical records. There are also, however, the following records of interest:

1. Secret/Restricted Data and below White Sands Missile Range administrative files, historian background files, technical reports, R&D files, and other records from the late 1940s into the early 1960s;

2. Secret and below Army Mapping Service intelligence data files from the 1940s and 1950s;

3. Secret and below U.S. Army Biological Warfare Laboratories head-quarters administrative files, technical reports, intelligence data files, publications, and R&D files from the late 1940s and 1950s;

4. Secret and below Army Chemical Center administrative files, operating program files, R&D files, technical reports, and publications from the 1940s and 1950s.[33]

Record Group 338 at the Boston Federal Records Center has about 3 million pages of records as of 2000, but they are almost exclusively un-classified *temporary* finance records.[34]

Record Group 156 contains records of the Office of the Chief of Ord-nance (1832–1962). At the College Park National Archives, RG 156 has more than 27.5 million pages of records, most of which are from World War II and earlier. Some regional National Archives have small RG 156 holdings that also are almost exclusively records from World War II and earlier. Postwar records at the College Park National Archives that have been reviewed for declassification and *processed* include:

1. Secret/Restricted Data and below Chief of Ordnance decimal and cor-respondence files from 1945–1954;

2. unclassified headquarters and field activity periodic histories and histor-ical summaries from 1945–1962 (copies of these also should be at the Military History Institute and Center for Military History discussed in the following section);

3. Secret and below agendas, minutes, reports, and other records of the Ordnance Technical Committee from 1945–1962;

4. Secret and below publication background papers and files from 1945–1954;

5. limited number of Secret and below technical reports from 1945–1954.

Postwar records that are still classified or that have been reviewed for de-classification but await possible re-review by the DOE under the Kyl Plan and then *processing* by the National Archives before being made available to the public include the following:

1. Secret/Restricted Data and below Chief of Ordnance decimal and cor-respondence files from 1955–1962;

2. Top Secret/Restricted Data and below reading and office files of General John Hinichs from 1958–1962;

3. Confidential through Secret/Restricted Data headquarters and field ac-tivity periodic histories and historical summaries from 1945–1962 (cop-

ies of these should also be at the Center for Military History and the Military History Institute discussed in the following section);

4. Secret and below publication background papers and files from 1955–1962;

5. Secret/Restricted Data and below Historian's Office annual reports on guided missiles from 1952–1958 and miscellaneous records on guided missiles from 1940–1962;

6. Secret and below Program Management Branch, R&D Division budget files, project files, program progress reports, and other records from 1945–1962;

7. Secret/Restricted Data and below Nuclear & Special Components Branch, R&D Division project control files and other records from the late 1940s to 1962;

8. Secret/Restricted Data and below Rocket Branch/Guided Missiles Systems Branch, R&D Division project control files, and other records on rockets and guided missiles from 1941–1962;

9. a wide range of Secret and below files of other offices under the R&D Division, including the Small Arms Branch, Tank & Automotive Branch, Artillery & Vehicle Systems Branch, and Infantry & Aircraft Weapons Systems Branch.

A few regional Federal records centers have very small RG 156 holdings, and it should be noted that RG 338 at the Washington National Records Center has some Office of the Chief of Ordnance records.

Record Group 175 contains the records of the Chemical Warfare Service (1918–1946) and the Chemical Corps (1946–1962). At the College Park National Archives, RG 175 has about 3.5 million pages of records. No other National Archives has any post–World War II RG 175 records. The *finding aids* are generally useful. The following postwar records have been reviewed for declassification but still require possible re-review by the DOE under the Kyl Plan and then *processing* by the National Archives before they will be available to the public:

1. Secret and below decimal files, station files, and miscellaneous files of the Chief Chemical Officer from 1946–1954;

2. Secret and below agendas, summary minutes, and reports of the Chemical Corps Technical Committee from 1935–1962.

Postwar records that are still classified or that have been reviewed for declassification but await possible re-review by the DOE under the Kyl Plan and then *processing* by the National Archives before being made available to the public include:

1. Secret and below decimal files, station files, and miscellaneous files of the Chief Chemical Officer from 1955–1961;
2. a limited number of Secret and below records from the late 1940s and early 1950s of the Army Chemical Center at Edgewood Arsenal and Chemical Corps Biological Department at Ft. Detrick, Maryland;
3. Secret and below History Office background files on human experimentation.

Record Group 175 at the Washington National Records Center has only about 15,000 pages of Chemical Corps records, all of which are classified. Among the important records that were at the Washington National Records Center but were withdrawn in recent years by the Chemical & Biological Defense Command are:

1. Secret and below files from 1955–1962 of the Research and Engineering Command and its successor, the Research and Development Command;
2. agendas, minutes, reports, and related documents from the late 1940s to the early 1960s of the Chemical Corps Research Council and its successor, the Chemical Corps Advisory Council;
3. agendas, minutes, reports, and related documents from the 1950s and early 1960s of the Committee (American Chemical Society) Advisory to the Chemical Corps and Committee (Society of American Bacteriologists) Advisory to the Chemical Corps;
4. agendas, minutes, and reports of United States/United Kingdom/Canada Tripartite Conferences and United States/United Kingdom/Canada/France Quadripartite Conferences from the 1950s and early 1960s;
5. periodic historical reports and summaries of Chemical Corps offices and commands from the late 1940s to the early 1960s. (Copies of these should also be at the Military History Institute and Center for Military History discussed in the following section.).

These withdrawn records are presumably now at either the Command Historian's Office, U.S. Army Soldier & Biological Chemical Command or the Edgewood Area Records Holding Area. Both of these repositories are discussed in the following section. A few regional Federal records centers have very small RG 175 holdings, and it should be noted that RG 338 at the Washington National Records Center has some Chemical Corps records.

Record Group 111 contains the records of the Office of the Chief Signal Officer (1866–1962). At the College Park National Archives, RG 111 has more than 30 million pages of records, the vast majority of which are from World War II and earlier. No other National Archives has any RG 111 holdings. The *finding aids* are generally good. Postwar records that have been reviewed for declassification and *processed* include:

1. Secret and below Chief Signal Officer decimal files from 1940–1948;
2. Secret and below Office of the Historian files on a wide variety of subjects from 1908–1962.

Postwar records that are still classified or that have been reviewed for declassification but await possible re-review by the DOE under the Kyl Plan and then *processing* by the National Archives before being made available to the public include:

1. Secret and Confidential Chief Signal Officer decimal files from 1949–1961;
2. Secret and Confidential intelligence reports from 1945–1948;
3. Secret and below files of the Army Electronics Warfare Policy Committee from 1956–1960;
4. Secret and below subject files of the Operations Planning Branch;
5. Secret and below subject files of the Electronics Warfare Branch from 1945–1953;
6. Secret and below subject files of the Communications Liaison Branch from 1942–1963;
7. Secret and below records of the Combined Communications Board from 1944–1948 and Joint Communications Board from 1944–1949;
8. Secret and below Mutual Security Branch foreign aid files from 1947–1956;
9. Secret and below Communications Services Division subject files from 1958–1962, control files from 1951–1955, and decimal files from 1945–1959;
10. Secret and below Avionics and Surveillance Branch project files from 1952–1958;
11. Secret/Restricted Data and below Research & Development Division files from 1943–1953 on nuclear weapons tests and Secret and below decimal files from 1949–1959;
12. Secret and below Special Projects Branch files from 1947–1954 and control files from 1951–1957.

There are no postwar records in RG 111 at the Washington National Records Center or any other Federal records center. It should be noted that RG 338 at the Washington National Records Center has some Office of the Chief Signal Officer records.

Record Group 407 contains the records of the Adjutant General's Office. At the College Park National Archives, RG 407 has more than 75 million pages of records, most of which are from World War II and earlier. The *finding aids* are generally good. Most of the postwar records have been reviewed for declassification and *processed* and these include:

1. Secret and below central general administrative files from 1945–1962;
2. Secret and below publications record set from 1945–1960;
3. Secret and below central decimal files from 1945–1954;
4. Secret and below Korean War Command Reports from 1949–1954;
5. Far East foreign occupied area intelligence reports.

A few regional National Archives have very small RG 407 holdings.

At the Washington National Records Center, RG 407 has fewer than 2.25 million pages of records as of 2000 (30% *permanent* and 70% *temporary*). No other Federal records center has any RG 407 holdings. As part of the P-2000 Project, about 490,000 pages of unclassified *permanent* records and 15,000 pages of classified *permanent* records will be transferred to RG 407 at the College Park National Archives by the end of 2001. Even if the classified *permanent* records have been reviewed for declassification by the time of their transfer, they will not be available to the public until they are possibly re-reviewed by the DOE under the Kyl Plan and then *processed* by the National Archives.

Record Group 112 has the records of the Office of the Surgeon General (1818–present). At the College Park National Archives, RG 112 has more than 12.5 million pages of records. Virtually all the records are unclassified or have been reviewed for declassification and *processed*. Although most of the records are from World War II and earlier, postwar records include the official histories into the 1970s and historians' background files used in writing these, medical unit annual reports and general reports from 1950–1969, and annual reports from 1941–1974 of the divisions within the Office of the Surgeon General. Some regional National Archives have very small RG 112 holdings.

Record Group 112 at the Washington National Records Center has almost 10 million pages of records as of 2000 (90% *permanent* and 10% *unappraised*). An unknown number of *permanent* records will be transferred to RG 112 at the College Park National Archives under the P-2000 Project. Records that are both eligible and not eligible for transfer by 2001 include:

1. Top Secret central subject files, geographic files, and 095 files from 1949–1950;

2. Secret and below central subject files, geographic files, and 095 files from 1945–1962;

3. Secret and below subject-numeric files from 1963 to the 1970s;

4. unclassified and classified records from the late 1940s to the 1970s of the Medical Research and Development Board and its successors, the Research and Development Division and the Army Medical Research and Development Command;

5. unclassified and classified reports on individual projects from the in-house medical research laboratories (for example, the Army Medical Research Laboratory and the Walter Reed Army Institute of Research) from the late 1940s to the 1970s;

6. unclassified and classified agendas, minutes, and reports of the Advisory Board of the Society of Medical Consultants from the late 1940s to the 1960s;

7. unclassified and classified outside R&D contract files and outside R&D contract progress reports from the late 1940s to the 1970s;

8. unclassified records of the Armed Forces Epidemiological Board from the 1960s and 1970s.

A few regional Federal records centers have very small RG 112 holdings.

### Army Records at Army Commands, National Defense University, Presidential Libraries, Library of Congress, and other Repositories

There are numerous Army commands around the world, and some have significant holdings with which researchers should be familiar. It should be noted, however, that the following list is not comprehensive as there is no information available on the holdings at some commands.

The Military History Institute at Carlisle Barracks has a large number of important collections. It can be contacted at 22 Ashburn Drive, Carlisle Barracks, Carlisle, PA 17013–5008; 717–245–3611; or carlisle-www.army.mil/usamhi. First, the Archives has a number of manuscript holdings, and the database can be searched on the homepage. Second, the Historical Reference Branch has the most complete collection of Army periodic and programmatic histories in existence. Many of the postwar histories are still classified. The database for the histories can be searched on the homepage. Third, there is the Senior Officer Oral History Program collection of oral history interviews. A small number are classified.

The Army War College Library at Carlisle Barracks also has some significant holdings in addition to a huge quantity of secondary literature. These include everything from organizational charts to theses written by students at Army educational institutions. The easiest means of determining what exists is to search one or more of the twenty-eight library bibliographies on the Carlisle Barracks homepage.

The Center for Military History has numerous important collections. It can be contacted at Building 35, 102 Fourth Avenue, Fort Lesley J. McNair, Washington, D.C. 20319–5058. In addition to a large quantity of secondary literature, there are several important collections. First, there are the two Historical Research Collections (one containing materials collected through 1984 and the other containing materials collected since 1984). Both are organized by the War Department Decimal System, and their files contain a wide range of records obtained by Army historians through the years, some of which are classified. The indexes to the two collections are at the Center. Second, there are the unpublished manuscripts and studies prepared through the years by Army historians in two Historical Manuscripts Collections (one containing items prepared through 1984 and the other containing items prepared since 1984) and the Chief of Military History Collection. Some of the unpublished manuscripts and studies are classified. The indexes to these are at the Center as well. Third, there are a substantial number of periodic and programmatic histories, and the Center has indexes to these. Fourth, there are the Vietnam Interview and Vietnam Interview Tape collections. The former consists of narrative reports prepared by combat historians largely on the basis of oral history interviews, while the latter consists of more than 1,000 audiotapes. Indexes for both are at the Center and on the Center's homepage (www4.army.mil/cmh). Sixth, there are JUST CAUSE and DESERT SHIELD/DESERT STORM Interview Tapes. The indexes are at the Center and on the homepage. Seventh, there are several specialized collections consisting of primary source documents, monographs, and other records relating to DESERT SHIELD and DESERT STORM, JUST CAUSE, RESTORE HOPE, and other subjects. Some of these collections have classified material. Indexes to them are at the Center. Eighth, there are copies of a substantial number of oral history interviews conducted by Army historians under the Senior Officer Oral History Program.

The Edgewood Area Records Holding Area at Aberdeen Proving Ground contains more than 10 million pages of records of the various commands that have been located at this facility through the years. Most of the records are classified, and apparently they span the period from World War II to the present. Further information about the record holdings or access to any records requires a FOIA or MDR request be submitted to Commander, U.S. Army Garrison, Aberdeen Proving Ground, ATTN: STEAP-IM-R, 5179 Hoadley Road, Aberdeen Proving Ground, MD 21010–5401.[35]

The Office of the Command Historian, U.S. Army Soldier and Biological Chemical Command has a large number of almost entirely classified records dating from the 1940s to the present. For information concerning the types of records and access, researchers should contact this office at the U.S.

Army Soldier & Biological Chemical Command, Bldg. E5101, 5183 Black-hawk Road, Aberdeen Proving Ground, MD 21010–5424.

The Army Intelligence and Security Command's Investigative Records Repository has almost 2 million records on individuals and organizations (as noted in the preceding section, some records from this repository have been transferred to RG 319 at the College Park National Archives). The date range of the records is unknown, but it is believed that they span from the 1930s to the present. There are two main indexes that the command uses to determine whether it holds records. The first is the Master Name Index that contains listings on individuals with at least one personal iden-tifying data (date of birth, place of birth, or social security number). The second is the Name Only/Impersonal Title Index for individuals with no personal identifying data or for organizations.[36] There is no public access to this facility or to the two indexes. A FOIA or MDR request must be submitted to the FOIA/Privacy Act Office, U.S. Army Intelligence and Se-curity Command, Fort George G. Meade, MD 20755–5995.

The Redstone Scientific Information Center (RSIC) in Huntsville, Ala-bama, has a huge number of records dating from the 1940s to the present relating primarily to aviation, rockets, and missiles. The holdings include 228,000 books; 2,270,000 technical reports; 2,600,000 patents; 1,000,000 American Institute of Aeronautics and Astronautics papers; 2,600 transla-tions; and journals. There are two databases for the technical reports, one listing the unclassified and declassified titles and the other listing the clas-sified titles.[37] The former database can be accessed by the public through the RSIC homepage at rsic3.redstone.army.mil/rsichome or in person at the Center.

The U.S. Army Aviation and Missile Command (AMCOM) in Huntsville has a small archives containing mostly classified records to which the public has no access. However, it does have an excellent homepage at www.redstone.army.mil/history, which contains some important unclassi-fied and declassified documents including chronologies of the Redstone Arsenal complex from World War II to the present, systems chronologies of a number of Army missiles, oral histories of many Missile Command/AMCOM commanders, and declassified histories of the Army satellite pro-gram and several early Army missiles. The quantity, nature, and *appraisal* status of holdings outside this archives are unknown.

Other commands that also have archives containing almost entirely clas-sified records to which the public has no access include the U.S. Army Space and Missile Defense Command and the headquarters of the Army Intelli-gence and Security Command.[38] The quantity, nature, and *appraisal* status of holdings at these two commands are not known.

The Truman Library has the personal papers of Earl Johnson (Assistant Secretary and Under Secretary of the Army from 1950–1954) and the personal papers of Frank Pace (Secretary of the Army from 1950–1953). Both collections are open.

As discussed in the section on National Defense University records, that institution has the personal papers of several Army general officers, including Maxwell Taylor, Lyman Lemnitzer, and Andrew Goodpaster. Many portions of these collections, however, are classified. A small quantity of General William Odom's papers from his tenure as Assistant Chief of Staff/ Intelligence from 1981–1985 is at the Manuscript Division of the Library of Congress. There is a good *finding aid*. However, virtually all the documents are still classified.

A large number of General MacArthur's personal papers from 1941 on are at MacArthur Memorial Library & Archives in Norfolk, Virginia. All have been microfilmed, and the microfilm is available through interlibrary loan or purchase. The archivist can be contacted by phone at 757–441–2695 or by fax at 757–441–5389.

Requests under the FOIA and MDR for records at a Federal records center or at an Army command can be submitted to the commanding officer of the command holding the records, or if there is any doubt as to which command holds the records, requests should be sent to Chief, Freedom of Information and Privacy Act Division, Information Systems Command, ATTN: ASQNS-OPF, Room 1146, Hoffman I, 2461 Eisenhower Avenue, Alexandria, VA 22331–0301.

### Army Air Forces (AAF) Records at the National Archives

Virtually all the AAF records are in one of several *record groups* at the National Archives. Record Group 18 contains the records of the AAF, and at the College Park National Archives there are more than 27.5 million pages of records in this *record* group. Some regional National Archives have RG 18 holdings, but they are almost exclusively World War II and prewar records.

Virtually all the records at the College Park National Archives have been reviewed for declassification and *processed*, and the *finding aids* to them are good. A few *entries* contain not only AAF records, but records from the early years of the U.S. Air Force. The postwar records include: (1) Top Secret and below correspondence and incoming and outgoing message files of the Commanding General; (2) Top Secret and below correspondence files, technical reports, and related materials of the Assistant Chief of the Air Staff, Material and Services; (3) Top Secret and below records of such advisory boards and committees as the Air Board and Scientific Advisory Group. There are no records in RG 18 at any Federal records center.

There are also some AAF records in RG 107 (Secretary of War) at the College Park National Archives. For the most part, these are in the *entries* containing records of the Assistant Secretary of War for Air. They have been reviewed for declassification and *processed*, and the *finding aids* to them are good. There are no records in Record Group 107 at any Federal records center.

Some AAF records are also in Record Group 341 (U.S. Air Force head-quarters) at the College Park National Archives. As an example, Entry #335 contains the voluminous Top Secret decimal correspondence files of the Assistant Chief of the Air Staff, Plans from 1942–1947. Entry #336 has the extensive Secret decimal correspondence files of this office for the same time period.

### AAF Records at Air Force Commands and the Library of Congress

As discussed in the section on Air Force records, there are a considerable number of AAF records at the U.S. Air Force Historical Research Agency at Maxwell Air Force Base, Alabama, and the Manuscript Division at the Library of Congress has several relevant collections.

### Ballistic Missile Defense Organization (BMDO) / Strategic Defense Initiative Organization (SDIO) Records

The only records of the BMDO (1993–present) and SDIO (1984–1993) at any National Archives or Federal records center are a small number of Secret and below chronological files of the Director of the SDIO from the 1980s in RG 330 at the Washington National Records Center. All the rest of the records of these two organizations must still be held by the BMDO. However, there is no information available on the quantity, nature, and *appraisal* status of such records.

It is not known whether the BMDO has any *permanent* pre-1975 clas-sified records subject to E.O. 12958. The FY 1996, FY 1997, FY 1998, and FY 1999 ISOO annual reports do not specifically list the BMDO as having declassified any records, but it is possible that its totals are included in the "All Others" section in these reports.

Requests under the FOIA or MDR should be submitted to the Office of General Counsel, Ballistic Missile Defense Organization, 7100 Defense Pentagon, Washington, D.C. 20301–7100.

### Bureau of Export Administration (BXA) / Office of Export Administration (OXA) / Office of Export Control (OXC) Records at the National Archives and Federal Records Centers

A large number of records of the BXA (1988–present) and its predeces-sors, the OXA (1987–1988) and OXC (1945–1987), are in RG 476 at the College Park National Archives and Washington National Records Center.

No other National Archives or Federal records center has any RG 476 holdings.

It is not known how many *permanent* pre-1975 classified records the BXA has subject to E.O. 12958. The FY 1996 ISOO annual report listed the Department of Commerce as having declassified more than 2.6 million pages, but it is not known whether any of these are BXA, OXA or OXC records. Subsequent ISOO annual reports have not listed either the Department of Commerce or the BXA as having declassified any records.

At the College Park National Archives, RG 476 has about 1.75 million pages of records. The *finding aids* are good. Records that have been reviewed for declassification and *processed* include:

1. Secret and below Director's case files from 1968–1971;
2. Confidential and below Director's commodity files from 1962–1974;
3. Secret and below Deputy Director's general correspondence files from 1969–1971;
4. Confidential and below Eastern Europe economic files from 1954–1959;
5. Confidential and below record set of publications from 1940–1974;
6. Secret and below export license case files from the 1950s and 1960s.

There are numerous records that are still classified, and these include the following:

1. Secret and below Soviet Bloc Technical Data and Exchange Program records from 1949–1979;
2. Secret and below Advisory Committee on Export Control files from 1969–1981;
3. Secret and below Operating Committee agendas and minutes from 1961–1977, document master files from 1955–1973, case files from 1950–1980, and subject files from 1958–1974;
4. Confidential and below Coordinating Committee for Multilateral Export Controls (COCOM) List review files from 1966–1973;
5. Confidential and below Export Committee files from 1953–1968;
6. Secret and below country files from 1950–1972;
7. Confidential and below Soviet Bloc economic files from 1938–1965;
8. Confidential and below export policy records from 1958–1967.

Record Group 476 at the Washington National Records Center has more than 3 million pages of largely classified records of the BXA and its predecessors as of 2000 (40% *permanent* and 60% *temporary*). As part of the P-2000 Project, about 170,000 pages of unclassified *permanent* records and

640,000 pages of classified *permanent* records will be transferred to RG 476 at the College Park National Archives by the end of 2001. Even if the classified records have been reviewed for declassification by the time of their transfer, they will not be available to the public until they are possibly re-reviewed by the DOE under the Kyl Plan and then *processed* by the National Archives. The records to be transferred include:

1. Secret and below Director's subject files from 1969–1979;
2. Secret and below Assistant Secretary for Export Administration and Deputy Assistant Secretary for Export Administration subject and country files from the early 1980s;
3. Secret and below Operating Committee subject files from 1961–1976 and case files from 1977–1985;
4. Secret and below policy planning subject files from 1947–1979;
5. Secret and below country control case files from 1950–1980;
6. Secret and below nuclear-related program commodity files from 1963–1980;
7. Secret and below consolidated compliance subject files/program operations files from 1948–1979;
8. Secret and below Industry Evaluation Board summary analyses from 1951–1974;
9. Secret and below China special trade files from 1956–1977;
10. Secret and below COCOM List review files from 1952–1975;
11. Secret and below strategic commodity policy and procedures files from 1958–1975;
12. Secret and below international lists and Commodity Control List (CCL) review files from the early 1960s to 1978.

Records that are not eligible for transfer to RG 476 the College Park National Archives by 2001 include:

1. Secret and below Assistant Secretary for Export Administration and Deputy Secretary for Export Administration subject and country files from the mid-1980s into the late 1990s;
2. Secret and below intelligence and investigative case files from the 1940s to the 1990s.

### BXA, OXA, and OXC Records Still at the BXA

The quantity, nature, and *appraisal* status of records still at the BXA are not known.

Requests under the FOIA and MDR for records at the Washington National Records Center or still at the BXA can be submitted to the Freedom of Information Officer, Bureau of Export Administration, Room 6881, U.S. Department of Commerce, Washington, D.C. 20230.

### Central Intelligence Agency (CIA) / Central Intelligence Group (CIG) / Strategic Services Unit (SSU) / Office of Strategic Services (OSS) Records at the National Archives

The CIA (1947–present) still holds almost all of its own records and some of its predecessors, the OSS (1942–1945), SSU (1945–1946), and CIG (1946–1947). There is only a very small number of records of these four agencies in three *records groups* at the College Park National Archives. No other National Archives or any Federal records center has any records of these agencies (the CIA has permission from NARA to use its own Agency Records Center to store inactive records instead of sending them to the Washington National Records Center).

The 1997 *Report of the Commission on Reducing and Protecting Government Secrecy* stated that the CIA has approximately 166 million pages of *permanent* pre-1975 classified records subject to E.O. 12958.[39] The CIA's proposed implementation plan under E.O. 12958 on file at the ISOO presumably also contains an estimate of the quantity of subject records, but it is marked "For Official Use Only," and the CIA will not permit the public to access it. In early 1999, the White House granted the CIA an exemption from automatic declassification of 94.5 million pages (60% of its subject records), which means that the CIA has a total of a little more than 157 million pages of *permanent* pre-1975 classified records.[40] The list of exempted files is itself classified. Of course, the use of "pages" is erroneous in part because some of the subject records and exempted records are nontextual records.

Progress in the declassification review program under E.O. 12958 has been slow, with the FY 1996 through FY 1999 ISOO annual reports crediting the CIA with declassifying approximately 5 million pages. However, the available evidence indicates that the CIA has not declassified this number of records but has instead only reviewed this quantity for declassification. Furthermore, the use of "pages" is erroneous in part because some of the records that have been declassified are nontextual records. As mentioned in the previous chapter, the CIA is one of the few agencies *redacting* in its declassification review program.

Record Group 226 contains OSS records, as well as a small number of those of the SSU and CIG. At the College Park National Archives, there are about 10 million pages of records in RG 226. Most of the records have been reviewed for declassification and *processed*, and the *finding aids* are good. Among the postwar records are: (1) selected intelligence reports, subject and correspondence files, field operations records, incoming and outgoing messages, and related records of the director of the SSU and CIG; (2) various records of the numerous offices, divisions, and branches in the SSU and CIG (for example, Office of the General Counsel, Communications Branch, Office of Research and Development, History Office, Secret Intelligence Branch, and Counter-Intelligence Branch).

Record Group 263 contains CIA records, as well as a small number from the SSU and CIG. In RG 263 at the College Park National Archives there are approximately 5 million pages of textual records and a large number of nontextual records. Records that have been reviewed for declassification and *processed* include:

1. approximately 800,000 images from the CORONA, ARGON, and LANYARD missions;

2. daily transcripts, summaries of monitored foreign radio broadcasts and teletypes of material for transmission to other government agencies of Foreign Broadcast Information Service files from 1947 and 1948, as well as transcripts of monitored broadcasts relating to the Vietnam War from 1957–1974;

3. a very limited number of DCI Historian histories, including the three-volume *The CIA: An Instrument of Government to 1950*; the five-volume *General Walter Bedell Smith as Director of Central Intelligence, October 1950-February 1953*; and the first nine volumes of *Organization and History of the Central Intelligence Agency*;

4. internal DCI Historian files from the 1940s and 1950s containing a wide range of documents from this and other offices;

5. CIA documents on the Cuban Missile Crisis;

6. *Estimates of Soviet Offensive Threat, 1976* (the Team A and Team B reports);

7. intelligence estimates from the late 1940s of the Office of Research and Estimates on a wide variety of subjects;

8. *National Intelligence Estimates* on Soviet military, political, and economic issues from 1950–1984;

9. analyses and reports from 1951–1975 concerning agricultural, economic, and industrial matters in the Soviet Union and Sino-Soviet bloc;

10. selected articles from 1955–1992 from *Studies in Intelligence*, an internal CIA publication;

11. small personal files of a few CIA and one State Department employee;

12. *Joint Army-Navy Intelligence Studies*;

13. *National Intelligence Surveys*;

14. Office of Current Intelligence *Country Studies*;

15. a very limited number of records from the principal directorates and the Office of the Director of Central Intelligence from 1947 into the 1970s;

16. ground photographs of various nations and regions taken from manned aircraft during the late 1950s to the early 1970s.

Approximately 1 million "pages" of these *Joint Army-Navy Intelligence Studies*, *National Intelligence Surveys*, *Country Studies*, records of the directorates and Office of the Director of Central Intelligence, and ground photographs were transferred to the College Park National Archives in late 1998 and, after *processing* there, were opened to the public in the fall of 1999. It must be noted, however, that approximately 80% of the textual records in this transfer are withdrawn in their entirety and many of the remaining 20% are *redacted*. Records that have been reviewed for declassification by the CIA and are currently undergoing *processing* by the National Archives include more than 4 million "pages" of Directorate of Operations reports from 1947–1955; Directorate of Intelligence reports from 1947 into the 1970s; records of the Office of the Director of Central Intelligence; abstracts of foreign scientific articles; translations of foreign language reports, journals, and media; early satellite photography analytical reports; ground photographs; and films (these records were transferred in October 1999).[41]

Record Group 262 contains the records of the Foreign Broadcast Information Branch (under the CIG from January–September 1947), Foreign Broadcast Information Service (under the CIG from November–December 1946), and the Foreign Broadcast Intelligence Service (under the Federal Communications Commission and War Department from 1941–1946). At the College Park National Archives, RG 262 has many thousands of sound recordings and about 1.5 million pages of textual records. The few postwar materials include a limited number of translations of monitored foreign broadcasts and daily reports of the Far Eastern, Latin American, and European Sections.

### CIA, CIG, SSU, and OSS Records at the CIA

With the exception of a few collections that are generally described in the recent *Records Management in the Central Intelligence Agency, A NARA Evaluation*[42] or in unclassified or declassified correspondence between the CIA and the JFK Assassination Records Review Board (located in RG 541 at the College Park National Archives), there is no information publicly available on the quantity, nature, and *appraisal* status of records at the CIA today.

This is true despite the fact that recently declassified CIA documents state that as of 1968 all the CIA facilities together held almost 251,500 c.f. of records (there is no breakdown by the individual facility holding the records, the individual office creating the records, or the *appraisal* status of the records), and as of 1969 the Agency Records Center alone held more than 100,000 c.f. of records. These records in the Agency Records Center were: (1) inactive records, (2) vital records (copies of active records necessary for continued operations in an emergency), (3) reserve stocks of intelligence reports and maps, (4) archival records (records of lasting value documenting the mission and functions of the agency). The breakdown by major office was as follows:

1. Director of Central Intelligence—1,630 c.f. of inactive records (51% *permanent* and 49% *temporary*); 117 c.f. of vital records; and 122 c.f. of reserve stocks;

2. Deputy Director/Intelligence—14,204 c.f. of inactive records (54% *permanent*, 7% *temporary*, and 39% *indefinite*); 7,694 c.f. of vital records; and 18,552 c.f. of reserve stocks;

3. Deputy Director/Plans—22,718 c.f. of inactive records (9% *permanent*, 2% *temporary*, and 89% *indefinite*); 697 c.f. of vital records; and 113 c.f. of reserve stocks;

4. Deputy Director/Security—21,605 c.f. of inactive records (8% *permanent*, 79% *temporary*, and 13% *indefinite*); 285 c.f. of vital records; and 314 c.f. of reserve stocks;

5. Deputy Director/Science and Technology—2,912 c.f. of inactive records (30% *permanent*, 66% *temporary*, and 4% *indefinite*); 361 c.f. of vital records; and 425 c.f. of reserve stocks;

6. Archives—884 c.f. of inactive records (all *indefinite*) and 7,553 c.f. of archival records.[43]

The CIA's *record schedules* provide that *permanent* records are eligible for transfer to the National Archives when fifty years old "pending CIA determination that continued Agency retention is not required." The NARA report concludes that this retention period "is no longer appropriate" and recommends it be reduced. More specifically, the NARA report recommends that most pre-1961 *permanent* textual records be transferred to the College Park National Archives by the end of 2003. With respect to *permanent* cartographic, photographic, and other nontextual records, it recommends that they be transferred when thirty years old or less because of their special preservation and conservation problems.

An important issue raised in the NARA report is the fact that the CIA has several thousands of electronic records systems, including ones for such critical records as finished intelligence products (for example, the *President's Daily Brief*), covert action files, and intelligence asset files. However, only about sixty such systems for "routine housekeeping functions" are covered by *records schedules*. The NARA report states in this regard that "without approved schedules, there is a serious risk that information of great value will not be preserved," and it recommends that as soon as possible *records schedules* be developed.

Requests under the FOIA and MDR for records at the College Park National Archives or at the agency itself should be submitted to the Freedom of Information Act/Privacy Act Office, Central Intelligence Agency, Washington, D.C. 20505. As noted in the previous chapter, the CIA Information Act of 1984 gives authority to the Director of Central Intelligence to exempt operational files of the Directorate of Operations, the Directorate of Science and Technology, and the Office of Security within the Directorate of Administration from the provisions of the FOIA (E.O. 12958 exempts them from the provisions of MDR). Although there is no information publicly available on even the number or percentage of these directorates' and office's files exempted, it is safe to assume that a large amount have been.[44] In the decennial review of the exemptions required under the statute, the Acting Director in 1995 removed the exemption for the Security Access Approval Files of the Office of Security and the following Directorate of Operations files: (1) administrative files of the defunct Office of Policy Coordination, (2) files on the inactive National Committee for a Free Europe and Asia Foundation projects. At the same time, several additional unnamed categories of Directorate of Operations files were placed on the exemption list.[45]

### Office of the Secretary of Defense (OSD) at the National Archives and Federal Records Centers

A large number of the OSD (1947–present) records are in RG 330 at the College Park National Archives and Washington National Records Center. No other National Archives or Federal records center has any RG 330 holdings.

The OSD estimates that it has about 25 million pages of *permanent* pre-1975 classified records subject to E.O. 12958. As of 1999, it had reviewed more than 3 million of these pages. There is no information available to the public on exactly which records have been reviewed or where they are.[46] In early 1999, the White House granted the OSD an exemption from automatic declassification for more than 7 million pages.[47]

At the College Park National Archives, there are about 12.5 million pages of records in RG 330. The *record group* doubled in size in January 1996 when approximately 6.25 million pages of *permanent* records were transferred from RG 330 at the Washington National Records Center under the P-1995 Project. The vast majority of these P-1995 Project records were classified and date from the late 1940s into the 1960s. In a 1996 report prepared by the OSD at the author's request, all the pre-1964 records in RG 330 at the Washington National Records Center were listed as having been systematically reviewed for declassification between 1980 and 1995. However, for reasons that are not entirely clear, the College Park National Archives cannot treat the pre-1964 classified records that came over under the P-1995 Project as having been reviewed for declassification. As a result, they are awaiting another review under the OSD's current program, possible re-review by the DOE under the Kyl Plan, and then *processing* by the National Archives before they will be available to the public.

The *finding aids* for RG 330 are useful in generally describing the contents, size, and dates covered of all the *entries*. For some collections transferred directly from the OSD in recent years, as well as the nearly 1 million pages of Research & Development Board records in Entry #341, there are also lists of folder titles by box.

Among the records that have been reviewed for declassification and *processed* at the College Park National Archives are:

1. Top Secret/Restricted Data and below Secretary of Defense decimal files from 1947–1954 (these files are arranged by the War Department Decimal System);

2. unclassified speeches and other papers of the Secretary and Deputy Secretary from 1969–1977 and audiotape recordings of speeches of various officials from 1961–1973;

3. Top Secret and below files of various Special Assistants to the Secretary of Defense from the late 1940s and early 1950s;

4. a limited number of Top Secret and below Assistant Secretary of Defense (Legal & Legislative Affairs) files from the late 1940s and early 1950s on legislative programs, review of military information for public dissemination, and other topics;

5. a limited number of Top Secret and below Assistant Secretary of Defense (Comptroller) and predecessor subject files, program budget files, budget administration files, program planning files, and other records from 1947 into the early 1950s;

6. a limited number of records of the executive office of the Assistant Secretary of Defense (International Security Affairs) and its predecessors, including Top Secret and below country files from 1950–1955, monthly country activity reports from 1950–1955, foreign ministers meeting records from 1950–1952, papers prepared by the Department of State from 1951–1954, and U.S. European Command effectiveness reports from 1953–1954;

7. a limited number of records of various offices under ASD (ISA) and its predecessors, including Top Secret and below Office of Military Assistance general decimal and project files from 1949–1953, Military Assistance Advisory Group activity reports from 1952–1953, Foreign Military Assistance Coordinating Committee files from 1949–1950, and State/Defense Military Information Control Committee files from 1949–1951; Top Secret and below Office of Programming & Control country files from 1949–1955 and supply operations reports from 1950–1956; and Top Secret and below Office of Special International Affairs subject files from 1949–1955;

8. a limited number of Top Secret and below files from the late 1940s and early 1950s of the Assistant Secretary of Defense (Manpower, Personnel & Reserve Affairs);

9. 1963–1974 files of the Southeast Asia Force Effectiveness and Intelligence Division under the Assistant Secretary of Defense (Program Analysis & Evaluation);

10. Top Secret/Restricted Data and below Research & Development Board records from 1947–1953, including Executive Secretariat subject files and committee and panel agendas, summary minutes, reports, subject files, and related documents;

11. final report and background papers for the U.S. side of the U.S./Russia Joint Committee on POW/MIAs;

12. Defense Prisoner of War/Missing in Action Office records relating to Korean War POWs and MIAs;

13. a limited number of Joint Intelligence Objectives Agency files from the mid-1940s to the early 1960s on foreign scientists brought to the United States under the PAPERCLIP program and its successor, the Defense Scientists Immigration Program.

Still-classified records at the College Park National Archives include the following:

1. Top Secret/Restricted Data and below Secretary of Defense National Security Council files and budget files from 1947–1970;

2. Top Secret and below Secretary of Defense policy documents from 1947–1949 (it is not known whether these duplicate what is in the Secretary of Defense decimal files for this period) and briefing books from 1947–1951;

3. Top Secret/Restricted Data and below Secretary of Defense records on guided missiles from 1958–1959 (it is not known whether these duplicate what is in the Secretary of Defense decimal files for this period);

4. Secret/Restricted Data and below transcripts of the 1957–1961 Secretaries' and Commanders' Conferences (the *SF-135* for this *accession* states that the Top Secret/Restricted Data and Top Secret transcripts for these conferences are filed in the Secretary of Defense 1963 decimal files);

5. Top Secret/Restricted Data and below general decimal and country decimal files of the Assistant Secretary of Defense (International Security Affairs) from 1954–1959 and 1961–1964;

6. several specialized collections of records apparently used by the ASD (ISA) and other high level officials, including Top Secret and below Paris Peace Talks administrative files from 1968–1970; Top Secret and below files from 1967–1968 on the USS Pueblo, congressional hearings on the Vietnam air war, and the EC-121 incident; Top Secret and below Operations Coordinating Board files from 1953–1960; Top Secret and below Berlin Task Force files from 1961; Top Secret and below Washington Foreign Ministers' Conference files from 1961; Top Secret and below Washington Ambassadorial Group/Military Subgroup files from 1961–1963; and Secret and below Steering Group files on individual countries from the early 1960s;

7. a wide range of records of the Assistant General Counsel under ASD (ISA), including Top Secret and below general subject files from 1957–1964; Top Secret and below files on POWs and war crimes from 1950–1962; Top Secret/Restricted Data and below files on disarmament and arms control from 1955–1970; Top Secret/Restricted Data and below files on the Mutual Security Agency, Mutual Security Program, Military Assistance Program, NATO, and status of forces agreements from 1949 into the late 1960s; Top Secret and below files on Korean Armistice violations from 1953–1958; Secret/Restricted Data and below country files, weapons production program files, R&D files, and Mutual Weapons Development program files from the 1950s and 1960s; Secret/Restricted Data and below Multilateral Force files from 1958–1965; Secret and below case files from 1955–1962; Secret and below offshore procurement files from the 1950s; and Secret and below files concerning outer space issues from the 1960s;

8. a wide range of records of other offices and divisions under the ASD (ISA), including but not limited to Secret and below Office of Military Assistance/Director of Military Assistance Military Assistance Program and Mutual Security Program subject files and reports from 1959 into the 1960s; Top Secret and below Strategic Trade & Disclosure Directorate files from 1950–1959; Secret and below Office of Foreign Economic Assistance files from the 1950s and early 1960s; Top Secret and below International Logistics Negotiation Division files from the 1950s and early 1960s; Top Secret and below Office of Foreign Military

Rights Affairs files from the 1950s; Secret and below Near East Office files on Iran from the 1960s; Secret/Restricted Data and below European Region Office files from 1953–1962 on missile deployment and submarine basing in, and nuclear cooperation with, the United Kingdom; and Secret/Restricted Data and below European Region Office files from 1958–1964 on missile deployments and high-level visits by U.S. and Western European officials;

9. Top Secret/Restricted Data and below agendas, minutes, and reports of the Armed Forces Policy Council from 1949–1950;

10. Top Secret/Restricted Data and below Assistant to the Secretary of Defense (Special Operations) and predecessor psychological planning records from 1948–1958 and subject files and country files of General Lansdale from 1957–1961;

11. a limited number of Top Secret and below Joint Intelligence Objectives Agency policy files and histories from the 1950s and early 1960s;

12. Top Secret and below incoming messages to the OSD from 1950–1960;

13. Top Secret and below National Military Command Center/Military Assistance Command Vietnam and National Military Command Center/Commander in Chief, Pacific messages from 1966–1969;

14. a wide range of Top Secret/Restricted Data and below project files from the 1960s of the Office of Organization & Management Planning under the Assistant Secretary of Defense (Administration), including but not limited to files on the National Military Command System, establishment of the Defense Intelligence Agency, disestablishment of the Assistant to the Secretary of Defense (Special Operations), missile gap, TFX, strategic mobility, and civil rights (from the *SF-135s*, these files appear to have all the key OSD incoming and outgoing correspondence);

15. Secret and below Assistant Secretary of Defense (Administration) committee management files from 1947–1973;

16. Top Secret and below Assistant Secretary of Defense (Legislative Affairs) transcripts of congressional hearings and related files from 1956–1968;

17. Top Secret and below files from 1957 to the late 1960s of the Directorate for Security Review under the Assistant Secretary of Defense (Public Affairs) relating to the prior review of official speeches and writings;

18. Top Secret and below Assistant Secretary of Defense (Public Affairs) Cuba information releases from 1962–1963;

19. a wide range of Assistant Secretary of Defense (Comptroller) and predecessor records, including Top Secret and below 5-Year Plans from 1961–1969, budget correspondence files from 1947–1961, Military Assistance Program and Mutual Security Program files from 1951–1960, project files from 1948–1959, and general subject files from 1949–1954; and Secret and below R&D files from 1958–1968;

20. Secret/Restricted Data and below Assistant Secretary of Defense (Supply & Logistics)/Assistant Secretary of Defense (Installations & Logistics) general subject files and decimal files from the late 1950s and early 1960s;

21. Secret and below reports and communications files from 1951–1961 of the Director for Telecommunications Policy under the Assistant Secretary of Defense (Installations & Logistics) and its predecessors;

22. a limited number of Secret and below Assistant Secretary of Defense (Health & Medical)/Assistant Secretary of Defense (Manpower) general subject files from the late 1950s and early 1960s;

23. a limited number of Top Secret/Restricted Data and below Assistant to the Secretary of Defense (Atomic Energy) subject files concerning weapons development, testing, custody, storage, dispersal, safety, bilateral agreements with other nations, disarmament proposals, congressional relations, and other topics from the late 1940s to the early 1960s; General Loper's speeches from 1955–1960; General Loper's Daily Activity Reports from 1954–1961; SALT Working Papers from 1973–1980; Fritz Kramer Geo-Strategic Assessments from 1973–1978; and numbered files concerning the assignment and discontinuance of code words for projects and operations from 1945–1967;

24. Top Secret/Restricted Data and below agendas, summary minutes, and related records of the 1955–1960 formal Military Liaison Committee meetings (for unknown reasons the agendas, summary minutes, and related records of the 1946–1954 formal Military Liaison Committee meetings are in RG 334 at the Washington National Records Center); summary minutes of the 1955–1962 informal Military Liaison Committee meetings; and Military Liaison Committee subject files from 1953–1962;

25. a limited number of Top Secret/Restricted Data and below Weapons Systems Evaluation Group reports, decimal files, project correspondence files, and working papers from 1949–1963;

26. a wide range of Research & Development Board records from 1947–1953, including Top Secret/Restricted Data and below Executive Secretariat subject files; Top Secret/Restricted Data and below subject files, agendas, and minutes of the Committee on Atomic Energy; and Secret/

Restricted Data and below subject files of the Committee on Aeronautics, Committee on Materials, Committee on General Sciences, Committee on Medical Sciences, Committee on Human Research, Committee on Chemical & Biological Warfare, and the Committee on Guided Missiles. (These records were transferred in 1996 as part of the P-1995 Project. It is not known whether they duplicate the Research & Development Board records in Entry no. 341 that have been available to the public for some years.);

27. Top Secret/Restricted Data and below agendas, summary minutes, reports, and subject files from 1954–1958 of the numerous technical advisory panels and coordinating committees that replaced the committees and panels of the Research & Development Board and advised the Assistant Secretary of Defense (Research & Development), Assistant Secretary of Defense (Applications Engineering), and their successor, the Assistant Secretary of Defense (Research & Engineering);

28. Secret/Restricted Data and below agendas and summary minutes from 1955–1958 of the Policy Council that advised the ASD (R&D), ASD (AE), and ASD (R&E);

29. Secret/Restricted Data and below general subject files and project reports of the Director of Defense Research & Engineering from 1959–1963;

30. a limited number of records of the Assistant Directors and Deputy Directors under the Director of Defense Research & Engineering and their predecessors under the ASD (R&D), ASD (AE), and ASD (R&E), including but not limited to the Secret/Restricted Data and below subject files from 1949–1961 of the Assistant Director (Tactical Missiles & Ordnance); Secret/Restricted Data and below subject files on individual missile systems, ad hoc and study group reports, transcripts of conferences, briefing and meeting files, and budget files of the Special Assistant for Guided Missiles from 1945–1960; Secret/Restricted Data and below monthly reports on intercontinental and intermediate-range ballistic missiles, anti-ballistic missiles, satellites, and related systems of the Special Assistant for Guided Missiles from 1955–1961; Secret and below subject files from the early 1960s of the Assistant Director (Engineering Management); Secret/Restricted Data and below subject files from 1960–1964 of the Deputy Director (Research & Engineering); and Secret/Restricted Data and below subject files from 1949–1961 of the Deputy Director (Tactical Aircraft Systems);

31. a small quantity of records of the various offices under the Director of Defense Research & Engineering and the predecessor offices under the ASD (R&D), ASD (AE), and ASD (R&E), including but not limited to the Secret/Restricted Data and below Office of Aeronautical Re-

search subject files from 1961 and meeting and conference files, general subject files, and ad hoc study group files from 1953–1960; Secret/Restricted Data and below Strategic Weapons Office subject files from 1958–1963; Secret/Restricted Data and below Office of International Programs subject files from 1954–1962; Secret and below Office of Communications-Electronics subject files from 1948 into the early 1960s; and Secret/Restricted Data and below Nuclear Programs Office subject files from 1954–1963;

32. Secret/Restricted Data and below agendas, minutes, and subject files of the OSD Ballistic Missiles Committee from 1955–1960;

33. Secret/Restricted Data and below Advanced Research Projects Agency Monthly Management & Quarterly Reports from 1958–1963 and program documents on ballistic missile defense from 1958–1964; and Secret and below files from 1958–1960 on Project VANGUARD, Army/Navy/Air Force satellite programs, and the Advisory Group on Special Capabilities;

34. a limited number of records of the various offices under the Advanced Research Projects Agency, including Secret/Restricted Data and below Nuclear Test Detection Office subject files and reports on Project VELA and other topics from the late 1950s and early 1960s and Secret and below Nuclear Test Detection Office files on the Saturn rocket from the late 1950s and early 1960s;

35. the vast majority of Secret and below Joint Intelligence Objectives Agency files from the mid-1940s to the early 1960s on foreign scientists brought to the United States under the PAPERCLIP program and its successor, the Defense Scientist Immigration Program.

There are more than 60 million pages of mostly classified records in RG 330 at the Washington National Records Center as of 2000 (80% *permanent* and 20% *temporary*). As part of the P-2000 Project, about 800,000 pages of unclassified *permanent* records and 3.4 million pages of classified *permanent* records will be transferred to RG 330 at the College Park National Archives by the end of 2001. Even if the classified records have been reviewed for declassification by the time of their transfer, they will not be available to the public until they are possibly re-reviewed by the DOE under the Kyl Plan and then *processed* by the National Archives. The records to be transferred include:

1. Top Secret/Restricted Data and below Toner Reports to the President from 1956–1960 (copies of these are presumably at the Eisenhower Library);

2. small collections of Top Secret/Restricted Data and below reading and speech files of Secretary of Defense Wilson from 1953–1957, Deputy Secretary of Defense Quarles from 1957–1959, and Secretary of Defense McElroy from 1957–1959 (it is not known whether these records duplicate what is in the Secretary and Deputy Secretary of Defense decimal files for these years);

3. Top Secret/Restricted Data and below decimal files of the Secretary of Defense, Deputy Secretary of Defense, and the Special Assistants thereto from 1955–1960 (these are arranged by the War Department Decimal System);

4. Top Secret and below Secretary of Defense/Military Assistance Command Vietnam and Secretary of Defense/Commander in Chief, Pacific briefing files from 1967;

5. Top Secret and below National Military Command Center/Military Assistance Command Vietnam and National Military Command Center/Commander in Chief, Pacific messages from 1969–1970;

6. Top Secret and below Special State-Defense Study Group historical documents from 1962–1965, and files relating to the 1966 long-range study on Communist China, the 1967 study on American strategy in the Near East and North Africa, the 1968 study on Latin America, and the 1968 study on future American overseas base requirements;

7. a limited number of Top Secret and below Senior Interdepartmental Group agendas, minutes, and meeting files from 1966–1968;

8. a limited number of Top Secret and below Vietnam Task Force files consisting of documents on the politico-military situation from 1968–1970, action papers to and from the White House from 1969–1971, miscellaneous papers on negotiations from 1967–1969, and background papers on U.S. policy from 1961–1967;

9. Secret and below POW/MIA Task Force files from 1965–1969;

10. Top Secret/Restricted Data and below general decimal files and country decimal files of the Assistant Secretary of Defense (International Security Affairs) from 1960 and 1965 and Project REDCOSTE files from 1966–1969;

11. Secret and Confidential Director of Military Assistance/Directorate for Security Assistance Operations, ASD (ISA) Military Assistance Program subject files, planning files, 5-year assistance plans, orders, progress reports, summary reports, status reports, and audits from the late 1950s to 1970;

12. Secret and below Policy Planning Staff, ASD (ISA) files on the Interdepartmental Psychological-Political Working Group from 1961–1965;

13. Top Secret/Restricted Data and below European Region Office, ASD (ISA) nuclear planning files from 1960–1970 concerning anti-ballistic missiles, medium-range ballistic missiles, the Multilateral Force, Special Committee on Nuclear Planning, Special Committee on Intelligence/ Data Exchange, and Working Group on Communications; and Top Secret/Restricted Data and below policy and subject files from 1958– 1970;

14. Secret and below Near East Region Office and Africa Region Office, ASD (ISA) policy and subject files from the late 1960s;

15. Top Secret/Restricted Data and below Assistant General Counsel, ASD (ISA) international negotiations/agreements files from 1952–1970 and subject files from 1957–1970;

16. Secret and below Programs Directorate, ASD (ISA) civic action and internal security reports from the 1950s to 1965;

17. Secret/Restricted Data and below Defense Advisor, U.S. Mission to NATO subject files from 1966–1968;

18. Top Secret/Restricted Data and below Assistant Secretary of Defense (Comptroller) subject files from 1961–1966;

19. Top Secret/Restricted Data and below Department of Defense Directives from 1958–1960;

20. Top Secret/Restricted Data and below Tactical Air Division, Assistant Secretary of Defense (Systems Analysis) subject files from 1961–1966;

21. Secret/Restricted Data and below NATO Division, ASD (SA) subject files from 1966–1968 and strategic programs files from 1965– 1970;

22. Top Secret and below Director of South East Asia Programs, ASD (SA) intelligence reports, studies, and related records from 1964–1967; and Secret and below Director of South East Asia Programs Presidential memos on Vietnam from 1972, CINPAC Reports, OPREPS, MAC-CORD Provincial Reports, Measurement of Progress Reports, MACV SEER Reports, CIRADS, CIA memos, CIA Weekly Situation Reports, and related records from 1967–1972;

23. Top Secret/Restricted Data and below Nuclear Weapons & Planning Division, ASD (SA) Project REDCOSTE files from 1970;

24. Top Secret/Restricted Data and below Directorate for Planning & Evaluation, ASD (SA) files on naval forces from 1966–1969;

25. a limited number of Secret/Restricted Data and below Assistant to the Secretary of Defense (Atomic Energy) subject files from 1957–1966 on atomic weapons, testing, storage, dispersal, safety, command & control, bilateral agreements, and congressional relations;

26. Top Secret and below Assistant Secretary of Defense (Installations & Logistics) chronological files from 1953–1959;

27. Secret/Restricted Data and below Defense Science Board Executive Committee files from 1961–1968, NATO Long Term Study Group files from 1966–1967, Subcommittee on Military Role in Space files from 1962–1963, and Subcommittee on DOD R&D files from 1963–1965;

28. Secret and below Defense Science Board files from 1958–1968 on the Tripartite Technical Cooperation Program;

29. a limited number of Top Secret and below Defense Special Projects Group plans & objectives files from 1970–1972 and R&D strategy files from 1969–1972;

30. Secret/Restricted Data and below chronological reading files from 1953–1957 of the Assistant Secretary of Defense (Research & Development);

31. Secret/Restricted Data and below chronological files and subject files from 1958 into the early 1960s of the Director of Defense Research & Engineering and the Deputy Directors and Assistant Directors thereunder;

32. Secret/Restricted Data and below DDR&E Presidential Science Advisory Committee files from 1959–1969;

33. Secret/Restricted Data and below DDR&E Tactical Missiles & Ordnance Division/Land Warfare Division and predecessor office project reports, studies, correspondence files, and related records from 1951–1970;

34. Secret/Restricted Data and below DDR&E Strategic Weapons Division project reports, studies, subject files, and related records from 1958–1970 primarily concerning ballistic missiles and ballistic missile defense;

35. Secret/Restricted Data and below DDR&E Chemical Technology Division subject files from 1960–1966;

36. Secret and below DDR&E Space Technology Division DOD/NASA Aeronautics & Astronautics Coordinating Board agendas, minutes, reports, and correspondence files from the 1960s; Secret and below DOD/NACA & DOD/NASA agreements from 1954–1964; Secret and below DOD/NASA Large Launch Vehicle Planning Group reports from 1961–1962 and files on individual launch vehicles, guidance, and propulsion from the 1960s; and Secret and below Tripartite Technical Cooperation Program-Subgroup M (Military Space Research) minutes, reports, and correspondence files from 1959–1969;

37. Secret/Restricted Data and below DDR&E Tactical Aircraft Division and predecessor office project reports, studies, subject files, and related records from 1955–1970 on individual aircraft, SST, engines, electronic systems, drones, surveillance, air-launched weapons, and related topics;

38. Secret/Restricted Data and below DDR&E Sea Warfare Systems Division project reports, studies, subject files, and related records from 1958–1966;

39. Secret/Restricted Data and below Advanced Research Projects Agency files on Projects VELA, AGILE, and JET BELT from the late 1950s into the early 1970s;

40. Secret and below ARPA Overseas Defense Research Office TIARA reports and other reports, studies and related records from the 1960s;

41. Secret/Restricted Data and below ARPA Nuclear Monitoring Research Office Salmon, Long Shot, and Shoal reports from 1962–1967; and Secret/Restricted Data and below subject files, program files, project files, JOWOG files, and related records from the 1960s;

42. Secret/Restricted Data and below ARPA Strategic Technology Division subject files, program files, project files, and related records from 1958–1970;

43. Secret/Restricted Data and below ARPA Tactical Technology Office subject files, program files, project files, and related records from 1958–1970;

44. Secret/Restricted Data and below ARPA Program Management Office subject files and program files from the late 1960s;

45. Secret/Restricted Data and below ARPA Advanced Engineering Office subject files and project files from the late 1960s;

46. Secret and below ARPA Research Development Field Unit Vietnam files from the 1960s.

There are numerous records that are not eligible for transfer to RG 330 at the College Park National Archives by 2001. In this regard, it should be recalled that the *permanent* OSD records of high-level officials and task forces are only eligible for transfer after forty years (all other records are eligible after thirty years). Moreover, many *accessions* contain *permanent* records that span several decades, and they are only eligible for transfer thirty or forty years after the date of the most recent record therein. Among the records not eligible for transfer by 2001 are:

1. Top Secret/Restricted Data and below decimal files from 1961–1997 of the Secretary of Defense, Deputy Secretary of Defense, and their

Special Assistants, Executive Secretaries, and Military Assistants (these files are arranged by the War Department Decimal System);

2. Top Secret/Restricted Data and below reading files of Secretary of Defense Gates from 1950–1960 and numbered files of Secretary of Defense Laird from 1969–1972;

3. Top Secret and below Secretary of Defense McNamara files on Vietnam, draft presidential memorandums, and guidance memorandums from 1961–1968; and Top Secret and below Secretary of Defense Clifford records on Vietnam from 1968–1969;

4. Top Secret/Restricted Data and below *DOD Weekly Reports* to the President from 1963–1967;

5. Top Secret/Restricted Data and below Joint Strategic Objectives Plan records of the Secretary of Defense, Deputy Secretary of Defense and their Military Assistants from 1969–1985;

6. Top Secret/Restricted Data and below multiaddressee memos signed by the Secretary of Defense and Deputy Secretary of Defense from 1948–1977;

7. Top Secret/Restricted Data and below Secretary of Defense Brown and Deputy Secretaries of Defense Duncan and Clayton signer's copies from 1977–1980;

8. Secret/Restricted Data and below Secretary of Defense and Deputy Secretary of Defense signer's copies from 1981 into the 1990s;

9. Top Secret and below files on Cuba and the Dominican Republic from 1963–1965 used by the Secretary of Defense and other high-level officials;

10. Top Secret/Restricted Data and below chronological files of Deputy Secretary of Defense Quarles from 1957–1959, chronological files of Deputy Secretary of Defense Gilpatric from 1961–1963, chronological files of Deputy Secretary of Defense Vance from 1964–1967, and chronological files of Deputy Secretary of Defense Nitze from 1967–1968;

11. Top Secret/Restricted Data and below Special Assistant to the Secretary of Defense and other Deputy Secretary of Defense chronological files from 1958 into the 1970s;

12. Top Secret/Restricted Data and below notes made by the Special Assistant to the Secretary of Defense and Deputy Secretary of Defense on the 1955–1962 Armed Forces Policy Council meetings, Joint Secretaries Meetings, and Staff Council Meetings;

13. Top Secret/Restricted Data and below agendas, summary minutes, and reports of the Armed Forces Policy Council from 1951 into the 1980s,

Joint Secretaries Meetings from 1950–1960, and Staff Council Meetings from 1951–1972;

14. Secret and below *Annual Defense Report* history books from 1988–1995;

15. Top Secret/Restricted Data and below Assistant to the Secretary of Defense (Special Operations) and predecessor chronological files from 1952–1961; Burma files from 1954–1957; Psychological Strategy Board files from 1951–1952; Indochina files from 1953–1954; Antarctica and OPERATION DEEPFREEZE files from 1954–1961; and miscellaneous files of General Lansdale from 1954–1963;

16. Top Secret and below Vietnam Task Force records, including but not limited to War Department/Navy Department/State Department/DOD cables from 1940–1968; White House/War Department/Navy Department/State Department/DOD/CIA memos, reports, studies and correspondence from 1945–1968; working files on the 1954 Geneva Conference; miscellaneous documents from 1954–1961 on U.S. aid programs; congressional correspondence files; and task force chronological files;

17. Top Secret/Restricted Data and below SALT Task Force records from 1968–1981, including but not limited to cables, messages, outside research reports, task force subject and policy files, White House/DOD/State/CIA memos and reports, draft agreements, U.S. statements, Soviet statements, joint statements, and copies of congressional testimony;

18. Top Secret/Restricted Data and below Mutual Balanced Forces Reduction Task Force files from 1970–1980;

19. Top Secret and below POW/MIA Task Force records from 1965–1982, including but not limited to individual case files, intelligence reports, and Interagency Group meeting files;

20. Top Secret/Restricted Data and below Department of Defense Directives, Instructions, and Transmittals from the late 1940s into the early 1990s;

21. Top Secret and below messages between the National Military Command Center and Military Assistance Command Vietnam/Commander in Chief, Pacific from 1971;

22. Top Secret and below Military Assistance Command Vietnam/Commander in Chief, Pacific telephone conference records from 1970–1972;

23. Top Secret/Restricted Data and below general decimal files and country decimal files of the Assistant Secretary of Defense (International Security Affairs) from 1966 into the 1980s;

24. Top Secret and below Deputy Under Secretary of Defense (Policy Support) and predecessor emergency planning files from 1964–1996;

25. Secret/Restricted Data and below chronological files and policy files of the Under Secretary of Defense for Policy from the 1990s;

26. a wide range of records of offices under ASD (ISA) and USDP, including but not limited to Secret and below foreign military rights affairs files from 1942–1995; Secret/Restricted Data and below reports of the Director of Net Assessment from the 1980s; Top Secret/Restricted Data and below external research reports from the 1960s and 1970s; Top Secret/Restricted Data and below National Security Council files from the late 1960s into the 1980s; Secret and below satellite and space files from the 1960s and 1970s; Secret and below censorship files from 1961–1981; Top Secret and below emergency planning files from 1964–1997; Top Secret/Restricted Data and below NATO High Level Group Meeting briefing books from 1977–1990; Top Secret/Restricted Data and below Senior Review Group files from 1970–1977; Secret and below Middle East Task Group meeting and negotiation files from 1966–1980; Secret/Restricted Data and below SALT, START, and INF files from the 1972 into the early 1990s; Secret and below Cooperative Threat Reduction files from 1983–1990; Secret and below Haiti special studies from 1983–1997; Secret/Restricted Data and below treaty files from the 1980s; Secret/Restricted Data and below U.S.S.R. nuclear affairs files from 1983–1991; Secret/Restricted Data and below Competitive Strategies Office files from 1973–1992; and Secret and below special operations and low intensity conflict chronological files from 1987–1991;

27. Top Secret/Restricted Data and below subject files, chronological files, and reading files of the Office of General Counsel from the 1950s into the 1980s;

28. a wide range of Top Secret/Restricted Data and below records of the Assistant Secretary of Defense (Comptroller) and the Deputy Assistant Secretaries and offices thereunder from the 1960s into the 1980s;

29. Top Secret/Restricted Data and below chronological files, policy files, and subject files of the Assistant Secretary of Defense (Systems Analysis) and Assistant Secretary of Defense (Program Analysis & Evaluation) from 1961 into the early 1990s;

30. a small number of records of various offices under ASD (SA) and ASD (PA&E), including but not limited to Top Secret/Restricted Data and below Naval Forces Division files from 1964–1973; Top Secret/Restricted Data and below Naval Threat Forces Working Group chairman's files from 1972–1973; Secret/Restricted Data and below Tactical Air Divi-

sion anti-tactical missile program case files from 1981–1987, tactical missile programs and technology development files from 1980–1992, OPERATION DESERT STORM Lessons Learned files from 1990–1991, Navy fleet air defense missile programs files from 1969–1990, and close air support gun weapons effective case files from 1969–1990; Secret/Restricted Data and below Strategic Defensive & Space Programs Division case files from 1987–1998; and Secret and below Force Structure Division case files from 1988–1994;

31. Top Secret/Restricted Data and below subject files, correspondence files, congressional testimony, and periodic reports of the Assistant to the Secretary of Defense (Atomic Energy) and its predecessor from 1948 into the early 1980s;

32. Secret/Restricted Data and below agendas and summary minutes of Military Liaison Committee meetings from 1960–1986; agendas and summary minutes of Military Liaison Committee/Atomic Energy Commission meetings from 1947–1974; and Military Liaison Committee subject files, correspondence files, annual reports, and monthly reports to the Joint Committee on Atomic Energy from 1947 into the early 1970s;

33. Secret/Restricted Data and below agendas, minutes, and reports of the Nuclear Weapons Council from the 1980s;

34. Secret/Restricted Data and below Assistant to the Secretary of Defense (Atomic Energy) subject files, briefing files, meeting files, and congressional testimony from the 1980s into the early 1990s;

35. a large number of records of the Assistant to the Secretary of Defense (Legislative Affairs) and the Deputy Assistant Secretaries and offices thereunder, including but not limited to Top Secret/Restricted Data and below transcripts of congressional hearings and related files from the late 1960s into the 1980s;

36. many records of the Assistant Secretary of Defense (Administration), including but not limited to Secret/Restricted Data and below strategic arms control files from 1974–1986 and offensive weapons and space systems files from 1967–1983;

37. Secret/Restricted Data and below policy files of the Assistant to the Secretary of Defense (Command, Control, Communications, and Intelligence) and its predecessors from 1953–1974;

38. Secret/Restricted Data and below chronological reading files of ASD (C3I) from the 1980s and early 1990s;

39. a large number of records of the Assistant Secretary of Defense (Public Affairs), Assistant Secretary of Defense (Installations & Logistics), As-

sistant Secretary of Defense (Health & Environment), Assistant Secretary of Defense (Manpower & Reserve Affairs), and the Deputy Assistant Secretaries and offices thereunder;

40. Secret and below chronological files of the Director of the Strategic Defense Initiative Organization from the 1980s;

41. Top Secret/Restricted Data and below Weapons Systems Evaluation Group reports, working papers, decimal files, and project correspondence files from the late 1940s into the early 1970s;

42. a limited number of Defense Special Projects Group records, including Secret and below tasking memos from 1966–1970; Division of Operations files from the early 1970s; Division of Logistical Support general R&D files from 1966–1970; and Division of Engineering R&D project files from 1969–1972 and science advisory committee files from 1966–1972;

43. Secret and below Defense Technology Security Administration chronological files and policy, plans and program files from the 1970s into the early 1990s;

44. Secret and below Defense Security Assistance Agency/Defense Security Cooperation Agency reports to Congress, foreign military sales files, policy files, program files, country files, and legal files from the 1970s into the 1990s;

45. Secret/Restricted Data and below agendas and summary minutes of the 1956–1975 meetings of the Defense Science Board and reports of various task forces and ad hoc groups thereunder from the same period;

46. Secret/Restricted Data and below meeting and conference files of the Director of Defense Research & Engineering and its predecessors from 1951–1973;

47. Top Secret/Restricted Data and below DDR&E policy files from 1959 into the 1980s;

48. Top Secret/Restricted Data and below DDR&E congressional correspondence and testimony files from the 1960s and 1970s;

49. Secret/Restricted Data and below chronological files from 1959 into the early 1990s of the DDR&E and the many Deputy Directors and Assistant Directors thereunder;

50. Secret/Restricted Data and below DDR&E Development Concept Papers from 1969–1973;

51. Top Secret/Restricted Data and below DDR&E files on NSSM 246 (Strategic Task Force) from 1976;

52. Top Secret/Restricted Data and below DDR&E files on the Conference of National Armaments Directors from 1972–1975;

53. Top Secret/Restricted Data and below DDR&E project case files from 1966–1979;

54. Secret/Restricted Data and below DDR&E *Weekly Reports* from 1978–1984;

55. Secret and below DDR&E Engineering Technology Office Tripartite Technical Cooperation Program files from 1961–1972 and files on guided bombs from 1967–1972;

56. Top Secret/Restricted Data and below DDR&E Electronics & Information Systems Office files on missile intelligence collection, the National Military Command System, airborne command posts, and command and control from the 1960s;

57. Top Secret and below DDR&E Electronic Warfare & Reconnaissance Office files on various aircraft and missile intelligence collection projects from the 1960s and early 1970s;

58. Secret/Restricted Data and below DDR&E Land Warfare Office files on armored vehicles, antitank and assault weapons, air defense weapons, tactical missiles, and other topics from the 1960s and early 1970s;

59. Secret and below DDR&E Environmental & Life Sciences Office files on herbicides in Vietnam from the 1960s and early 1970s;

60. Secret/Restricted Data and below DDR&E Strategic & Space Systems Office files from the 1960s on NASA programs, Manned Orbiting Laboratory, Titan III, navigation satellites, and the *Military Plans for Using Space to Improve National Security* report;

61. Secret and below DDR&E Strategic & Space Systems Office files on the Global Positioning System from 1973–1975, Navigation Working Group meetings from 1974–1975, and navigation satellite transit from 1970–1974;

62. Secret/Restricted Data and below chronological files of the Director and Deputy Director of the Advanced Research Projects Agency from the 1960s into the 1980s;

63. miscellaneous Secret/Restricted Data and below ARPA program files from 1958–1989;

64. miscellaneous Secret/Restricted Data and below ARPA documents from 1960–1977 concerning Comprehensive Test Ban Treaty and Mutual Balanced Forces Reduction issues;

65. a wide range of files of the ARPA Tactical Technology Office, including but not limited to Secret and below files from 1968–1972 on Project

QUIET HELICOPTER; and Secret/Restricted Data and below studies from 1969–1980 on target acquisition and outside R&D studies from the 1960s into the 1980s on various aspects of land warfare;

66. a limited number of records of the ARPA Program Management Office, including but not limited to Secret and below R&D funding records from the 1960s and 1970s;

67. a limited number of Secret/Restricted Data and below ARPA SALT Support Group files from 1960–1977;

68. a limited number of Secret/Restricted Data and below ARPA Strategic Technology Office files from the 1960s and 1970s;

69. a limited number of Secret and below records of the ARPA Technology Assessment Office, including but not limited to external research reports from the 1960s and 1970s on China, psychological operations, Nixon Doctrine, and other topics;

70. a limited number of records of the ARPA Ocean Control Office, including but not limited to Secret/Restricted Data and below files from the 1970s and 1980s on various aspects of naval warfare;

71. Secret and below ARPA Materials Science Office R&D studies, program documents, and other records from the 1960s into the 1980s;

72. a limited number of Secret/Restricted Data and below ARPA Nuclear Monitoring Research Office R&D studies, program documents, and other records from the 1970s and 1980s.

A large number of Robert McNamara's papers from his tenure as Secretary of Defense are in RG 200 (National Archives gift collections) at the College Park National Archives. It is not known whether these are duplicates of what is in RG 330 at the Washington National Records Center. There is an excellent *finding aid* that lists all the folder titles by box. However, a large number of documents are still classified.

### OSD Records at the OSD, Presidential Libraries, Library of Congress, and other Institutions

The OSD does not have any central records storage facility or archives. There is no information publicly available regarding the quantity, nature, and *appraisal* status of records still at the OSD.[48]

Several presidential libraries have relevant holdings. The Truman Library has the personal papers of Felix Larkin (General Counsel from 1947–1951) and the personal papers of John Ohly (various positions in the War Department and DOD from 1940–1949), both of which are open. The personal papers of Neil McElroy (Secretary of Defense from 1957–1959) and the personal papers of Donald Quarles (various positions within DOD during the 1950s) are at the Eisenhower Library, and both are open. The Kennedy Library has the personal papers of Roswell Gilpatric (Deputy Secretary of Defense from 1956–1967) and microfilm copies of the 1961–1963 cables, numerical files, and correspondence files of Robert McNamara (Secretary of Defense from 1961–1968), both of which are open. At the Johnson Library there are the personal papers of Clark Clifford (Secretary of Defense from 1968–1969), Alain Enthoven (Assistant Secretary of Defense [Systems Analysis] from 1960–1969), and Morton Halperin (Deputy Assistant Secretary of Defense [International Security Affairs] and National Security Council staff member from 1968–1969). However, only the Clifford papers are open. The Reagan Library has the personal papers of Fred Ikle (Under Secretary for Policy from 1981–1989), but they are not open.

A large number of General George Marshall's papers, including some from his service as Secretary of Defense, are available at the George C. Marshall Research Foundation in Lexington, Virginia. The library and archives section can be contacted at 540–463-7103, ext. 230. There is an extensive collection of Secretary of Defense Caspar Weinberger's papers at the Manuscript Division at the Library of Congress. Because of their classification and restrictions imposed by him when donated to the institution, however, they are not open. A limited number of papers of General Edward Lansdale are at the Hoover Institution at Stanford University. The collection is open, although the OSD apparently has withdrawn many items.

Requests under the FOIA or MDR for records at the Washington National Records Center or at the OSD should be submitted to the Office of the Secretary of Defense (Public Affairs), ATTN: Directorate for Freedom of Information and Security Review, Room 2C757, Pentagon, Washington, D.C. 20301–1400.

### Defense Civil Preparedness Agency (DCPA) / Office of Civil Defense (OCD) / Office of Emergency Planning (OEP) / Office of Civil and Defense Mobilization (OCDM) / Federal Civil Defense Administration (FCDA) / Office of Defense Mobilization (ODM) / National Security Resources Board (NSRB) Records at the National Archives and Federal Record Centers

The vast majority of records of the DCPA (1972–1979), OCD (1961–1972), OEP (1961–1973), OCDM (1958–1961), FCDA (1950–1958), ODM (1950–1958), and NSRB (1947–1953) are in several *record groups* at the College Park National Archives and Washington National Records Center.

Record Group 304 has records of the OCDM. At the College Park National Archives, RG 304 contains about 2 million pages of records. Among the records that have been reviewed for declassification and *processed* are:

1. Top Secret and below office files of the Chairman and Vice Chairman of the NSRB from 1947–1953 and various records of the Administrative and Coordinating Staff and Mobilization Planning Staff of the NSRB from 1947–1953;

2. Top Secret and below records of the ODM from 1950–1958, including the Central Files from 1950–1953;

3. Secret and below OCDM Central Files from 1960;

4. Top Secret/Restricted Data and below files of the Technical Liaison Division, Office of the Secretary of the Army (Civil Defense), from 1951–1958.

Some regional National Archives have small RG 304 holdings. No Federal records center has any RG 304 holdings.

Record Group 396 contains records of the OEP. At the College Park National Archives, RG 396 has about 500,000 pages of records. Most of the records at the College Park National Archives are unclassified or have been reviewed for declassification and *processed*, and they include:

1. Secret and below central files and subject files of the Directors of the FCDA, OCDM, and OEP from 1950–1973;

2. Secret and below FCDA, OCDM, and OEP committee files from 1957–1963;

3. Secret and below subject files of the Assistant Directors of the FCDA and OCDM from 1958–1961;

4. Secret and below subject files of the Deputy Director of the OEP from 1962–1963;

5. Secret and below files of the Resource Analysis Division of the FCDA and OCDM from 1951–1961;

6. Secret and below miscellaneous records of the OCDM, FCDA, OCDM, and their predecessors from 1944–1962;

7. Secret and below subject files of the Office of General Counsel of the ODM, OCDM, and OEP from 1952–1964;

8. censorship planning records from World War II to 1953.

Some regional National Archives have small RG 396 holdings. There are no relevant records in RG 396 at any Federal records center.

Record Group 397 contains the records of the DCPA. At the College Park National Archives, RG 397 has more than 1 million pages of records that are entirely unclassified or have been reviewed for declassification and *processed*. The records include:

1. correspondence files of the Director of the DCPA from 1973–1979;

2. various reports, studies, program records, and planning records from the early 1950s into the early 1970s of the Plans and Operations Directorate of the OCD and the equivalent offices under the OCDM and FCDA.

No regional National Archives or any Federal records center has RG 397 holdings of interest.

### Defense Information Systems Agency (DISA) / Defense Communications Agency (DCA) Records at the National Archives and Federal Record Centers

A large number of records of the DISA (1991–present) and DCA (1961–1991) are in RG 371 at the College Park National Archives and the Washington National Records Center. No other National Archives or Federal records center has any RG 371 holdings.

It is not known how many *permanent* pre-1975 classified records the DISA holds subject to E.O. 12958. The FY 1996, FY 1997, FY 1998, and FY 1999 ISOO annual reports have not specifically listed the DISA as having declassified any records, although its totals may be included in the general "All Others" category in these reports.

Record Group 371 at the College Park National Archives has less than 250,000 pages of records. All have been reviewed for declassification and *processed*, and they include:

1. Secret and below speech and briefing files from 1960–1970;

2. Secret and below budget, planning, and operations files from 1960–1968;

3. Secret and below budget formulation and execution files from 1963–1970;

4. Secret and below program management files from 1963–1964;

5. Secret and below satellite communications program management files from 1962–1964.

Record Group 371 at the Washington National Records Center has about 3.5 million pages of almost completely classified records as of 2000 (50% *permanent*, 25% *temporary*, and 25% *unappraised*). As part of the P-2000 Project, about 48,000 pages of unclassified *permanent* records and 370,000 pages of classified *permanent* records will be transferred to RG 371 at the College Park National Archives by the end of 2001. Even if the classified records have been reviewed for declassification by the time of their transfer, they will not be available to the public until they have been possibly re-reviewed by the DOE under the Kyl Plan and then *processed* by the National Archives. The records to be transferred include:

1. Secret and below Director's reading files from 1961–1972;
2. selected historian source files from the 1960s;
3. Confidential and below Deputy Chief of Staff/Plans program and miscellaneous files from 1961–1966;
4. Secret and below files concerning commercial communications from 1961–1966;
5. Secret and below Deputy Chief of Staff communication summaries from 1962–1967;
6. Secret and below agendas, minutes, and reports of the Military Communications-Electronics Board from the 1960s;
7. Secret and below Canada/United Kingdom/United States status reports from the 1950s.

Records not eligible for transfer to RG 371 the College Park National Archives by 2001 include:

1. Secret and below administrative files, messages, publication record sets, reports, R&D project files, historical background material files, satellite communications program management files, survival study files, simulation study files, program files, project files, operational plans and implementation files, and historian source files from 1961 into the 1980s;
2. Top Secret and below National Military Command System Support Center/Command & Control Technical Center technical library publications and technical and analytical support files from 1968–1982.

### DISA and DCA Records at the DISA

The DISA does not have a central records storage facility or archives. There is no information publicly available on the quantity, nature, and *appraisal* status of the records still at the DISA.[49]

Requests under the FOIA and MDR for records at the Washington National Records Center or still at the DISA should be submitted to the Defense Information Systems Agency, ATTN: RGC/FOIA Officer, 701 S. Courthouse Road, Arlington, VA 22204–2199.

### Defense Intelligence Agency (DIA) and Predecessor Agency Records at the National Archives and Federal Records Centers

A large quantity of DIA (1961–present) records are in RG 373 at the College Park National Archives and Washington National Records Center. No other National Archives or Federal records center has any RG 373 holdings.

The DIA originally estimated in 1995 that it had a little over 21 million pages and 280,000 cans of aerial film subject to E.O. 12958.[50] This initial figure was evidently low, as in early 1999 the White House granted the DIA an exemption from automatic declassification of a little over 26 million pages (38%) of its subject records. However, it is not clear whether this means 26 million pages of textual records are exempted or 10,400 c.f. of textual records and aerial films are exempted. In any event, this means that the DIA either has about 67 million pages of *permanent* pre-1975 classified textual records or that the DIA has 26,800 c.f. of *permanent* pre-1975 classified textual records and aerial films.

With respect to progress in its declassification review program, the FY 1996 ISOO annual report stated that the DIA had declassified almost 22 million pages. These were in fact aerial films and not textual records, and it is not known why "22 million pages" was used.[51] Subsequent ISOO annual reports have not specifically listed the DIA as having declassified any records, although its totals may be included in the "All Others" category in these reports.

At the College Park National Archives, RG 373 has fewer than 250,000 pages of textual records (there is also a large number of maps, charts, and photographs). The textual records are unclassified documents captured during the Grenada invasion and Secret and below files and reports collected by Edgewood Arsenal from 1920–1950 on foreign developments on chemical, biological, and radiological warfare.

At the Washington National Records Center, RG 373 contains 112,000 c.f. of almost entirely classified DIA and pre-DIA records as of 2000 (20% *permanent* and 80% *temporary*). Many of these records are aerial films. As part of the P-2000 Project, about 2,161 c.f. of classified *permanent* records will be transferred to RG 373 at the College Park National Archives by the end of 2001. Even if they have been reviewed for declassification by the time of their transfer, none will be available to the public until they are possibly re-reviewed by the DOE under the Kyl Plan and then *processed* by the National Archives. Textual records to be transferred include:

1. Top Secret and below intelligence reports of the War Department's Intelligence Division, Army's Intelligence Division, and the Assistant Chief of Staff/Intelligence of the Army from 1940–1953;

2. Secret and below Army intelligence reports from 1963;

3. Secret and below Navy intelligence reports from the 1940s into the early 1960s and attaché reports from the late 1940s to 1959;

4. Secret and below Air Force Air Intelligence Center reports from 1960–1963;

5. Confidential and below Army Air Forces/Air Force files on POW and forced labor camps in Eastern Europe, Korea, and the Soviet Union from 1944–1957;

6. Secret/Restricted Data and below *DOD Intelligence Reports* from 1965;

7. Secret and below Director's correspondence files from 1961–1980;

8. Secret and below files concerning foreign visitors and foreign liaison issues from 1967 until the mid-1970s;

9. Secret and below reports on convicted espionage agents from 1957–1973;

10. Secret and below POW/MIA Division chronological files, messages, reading files, photographs, films, and related records from the 1960s into the 1980s.

Among the records that are not eligible for transfer to the College Park National Archives by 2001 are:

1. Top Secret and below Specific Intelligence Collection Files from the 1960s;

2. Secret and below Director and Deputy Director correspondence files and chronological files from the 1980s to 1995;

3. Top Secret/Restricted Data/Sensitive Compartmented Information and below texts, outlines, background materials, and visual aids used in intelligence briefings of the Chairman of the Joint Chiefs of Staff and the Secretary of Defense from 1961 into the 1990s;

4. Secret and below Latin American military personnel biographic files from 1945–1980;

5. Top Secret/Restricted Data and below target jackets and target intelligence materials from the 1960s into the 1980s;

6. Secret and below records of an unnamed advisory committee to the DIA from 1966–1987;

7. Secret and below *DOD Intelligence Reports* from 1966–1999;

8. Secret/Restricted Data and below Internal Intelligence Policy files from the 1960s into the 1990s on weapons systems, individual nations, U.S. government agencies, and specific operations;

9. Secret and below Foreign Liaison Division country folders from the mid-1970s into the 1980s;

10. a huge quantity of Secret and below aerial films from the 1940s into the 1990s (although a few are *permanent*, the vast majority are *temporary*).

As noted in the section on National Imagery and Mapping Agency records, the records of the DIA's Mapping, Charting, and Geodetic Directorate (1963–1972) are in RG 456 at the College Park National Archives and Washington National Records Center.

### DIA Records at the DIA

The only information available on the quantity, nature, and *appraisal* status of records still at the DIA is contained in a June 1996 NARA report, *A Nara Evaluation–Disposition of Production Records of the Defense Intelligence Agency.*[52] This report states that the DIA Library receives the record copy of each DIA periodic and ad hoc intelligence publication and that under the DIA *records schedule*, these record copies are *permanent* records. With the exception of the Secret and below *DOD Intelligence Reports* noted in the preceding section, however, none have been transferred to the College Park National Archives or Washington National Records Center. The report does not give the quantity of the Library's holdings of these intelligence publications, but they certainly must be massive.

Requests under the FOIA and MDR for records at the Washington National Records Center or at the DIA should be submitted to the Defense Intelligence Agency, ATTN: RTS-1, Washington, D.C. 20340–3299.

### Defense Special Weapons Agency (DSWA) / Defense Nuclear Agency (DNA) / Defense Atomic Support Agency (DASA) / Armed Forces Special Weapons Project (AFSWP) Records at the National Archives and Federal Records Centers

There are a small number of records of DSWA (1996–1998) and its predecessors, the DNA (1971–1996), DASA (1958–1971), and AFSWP (1947–1958), in RG 374 at the College Park National Archives and Washington National Records Center.[53] No other National Archives or Federal records center has any RG 374 holdings.

DNA estimated in 1995 that it had approximately 35 million pages of *permanent* pre-1975 classified records, but that 90% of them were not subject to E.O. 12958 because they contained both National Security Information and Restricted Data or Formerly Restricted Data.[54] The FY

1996, FY 1997, and FY 1998 ISOO annual reports do not credit the DSWA with declassifying any records (although its totals may be included in the "All Others" category in these reports). The FY 1999 ISOO annual report lists the Defense Threat Reduction Agency as declassifying 1.7 million pages, but it is not known which records these are or where they are.

At the College Park National Archives, RG 374 has about 2 million pages of Manhattan Engineer District, AFSWP, DASA, and DNA records. There is a fairly helpful *finding aid*, and for some *entries* there are lists of folder titles by box. Among the records that have been reviewed for declassification and *processed* are:

1. official histories of the Manhattan Engineer District (these are on microfilm and, except for a few volumes, are available in their entirety);
2. Secret/Restricted Data and below subject correspondence files of the Office of the Deputy Chief (Navy) from 1947–1954;
3. Secret/Restricted Data and below correspondence and related documents from 1948–1953 of the Test Division concerning special operations conducted to test atomic weapons;
4. Office of the Historian reports from 1943–1948.

There are a number of records that are still classified, and they include the following:

1. Secret/Restricted Data and below Commanding General decimal files from 1947–1954;
2. Secret/Restricted Data and below Weapons Development Division records from 1948–1953 relating to the development, production, operational evaluation, and standardization of atomic weapons;
3. Secret and below Security Division Counter Intelligence Investigative files from 1947–1952 and subject files from 1952–1954;
4. Secret/Restricted Data and below records of Joint Task Force 1 relating to OPERATION CROSSROADS from 1946–1948; Joint Task Force 2 from 1965–1968; Joint Task Force 3 relating to OPERATION GREENHOUSE from 1949–1952; Joint Task Force 7 relating to OPERATIONS SANDSTONE, CASTLE, and IVY from 1947–1948 and 1952–1955; and Joint Task Force 132 relating to OPERATIONS WINDSTORM and IVY from 1949–1952;
5. Secret/Restricted Data and below Weapons Effect Test Group R&D reports from 1951–1960;
6. Top Secret/Restricted Data and below technical reports from 1947–1972;

7. Secret/Restricted Data and below Deputy Director for Science and Technology committee files from 1970–1972 and R&D files from 1963–1972;

8. Secret/Restricted Data and below Comptroller files from 1961–1968;

9. Secret/Restricted Data and below AFSWP histories from 1947–1958 and DASA histories from 1959–1969;

10. Secret/Restricted Data and below Sandia Base correspondence files from 1945–1950;

11. Secret/Restricted Data and below Sandia Base general administrative files and publication record sets from 1951–1954;

12. Secret/Restricted Data and below Sandia Base decimal files, directives, publications, and miscellaneous files from 1955–1969.

There are about 4.5 million pages of mostly classified AFSWP, DASA, and DNA records in RG 374 at the Washington National Records Center as of 2000 (15% *permanent*, 15% *temporary*, and 70% *unappraised*). As part of the P-2000 Project, about 350,000 pages of classified *permanent* records will be transferred to RG 374 the College Park National Archives by the end of 2001. Even if they have been reviewed for declassification by the time of their transfer, none will be available to the public until they are possibly re-reviewed by the DOE under the Kyl Plan and then *processed* by the National Archives. The records to be transferred include:

1. Top Secret/Restricted Data and below Deputy Director for Science & Technology files on SALT, Comprehensive Test Ban Treaty, and Threshold Test Ban Treaty from the 1970s;

2. Secret/Restricted Data and below headquarters publications and emergency planning files from the late 1960s.

Among the records that are not eligible for transfer to RG 374 at the College Park National Archives by 2001 are:

1. Secret/Restricted Data and below AFSWP and DASA Central Files from 1955–1962;

2. Secret/Restricted Data and below files from the 1940s into the 1960s of various directorates at headquarters and Sandia, including the Comptroller, Office of General Counsel, and Intelligence and Security;

3. Secret/Restricted Data and below files of many Joint Task Forces from the 1940s into the 1970s;

4. Secret/Restricted Data and below AFSWP and DASA technical publications from 1947 into the 1970s;

5. Secret/Restricted Data and below Joint Atomic Information Exchange Group (United States/United Kingdom) files from the 1950s into the 1990s.

### DSWA, DNA, DASA, and AFSWP Records at the Defense Threat Reduction Agency

The majority of records are at the former DSWA headquarters in Alexandria, Virginia, and the former DSWA Field Command in Albuquerque, New Mexico. The only information publicly available on the quantity and types of records held at these two facilities is that concerning *permanent* pre-1975 classified records, which is set forth in the November 1995 proposed implementation plan submitted to the ISOO. Among others, this plan describes the following holdings: (1) 3.25 million pages of Joint Nuclear Weapons Publications System works, (2) 600,000 pages of annual histories, (3) 450,000 pages of Nuclear Weapons Quantitative Histories, (4) 3 million pages of Development of Nuclear Weapons/Systems and Stockpile Reports, (5) 3.8 million pages of safety awareness protective training materials and audiovisual training materials, (6) 500 c.f. of nuclear test films and photos, (7) 3 million pages of Joint Nuclear Atmospheric Test Data Repository records, (8) 19.75 million pages of weapons effects test records.

There are two libraries containing specialized collections that are open to the public by appointment. One is the Nuclear Test Personnel Review (NTPR) program library at the former DSWA headquarters in Alexandria, Virginia. The NTPR program was established by the DNA in 1978 to accomplish several goals, including identifying all Department of Defense military and civilian personnel who participated in atmospheric tests between 1945 and 1962, publishing an unclassified history of each atmospheric test involving Department of Defense personnel, declassifying all possible nuclear test-related documents, providing estimates of radiation exposures, and identifying and notifying those personnel who received higher radiation doses than those under current federal guidelines and offering them free medical examinations at U.S. government hospitals. Holdings at the NTPR library include the histories,[55] the primary source documents used in writing them, and radiation dosimetry information on individuals. With the exception of individual radiation dosimetry information records (which fall under the protection of the Privacy Act) and a small number of still classified documents, the records are available for public review.

The second library is the Armed Forces Radiobiology Research Institute Technical Library located on the grounds of the National Naval Medical Center in Bethesda, Maryland. All the holdings relate to the general subject of radiobiology (for example, human and animal experiments involving radioactive substances and the effect of fallout) and are entirely unclassified or declassified. There are more than 2,000 printed reports of various government agencies and contractors (for example, the Atomic Energy Commission, Los Alamos Laboratory, University of California Radiation Laboratory, and Lovelace Foundation), and more than 10,000 reports from these agencies and contractors on microfiche. Unfortunately, there is no catalog or index to the collection. One has to browse through the stacks or microfiche holder to find items of interest, although this task is made somewhat easier by the fact most reports of each individual agency or contractor are filed together.

Requests under the FOIA and MDR for records at the Washington National Records Center or at the headquarters or field command should be submitted to the Freedom of Information Act Officer, Defense Threat Reduction Agency, FOIA Division, 45045 Aviation Drive, Dulles, VA 20166–7517.

### Department of Energy (DOE)/Energy Research and Development Administration (ERDA)/Atomic Energy Commission (AEC)/Manhattan Engineer District (MED) Records at the National Archives and Federal Records Centers

Only a small number of records of the MED (1943–1946) and its successors, the AEC (1947–1974), ERDA (1974–1977), and DOE (1977–present), are in four *record groups* at the National Archives and Federal records centers. As discussed in the following section, the vast majority are at the DOE headquarters, operations offices, and laboratories. In its 1995 publication, *Human Radiation Experiments: The Department of Energy Roadmap to the Story and the Records,* the DOE estimated that its textual records holdings total approximately 8 *billion* pages (560 *miles*). This publication gives no estimate of the quantities of photographs, films, and other nontextual records.[56]

The situation with respect to declassification review under E.O. 12958 is confused. The vast majority of classified individual records, as well as collections of classified records, contain both National Security Information and Restricted Data or Formerly Restricted Data and thus are exempt from the operation of the order. Although the DOE itself has apparently never published an estimate of the number of its *permanent* pre-1975 classified records, the 1997 *Report of the Commission on Protecting and Reducing Government Secrecy* contains an estimate of 230 million pages.[57] Regardless of the quantity, the DOE's progress under its declassification review program has been slow. The FY 1996, FY 1997, FY 1998, and FY 1999 ISOO annual reports list the DOE as having declassified a total of 6.2 million pages. However, there is no information available to the public on which records these are or where they are. It is possible that some of the 6.2 million pages are other agency records that the DOE is re-reviewing under the Kyl Plan (the DOE is devoting most of its limited declassification review resources to the re-review of other agency records under the Kyl Plan and there is very little review of its own records).[58]

There are fewer than 250,000 pages of MED records in RG 77 at the College Park National Archives, and most are from the files in General Groves's Washington, D.C., office.[59] No other National Archives has any relevant RG 77 records. The majority have been reviewed for declassification and *processed*, and they include:

1. a small quantity of General Groves's Top Secret and below files and individual documents;
2. a limited number of Secret and below decimal files;
3. a very small number of security and investigation files.

Still-classified records include:

1. Top Secret and below Madison Square Area Office reading files and miscellaneous records from 1943–1945;
2. Top Secret and below records of Columbia University's Division of War Research from 1942–1945.

There are no relevant records in RG 77 at any Federal records center.

As mentioned in the section on Defense Special Weapons Agency records, RG 374 at the College Park National Archives has the official histories of the MED on microfilm. Most are declassified in their entirety. The few volumes dealing with weapons research and related topics have been declassified in part only in recent years and are available in *redacted* form from the archivists in the Modern Military Branch.

Record Group 326 contains the records of the AEC, and there are approximately 2.5 million pages of records in this *record group* at the College Park National Archives. The *finding aids* are usually very good, listing all the folder titles by box. Among the records that have been reviewed for declassification and *processed* are:

1. Secret/Restricted Data and below office files of Commissioners Lilienthal, Waymack, Bacher, Pike, Strauss, and Dean;
2. Secret/Restricted Data and below summary minutes of the 1946–1961 Commission meetings and the index to these meetings;
3. Secret/Restricted Data and below Division of Security files on the J. Robert Oppenheimer security clearance revocation hearing held in 1954;

4. Secret/Restricted Data and below agendas, minutes, and reports of the 1947–1974 General Advisory Committee meetings;

5. Top Secret/Restricted Data and below 1947–1958 Executive Secretariat files;

6. Secret/Restricted Data and below Division of Biology and Medicine files from 1953–1964 on fallout monitoring and studies, general correspondence files from 1956–1975, and central subject files from 1947–1975;

7. Secret/Restricted Data and below Division of Raw Materials general files from 1947–1969;

8. Secret/Restricted Data and below reading file of the Director, Division of Reactor Development and Technology from 1959–1969;

9. Secret/Restricted Data and below files from 1942–1965 of the Argonne National Laboratory and its predecessor, the University of Chicago's Metallurgical Laboratory;

10. Secret/Restricted Data and below miscellaneous records from 1943–1958 dealing with personnel security;

11. Secret/Restricted Data and below Division of International Affairs records regarding the formation of the International Atomic Energy Agency from 1954–1957.

There are a large number of records that are still classified, and among them are the following:

1. Secret/Restricted Data and below office files of Commissioners Floberg, Vance, Bunting, Glennan, Williams, McCone, Libby, and Smyth;

2. Secret/Restricted Data and below records of the Chairman of the AEC on the Operations Coordinating Board from 1953–1961;

3. Secret/Restricted Data and below verbatim minutes of the 1954–1957 Commission meetings (the DOE's History Division states that these are the only verbatim minutes ever prepared);

4. Secret/Restricted Data and below Controller's Office budget estimates and related records from 1946–1954;

5. Secret/Restricted Data and below Office of Operations Analysis and Forecasting files on fiscal, intergovernmental, and international matters from 1951–1963;

6. Secret/Restricted Data and below MED/AEC files relating to the K-25 plant from 1944–1948;

7. Secret/Restricted Data and below MED/AEC decimal correspondence files and classified mail and records correspondence from 1946–1950;

8. Secret/Restricted Data and below MED/AEC decimal correspondence files regarding the X-10 reactor from 1945–1948;

9. Secret/Restricted Data and below MED/AEC Madison Square Area Office/New York Operations Office correspondence files from 1942–1951;

10. Secret/Restricted Data and below MED/AEC records relating to MED correspondence from 1942–1949;

11. Secret/Restricted Data and below MED/AEC diaries concerning Oak Ridge operations from 1943–1972;

12. Secret/Restricted Data and below Madison Square Area Office miscellaneous files from 1943–1945;

13. Secret/Restricted Data and below records of the Columbia University Division of War Research from 1942–1945;

14. Secret/Restricted Data and below Reactor Safeguard Committee correspondence files from 1947–1953;

15. Secret/Restricted Data and below Division of Research correspondence files on physical research programs and policies from 1946–1957;

16. Secret/Restricted Data and below records of the Missile Projects Branch, Division of Reactor Development from 1956–1962;

17. Secret/Restricted Data and below Division of Military Applications reports on OPERATION SANDSTONE from 1948–1949;

18. Secret/Restricted Data and below Division of Military Applications semiannual project histories of the Iowa Ordnance Plant and Iowa Army Ammunition Plant from 1954–1971;

19. Secret/Restricted Data and below Assistant for Military Arrangements, Division of International Affairs correspondence files from 1959–1965;

20. Secret/Restricted Data and below Asian-American Branch, Division of International Affairs correspondence files from 1964–1966;

21. Secret/Restricted Data and below Division of International Affairs correspondence files regarding technical exchanges and liaison programs with the United Kingdom and Canada from 1955–1963;

22. Secret/Restricted Data and below History Division records on disarmament and arms control from 1953–1963.

Record Group 326 at the East Point National Archives has 6.5 million pages of records. Since this facility cannot store classified documents, all the records were either originally unclassified or have been declassified. Important records include:

1. Oak Ridge National Laboratory correspondence files, technical reports, and other records, including those of the Reactor Division from 1955–

1967, the Research Division from 1944–1966, and the Research & Development Division from 1944–1966;

2. a limited number of MED/AEC Central Files from 1943–1950;

3. a limited number of correspondence files and technical reports of the New York Operations Office from 1943–1949;

4. correspondence files, budget files, press releases, project history files, and technical reports from 1950 into the early 1970s of the Technical Production Division, Savannah River Plant, and the E.I. du Pont de Nemours & Co.;

5. correspondence files, contract files, budget files, and technical and progress reports of Columbia University from 1942–1947, Tennessee Eastman Corporation from 1942–1947, Linde Air Products from 1942–1947, and General Electric Company from 1955–1962.

It should be noted that many of these and other collections that were transferred from Oak Ridge to the East Point National Archives in the 1960s are incomplete and have been broken up permanently. When the transfers initially occurred, all the classified records were removed and kept at Oak Ridge, where they underwent declassification review in the early 1970s. The declassified documents were then forwarded to the East Point National Archives, and the documents that could not be declassified remained at Oak Ridge. When the declassification procedures were found deficient several years later, all the declassified records were recalled from the East Point National Archives and underwent another review. Those that survived this second review were eventually returned to the East Point National Archives. As described in the following section, it is unclear what happened at Oak Ridge to all the documents that were never declassified or were subsequently reclassified.[60] Some other regional National Archives have very small RG 326 holdings.

Record Group 326 at the Washington National Records Center has almost 32.5 million pages of largely classified records as of 2000 (2% *permanent*, 38% *temporary*, and 60% *unappraised*). Unfortunately, because the vast majority of the records are *temporary* or *unappraised* the *SF-135s* do not contain detailed descriptions of the records, and it is impossible to determine the exact contents of the *accessions*. As part of the P-2000 Project, only 107,000 pages of unclassified and classified *permanent* records will be transferred to RG 326 at the College Park National Archives by the end of 2001. Records that are not eligible for transfer to the College Park National Archives by 2001 include:

1. Secret/Restricted Data and below office files of Commissioners Tape, Thompson, Nabrit, Costagliola, Johnson, Ramey, Ray, Seaborg, and Palfrey;

2. Secret/Restricted Data and below files of Chairmen Ray and Schlesinger on agency policy and procedures;

3. Secret/Restricted Data and below Office of General Counsel subject files, contract files, and correspondence files from 1947 into the 1960s;

4. Secret/Restricted Data and below Division of Raw Materials correspondence files and R&D reports from 1947–1970;

5. Secret/Restricted Data and below Division of Research correspondence files from 1947 into the early 1970s;

6. Secret/Restricted Data and below Division of Production correspondence files from 1947 into the early 1970s;

7. Secret/Restricted Data and below Division of International Affairs correspondence files from 1947 into the 1960s;

8. a limited number of Secret/Restricted Data and below subject files and correspondence files from 1946–1975 of the AEC's Division of Military Application and its successor under ERDA, the Office of Military Application;

9. a limited number of Division of Politico-Military Affairs correspondence files from 1950–1974;

10. a large number of Secret/Restricted Data and below records concerning a wide range of subjects acquired by the History Division from other AEC offices;

11. Secret/Restricted Data and below duplicates of AEC records at the Eisenhower, Kennedy, Johnson, and Nixon Presidential Libraries;

12. Secret/Restricted Data and below scientific and technical reports from 1942 into the 1960s (these probably duplicate what is in the Office of Science and Technology Information);

13. a large number of Kellex Corporation records from 1942–1946.

Every regional Federal records center has RG 326 holdings as of 2000, which vary in size considerably. The records are almost entirely unclassified or declassified and are primarily personnel, finance, contract, safety, radiation exposure or health records. The one exception is RG 326 at the Dayton Federal Records Center that has Confidential laboratory notebooks.[61]

Record Group 430 contains the records of the ERDA, but there are no records in this *record group* at the College Park National Archives. A few regional National Archives have very small RG 430 holdings.

At the Washington National Records Center, RG 430 has about 6 million pages of both ERDA and AEC records as of 2000 (4% *permanent*, 48% *temporary*, and 48% *unappraised*). The few records that concern national security issues include:

1. a very limited number of Secret/Restricted Data and below correspondence files from 1954–1976 of the AEC's Division of Intelligence and its successor under ERDA (these, as well as the small number of records noted below in RG 434 at the Washington National Records Center, are the only records of this office ever located by the author);
2. a limited number of Secret/Restricted Data and below subject correspondence files from 1962–1976 of the AEC's Division of Military Application and its successor under ERDA.

As part of the P-2000 Project, only about 25,000 pages of unclassified and classified *permanent* records will be transferred to RG 430 at the College Park National Archives by the end of 2001.

All the regional Federal records centers except Dayton and Ft. Worth have RG 430 holdings as of 2000, which vary in size considerably. The records are entirely unclassified or declassified and are mostly personnel, finance, contract, safety, radiation exposure, or health records.[62]

Record Group 434 contains the records of the DOE. At the College Park National Archives, the few records in RG 434 do not concern national security issues. A few regional National Archives have very small RG 434 holdings.

At the Washington National Records Center, RG 434 contains almost 50 million pages of largely classified DOE, ERDA, and AEC records as of 2000 (10% *permanent*, 70% *temporary*, and 20% *unappraised*). No *permanent* records will be transferred to RG 434 at the College Park National Archives under the P-2000 Project. Records not eligible for transfer to the College Park National Archives by 2001 include:

1. a limited number of Secret/Restricted Data and below subject correspondence files and R&D files of the AEC's Division of Military Application and its successors under the ERDA and DOE from 1951 to the early 1980s;
2. many Top Secret and below files of the Division of Security from the late 1940s into the 1970s;
3. a very limited number of Secret/Restricted Data and below correspondence files of the AEC's Division of Intelligence and its successors under the ERDA and DOE from 1955–1980 (as mentioned earlier, these and the very small number of records in RG 430 at the Washington National Records Center are the only records of this office ever located by the author).

All the regional Federal records centers except St. Louis and Kansas City have RG 434 holdings as of 2000, which vary in size considerably. With two exceptions, the records are entirely unclassified or declassified and are primarily personnel, contract, finance, safety, radiation exposure or health records. The first exception is the Dayton Federal Records Center, which has Confidential laboratory records. The second is the San Bruno Federal Records Center, which has the largely unclassified administrative records from the Lawrence Livermore National Laboratory, and unclassified and declassified program and policy files from the former University of California Radiation Laboratory (now the Ernest Orlando Lawrence Berkeley National Laboratory).[63] Good descriptions of some of the latter's collections are contained in *Human Radiation Experiments: The Department of Energy Roadmap to the Story and the Records*.

As mentioned in the section on Office of the Secretary of Defense records, RG 330 at the Washington National Records Center has the classified agendas and minutes of all the Atomic Energy Commission/Military Liaison Committee meetings from 1947 to 1974.

### DOE, ERDA, AEC, and MED Records at DOE Headquarters, DOE Operations Offices, DOE Laboratories, Presidential Libraries, and Other Repositories

As noted earlier, in 1995 the DOE estimated that its headquarters, operations offices, and laboratories held an estimated 8 *billion* pages of textual records and an unknown quantity of photographs, films, and other nontextual records. There is a much smaller number of records at some presidential libraries and other repositories. The known holdings at each will be addressed in turn.

One of the major impediments to determining record holdings at the DOE facilities is poor records management practices through the years. These practices were first identified in a 1988 NARA report, *Evaluation of the Records Management Program of the Department of Energy*. Among other things, the report concluded that there were some parts of the department that were not adequately documenting their decisions and activities, the existing *records schedules* were incomplete and difficult to apply, there was a huge backlog of *unappraised* records, and some managers and scientists were comingling department records with personal records and removing all of them when they terminated employment. The report also contained a number of recommendations to correct the problems.[64] A follow-up General Accounting Office report in 1992, *DOE Management, Better Planning Needed to Correct Records Management Problems*, found improvements in some areas but still concluded overall there were significant problems.[65] In *Human Radiation Experiments: The Department of Energy Roadmap to the Story and the Records*, the DOE admitted that "systematic knowledge about where specific records are or what records are available for a particular organization is spotty at best." Unfortunately, as of 2000, many of these problems still exist and numerous NARA recommendations from 1988 remain to be implemented.

Both the DOE headquarters in Washington, D.C., and the DOE facility in Germantown, Maryland, have internal records storage facilities that contain a large number of AEC, ERDA, and DOE records. The vast majority of these records are classified. They are under the control of the office that generated the records or its successor.

The History Division in Germantown should be contacted concerning *finding aids* to records in its custody (History Division, Department of Energy, AD-35 Germantown, Washington, D.C. 20545, 301–903–5431). All of the records are classified and they include:

1. Office of Scientific Research and Development (OSRD) historical documents and miscellaneous MED and OSRD materials;

2. Executive Secretariat files from 1959–1974;

3. summary minutes of the 1962–1974 Commission meetings;

4. AEC progress reports to the Joint Committee on Atomic Energy from 1947–1974;

5. periodic reports of AEC divisions to the General Manager;

6. periodic reports of the General Manager to the Commission;

7. General Manager subject and reading files from 1947–1974;

8. selected Division of Military Application files from the late 1940s to the early 1970s;

9. files on the nuclear navy and naval reactors;

10. AEC Division of Production files;

11. files on Lawrence Livermore National Laboratory nuclear testing;

12. security files on Edward Teller;

13. AEC historical documents;

14. files on the SALT talks;

15. documents cited in the published histories of the AEC ("footnote files");

16. AEC Division of International Affairs files on NATO and other topics;

17. civil defense files from 1952–1960;

18. Kellex records;

19. ERDA reading files, official files, locator files, current history files, miscellaneous files, and R&D plans;

20. files of DOE Secretaries Schlesinger, Deutch, and O'Leary, including secretarial briefing books;

21. files of the DOE Under Secretary and Office of the Special Assistant;

22. DOE files on the *Progressive* case;

23. DOE Office of Defense Programs periodic program reports, central files, chronological files, and miscellaneous documents;

24. DOE congressional testimony files;

25. DOE files on Chernobyl;

26. DOE Persian Gulf history collection;

27. Albuquerque weapons incidents files.

The DOE has eight operations offices (Albuquerque, New Mexico; Chicago, Illinois; Idaho Falls, Idaho; Las Vegas, Nevada; Oak Ridge, Tennessee; Oakland, California; Richland, Washington; and Savannah, Georgia) and three field offices (Golden, Colorado; Columbus, Ohio; and Rocky Flats, Colorado). Except for Oak Ridge and Nevada, there is no information publicly available about the record holdings at the operations offices and field offices.[66] The Oak Ridge Operations Office has about 17.5 million pages of records in a single vault, and many of them are fragments of collections at other sites (including the East Point National Archives, as explained earlier) or are in artificial collections. The date range is from the earliest days of the MED to the present. There are few *finding aids*.[67] Descriptions of a few of the records are in *Human Radiation Experiments: The Department of Energy Roadmap to the Story and the Records*. The Nevada Operations Office runs the Coordination and Information Center in Las Vegas that was established in 1981 to collect, preserve, and distribute to the government and public records on U.S. nuclear testing. There are now more than 310,000 originally unclassified and declassified documents concerning human radiation experiments and nuclear testing. Inquiries should be directed to the Coordination and Information Center, Bechtel, Nevada, P.O. Box 98521, Las Vegas, NV 89193–8521, 702–295–1628. There is no information available on the other holdings of the Nevada Operations Office.

There are more than thirty DOE laboratories and facilities around the country, and those that were or are currently engaged in a substantial amount of national security-related work include the Argonne National Laboratory (ANL), Ernest Orlando Lawrence Berkeley National Laboratory (LBNL), Brookhaven National Laboratory (BNL), Idaho National Engineering and Environmental Laboratory (INEEL), Knolls Atomic Power Laboratory (KAPL), Los Alamos National Laboratory (LANL), Lawrence Livermore National Laboratory (LLNL), Oak Ridge National Laboratory (ORNL), Sandia National Laboratories (SNL), Hanford, Nevada Test Site, Pantex, Paducah, Portsmouth, Fernald, Mound, and Savannah River Site. Some of these have large numbers of records stored on site while others have very few.

The ANL stores records on site, but the total quantity is unknown.[68] Descriptions of some of the records are in *Human Radiation Experiments: The Department of Energy Roadmap to the Story and the Records*. Through the years, the ANL has also transferred a number of records to RG 326, RG 430, and RG 434 at the Chicago Federal Records Center. Inquiries about the records at the two repositories should be directed to the Records Management Office, Argonne National Laboratory, Argonne, IL 60439.

The LBNL stopped performing classified work in the 1960s and, as mentioned earlier, almost all of its originally unclassified and declassified records from this period are in RG 434 at the San Bruno Federal Records Center (an unknown number of its classified records that were either reviewed and not declassified or never reviewed are at LLNL). The DOE acknowledges that of all the laboratories nationwide, the LBNL has the best intellectual control of its records, and there are excellent *finding aids* to them. Descriptions of many of the records are in *Human Radiation Experiments: The Department of Energy Roadmap to the Story and the Records*. Inquiries concerning the records and access thereto can be directed to the Archives and Records Office, Lawrence Berkeley National Laboratory, Berkeley, CA 94720.

The INEEL stores records on site, but the total quantity is unknown. Descriptions of some of the collections are in *Human Radiation Experiments: The Department of Energy Roadmap to the Story and the Records*. The INEEL also has transferred a large number of records to RG 326, RG 430, and RG 434 at the Seattle Federal Records Center. Inquiries about the records at the two repositories should be directed to INEEL, Central Facilities Area (CFA), Room 191, Building CFA-690 RESL, Idaho Falls, ID 83401.

The LANL has never transferred records to any National Archives or Federal records center, notwithstanding the fact that the above-mentioned 1988 NARA report recommended that an extensive photographic collection, small archival collection, and the oldest Laboratory Director's files be transferred to the National Archives. All of the LANL's records that still exist are stored on site at one of three locations. The first is the Records Center, which holds approximately 60 million pages of mostly classified records.[69] Important collections include: (1) Laboratory Director's files from 1943 to the present, (2) a portion of the LANL central files established by the Communications and Records Management Office, (3) laboratory progress reports from 1945–1975, (4) laboratory notebooks from 1942–1990, (5) portions of the records of some laboratory divisions, including the central administrative files of the J-Division (Weapons Testing) from 1946–1963.[70] The *finding aids* are good for many of the collections and unclassified *finding aids* are apparently available to the public. Inquiries about the records and *finding aids* at the Records Center should be directed to the Information & Records Management Group, CIC-10, MS-C322, Los Alamos National Laboratory, P.O. Box 1663, Los Alamos, NM 87545.

The second location of records is the divisions themselves. Some have apparently retained most or all of their records, and undoubtedly the vast majority of these are classified.[71] The quantity of records still held by the various divisions is unknown. The third location where records are held is the Los Alamos Reports Library. This library holds more than 17.5 million pages of technical reports from 1943 to the present, many of which are classified.[72] Whatever indexes or catalogues exist to the holdings are not available to the public.

The LLNL stores on site all of its records that still exist, with the exception of a small number of largely unclassified administrative records transferred to RG 434 at the San Bruno Federal Records Center. The on-site record holdings have been estimated to be about 95 million pages.[73] The vast majority of the records must be classified, and it is unknown what *finding aids* exist. Descriptions of a few records are in *Human Radiation Experiments: The Department of Energy Roadmap to the Story and the Records*. Inquiries about records and *finding aids* can be directed to Records Management Group, Lawrence Livermore National Laboratory, 7000 East Avenue, Livermore, CA 94550–9234.

The ORNL stores records at several locations at the facility, but the total quantity is unknown.[74] Descriptions of some of the records are in *Human Radiation Experiments: The Department of Energy Roadmap to the Story and the Records*. Some of the ORNL's records are at the Oak Ridge Operations Office, and through the years the ORNL has also transferred some records to RG 326, RG 430, and RG 434 at the East Point National Archives. Inquiries about records and *finding aids* should be directed to the Records Management Office, Oak Ridge National Laboratory, Building 4500N, MS 6285, Oak Ridge, TN 37831.

The SNL has never transferred records to any National Archives or Federal records center, and all of its records that still exist are stored on site. The total quantity is estimated to be about 230 million pages, and the vast majority must be classified.[75] It is not known what *finding aids* exist. Inquiries about records and *finding aids* can be directed to Community Involvement and Issues Management, Sandia National Laboratories, P.O. Box 5800, Albuquerque, NM 87185–1313.

Hanford's records are stored on site, at the Richland Operations Office, and at the Pacific Northwest Laboratory. The quantities at each location are unknown. Descriptions of some of the records are in *Human Radiation Experiments: The Department of Energy Roadmap to the Story and the Records*. Through the years, Hanford has also transferred a number of records to RG 326, RG 430, and RG 434 at the Seattle Federal Records Center. Inquiries about the records at these various repositories can be directed to the Records Management Officer, Richland Operations Office, Department of Energy, 2770 University Drive, Richland, WA 99352.

There is no information available on the record holdings at Pantex, Savannah River Site, Nevada Test Site, Paducah, Portsmouth, Fernald, Mound, the KAPL or the BNL.

With respect to relevant holdings at presidential libraries and other repositories, some of Lewis Strauss's papers are at the Hoover Library. A detailed *finding aid* is available. All the materials are open, although the DOE withdrew about 3,000 pages some years ago when it conducted a declassification review. These withdrawn items are in the custody of the Office of Presidential Libraries at the National Archives in downtown Washington, D.C. The Truman Library has the personal papers of Sumner Pike (AEC Commissioner from 1946–1951) and they are open. The personal papers of John McCone (AEC Commissioner from 1958–1961) are at the Eisenhower Library and they are open. At the Reagan Library are the personal papers of John Herrington (Secretary of Energy from 1985–1989), but very little of the collection is open. The papers of Dixie Lee Ray (AEC Commissioner during the 1960s) are at the Hoover Institution at Stanford University. A detailed *finding aid* is available. They are open, although the DOE withdrew many items some years ago when it performed a declassification review. It is not known where the withdrawn records are, but it is possible that they were placed in her office files, which are in RG 326 at the Washington National Records Center.

Requests under the FOIA and MDR for records at Federal records centers or at the DOE should be submitted to the facility holding the records or to the Freedom of Information Act/Privacy Act Division, Office of General Counsel, Department of Energy, 1000 Independence Avenue, S.W., Washington, D.C. 20585.

### Federal Bureau of Investigation (FBI) Records at the National Archives and Federal Records Centers

There is only a very small number of FBI records in RG 65 at the College Park National Archives and Washington National Records Center. No other National Archives or Federal records center has RG 65 holdings.

Under E.O. 12958, the FBI in 1995 received a blanket exemption from automatic declassification of all of its *permanent* pre-1975 classified records on the basis that their disclosure would violate the Privacy Act (the FBI never estimated how many records it has in this category, but it must be many hundreds of millions of pages considering the total number of *permanent* records). The blanket exemption is contained in a Memorandum of Understanding between the directors of the ISOO and the FBI, which was apparently later approved by the Assistant to the President for National Security Affairs.[76] Because of this, the FBI has not had any declassification review program under the order.

The main filing system used at all FBI offices and that contains the overwhelming majority of records is the Central Records System. Established in 1921, there is a separate classification number in this system for each major violation of federal law and several administrative matters, and more than 300 have been used (some are obsolete now). Classification numbers of importance include: 65 (Espionage), 100 (Domestic Security), 105 (Foreign Counterintelligence), 117 (Atomic Energy Act), 121 (Loyalty of Government Employees), 140 (Security of Government Employees). Through the years, several other filing systems have also been used to hold especially sensitive material, including "June Mail" and "Do Not File." Headquarters and field offices have also developed more than 100 different types of indexes to records in the Central Records System. As an example, five electronic surveillance indexes exist, and each covers electronic surveillance records for a different time period.

Researchers should note that there are two publications that are useful in learning about FBI filing systems and record-keeping practices: *Appraisal of the Records of the Federal Bureau of Investigation, A Report to Hon. Harold H. Greene, United States District Court for the District of Columbia* (Washington, D.C.: National Archives and Records Administration and Federal Bureau of Investigation, November 9, 1981)[77] and *Unlocking the Files of the FBI: A Guide to Its Records and Classification System* (Wilmington: Scholarly Resources, Inc., 1993). The first is a huge two-volume report prepared pursuant to the court's order in a suit brought by the American Friends Service Committee against the National Archives and the FBI for unauthorized and improper destruction of FBI records. It contains a wealth of information on the history of the different FBI filing systems and indexes and record management practices, and describes in detail the examination of selected FBI records by National Archives personnel and the draft *records schedule* based thereon (this was ultimately approved by the court in 1986 with some modifications). The second publication summarizes key sections of the 1981 report, describes the new classification numbers created since then, and discusses the meaning of the many abbreviations and symbols found in FBI reports and other FBI records. All in all, it is much more accessible and easier to use than the 1981 report itself.

At the College Park National Archives, RG 65 has more than 3 million pages of records but only a very small number are from the postwar period. These are primarily Class 199 (Foreign Counterintelligence and Terrorism) headquarters and field offices files from 1981–1990 on the Committee in Solidarity with the People of El Salvador, which are almost entirely classified.

At the Washington National Records Center, RG 65 has almost 15 million pages of records as of 2000 (30% *permanent* and 70% *temporary*). It is not known whether under the P-2000 Project any *permanent* records will be transferred to RG 65 at the College Park National Archives. The great majority of files concern audits and other administrative matters, but there are also the following records of interest:

1. Confidential electronic surveillance index of individuals whose names are mentioned in intercepted conversations from 1960–1975;
2. Secret 121 (Loyalty of Government Employees) files from 1948–1973;
3. Top Secret numerical abstracts from 1936–1979 that are only described on the *SF-135s* as being security-related.[78]

### FBI Records at the FBI

The FBI holds almost all of its records that still exist. In this regard, the FBI estimates that at its headquarters, field offices, and overseas offices there is the staggering total of 16.25 *billion* pages of textual records (1,231 *miles*). Approximately 25% of these records have been scheduled as *permanent*. There is no estimate of the quantity of photos, films, sound recordings, electronic records, and other nontextual records the FBI holds.[79]

For most *permanent* records, the FBI *records schedule* permits their transfer to the National Archives in ten-year blocks when they are fifty years old. There are probably many *permanent* records at the FBI that are now eligible for transfer to the National Archives under this criterion. Why they have not been transferred is unknown.

At FBI headquarters, the Freedom of Information Act/Privacy Act Office maintains a small reading room that researchers can use by appointment. This reading room contains more than 200 different declassified files that the FBI believes to be of particularly great interest to the public. A list of the files in the reading room is on the FBI's homepage (fbi.gov), and a few files can also be viewed on the homepage.

The FBI over the years, of course, has declassified many more files than are in the reading room, but any FBI indexes of such files that exist are not available to the public. To learn what files have already been declassified, a researcher can go to the "Secret No More" website (www.crunch.com) and find a partial list. Regardless of how a researcher learns that a file has already been declassified, the researcher must then submit a FOIA or MDR request to examine it if it is not in the reading room.[80]

Requests under the FOIA and MDR should be submitted to the field office holding the records or the Freedom of Information Act/Privacy Act Section, Federal Bureau of Investigation, 9th & Pennsylvania Avenues, N.W., Washington, D.C. 20535. A researcher must furnish an obituary or similar proof of death for the FBI to process a request for a file on a deceased person (special permission forms must be furnished with a request for a file on a living person). Along these lines, researchers should anticipate what other names might appear in the file they are requesting and, where possible, furnish proofs of death for these individuals. Without these additional proofs of death, the FBI will *redact* the names (the FBI should keep a database of proofs of death, but it does not). It should also be noted that requests for 500 pages or fewer receive top priority in processing.

### High Commissioner for Germany (HICOG) Records at the National Archives

Record Group 466 contains the records of HICOG (1949–1955) and its predecessors, and at the College Park National Archives, RG 466 has more than 8.75 million pages of records. No other National Archives or any Federal records center has any RG 466 holdings. The *finding aids* are good. Virtually all the records have been reviewed for declassification and *processed*, and they include:

1. Top Secret and below files of the High Commissioner from 1949–1952;
2. Top Secret and below files of the Executive Director from 1947–1955;
3. Office of General Counsel files from 1947–1955;
4. U.S. Secretariat, Allied High Commission files from 1947–1955;
5. U.S. Element, Military Security Board files from 1947–1955;
6. U.S. Element, Extradition Board files from 1947–1955;
7. files from 1947–1955 of the four Regional Land Commissioners.

### Records of International Commands and Organizations in Which the U.S. Military Has Participated at the National Archives and Federal Records Centers

Record Groups 331 and 333 at the College Park National Archives contain records of international commands and organizations in which the United States military has participated. No other National Archives or any Federal records center has any RG 331 or RG 333 records.

With respect to the declassification review of records under E.O. 12958, the only apparent review conducted thus far has been by the Air Force of the North American Air Defense Command records in RG 342 at the Washington National Records Center.

Record Group 331 at the College Park National Archives has World War II and postwar Allied operational and occupational headquarters records. At the College Park National Archives, RG 331 has approximately 45 million pages of records. The *finding aids* are very good. Virtually all the records have been reviewed for declassification and *processed*, and postwar records include:

1. Allied Military Government in Trieste (1947–1954) records, including but not limited to Chief of Staff subject-numeric files from 1947–1954, Planning and Advisory Staff subject-numeric files from 1947–1954, and Allied Secretariat reports and incoming and outgoing messages from 1947–1954;

2. a huge number of records of the General Headquarters, Supreme Commander for the Allied Powers (1945–1952), General Headquarters, Far East Command (1947–1957), and General Headquarters, United Nations Command (1950-present), including but not limited to central decimal files from 1945–1952; general administrative files from 1951–1952; SCAP instructions to the Japanese from 1945–1952; Deputy Chief of Staff subject files from 1945–1952; Assistant Chief of Staff, G-2 Civil Intelligence Section subject files from 1945–1952; Assistant Chief of Staff, G-3 subject files from 1945–1950; and Assistant Chief of Staff, G-4 decimal files from 1946–1950;

Record Group 333 contains records relating to U.S. participation in international military agencies. At the College Park National Archives, RG 333 has about 1 million pages of records. The *finding aids* are very good, listing the complete folder titles in most *entries*. Among the records that have been reviewed for declassification and *processed* are:

1. Top Secret and below Joint U.S./Brazil Military Commission records, including but not limited to decimal correspondence files of the U.S. Army section from 1946–1962;

2. Top Secret and below General Headquarters, United Nations Command (1950–present) records, including but not limited to central decimal correspondence files from 1951–1955; daily statistical summaries of unit strengths, battle casualties, and prisoners of war from 1951; J-2 subject correspondence files and country files from 1950–1955; Military Armistice Commission correspondence files and daily journals from 1951–1957, messages from 1951–1953, records of armistice observer and inspection teams from 1953–1957, minutes of headquarters meetings and secretaries meetings from 1953–1981, minutes of security officers meetings from 1954–1978, minutes of Neutral Nations Supervisory Commission from 1953–1981, and minutes of Joint Observer Teams meetings from 1953–1967; and Repatriation Group decimal correspondence files and daily journals from 1953–1954.

There are a large number of still-classified records, and they include the following:

1. Top Secret and below records of the United States Section of the Permanent Joint Board on Defense—United States and Canada, including subject-numeric files from 1941–1956 and case files on the development and implementation of joint defense plans from 1941–1956;

2. Top Secret and below Southeast Asia Treaty Organization records, including but not limited to memorandums, reports and other issuances of the Secretary-General from 1967–1974, of the Council from 1968–1972, of the Council Representatives from 1969 and 1972–1977, of the Military Planning Office from 1963 and 1965–1973, and of the Intelligence Committee from 1972–1973; transcripts of the Council meetings from 1965–1975; reports of the military advisors from 1962–1972; and reports of expert study groups from 1969–1973;

3. Top Secret and below Central Treaty Organization records, including but not limited to Combined Military Planning Staff numbered papers and background materials for the same from 1956–1979 and training and operational exercise reports from 1963–1979; and U.S. Element reports, issuances, messages, and other records from 1959–1979;

4. Top Secret and below case files and general administrative files of the U.S. Military Representative, Supreme Headquarters Allied Powers Europe from 1952–1962.

As described in the section on Air Force records, RG 342 at the Washington National Records Center has some records of the North American Air Defense Command. Additionally, as discussed in the section on Army records, RG 338 at the College Park National Archives has some United Nations Command records. Lastly, as set forth in the sections on interservice agency records and records of joint, specified, and unified commands, there are also a small number of records of the North American Air Defense Command/North American Aerospace Defense Command in RG 334 at the Washington National Records Center and records of the United Nations Command in RG 349 at the College Park National Archives.

### Records at International Commands and Organizations in which the United States Military Currently Participates

The quantity, nature, and *appraisal* status of records at the North American Aerospace Defense Command are unknown.

### Records of Interservice Agencies at the National Archives and Federal Records Centers

Record Group 334 contains the records of interservice agencies, and at the College Park National Archives, RG 334 has about 25 million pages of records. No other National Archives has any RG 334 holdings. The *finding aids* are good, but it is difficult to determine from them exactly which records have been reviewed for declassification and *processed* and which have not. The records include:

1. Top Secret and below records of the Joint U.S. Military Advisory Group, China from 1948–1949; Joint U.S. Military Advisory Group, Europe from 1949–1953; and Joint U.S. Military Advisory Group, Greece from 1947–1952;

2. Top Secret and below records of Military Assistance Advisory Groups to Belgium Luxembourg (1950–1954), Brazil (1953), Cambodia (1955–1964), Denmark (1950–1954), Ethiopia (1955–1958), France (1949–1954), Indonesia (1958–1964), Iran (1942–1953), Italy (1949–1954), Japan (1954), Korea (1952–1954), Laos (1962), Libya (1958–1960), Netherlands (1950–1954), Norway (1949–1954), Philippines (1949–1961), Portugal (1950–1954), Spain (1952–1964), Thailand (1957–1961), Turkey (1947–1954), United Kingdom (1949–1961), Uruguay (1955–1962), and Yugoslavia (1952–1958);

3. Top Secret and below State/Defense Military Information Control Committee activity reports from 1951–1959; secretariat correspondence with the U.S. Mission to NATO and European regional organizations from 1953–1963; weekly political and economic summaries prepared for NATO from 1951–1964; intelligence summaries prepared for NATO from 1951–1964; and intelligence summaries prepared for the Inter-American Defense Board from 1957–1962;

4. Top Secret and below State-War-Navy Coordinating Committee/State-Army-Navy-Air Force Coordinating Committee subject correspondence files, numbered policy papers, and numbered memorandums from 1947–1949 and summaries of actions and decisions from 1944–1947.

Record Group 334 at the Washington National Records Center has more than 27.5 million pages of mostly classified records as of 2000 (15% *permanent* and 85% *temporary*). No other Federal records center has any RG 334 holdings. It is not known how many *permanent* records will be transferred to RG 334 at the College Park National Archives under the P-2000 Project. Records that are both eligible and not eligible for transfer by 2001 include:

1. Top Secret and below files of Military Assistance Advisory Groups to numerous countries from the 1950s into the early 1970s;

2. Top Secret/Restricted Data/Single Integrated Operational Plan/Extremely Sensitive Information U.S. European Command headquarters mobilization, operations, and emergency planning files from the 1960s;

3. other Top Secret/Restricted Data and below U.S. European Command headquarters records, including but not limited to incoming and outgoing messages from 1954 into the 1960s; joint command case files from 1952 into the 1970s; general administrative files from 1957 into the 1970s; publication background files from 1957 into the 1970s; EOF files from 1955 into the 1970s; and emergency planning files from the 1950s;

4. Top Secret/Restricted Data and below General Headquarters, Far East Command records, including but not limited to OPERATION JIGSAW files from 1955 and general administrative files, emergency planning files, command report files, unit history files, publication record sets, and intelligence administrative files from 1953–1957;

5. records of various commands under General Headquarters, Far East Command, including but not limited to Top Secret/Restricted Data and below Strategic Operations Force, Far East general administrative files, unit history files, organization planning files, emergency planning files, and other records from 1954–1957; Top Secret and below U.S. Forces Korea headquarters general administrative files from the 1950s; and Secret and below Combined Command for Reconnaissance Activities, Far East publications, general administrative files, and intelligence report files from 1954;

6. Secret/Restricted Data and below Continental Air Defense Command headquarters records, including but not limited to regulations, staff memos, manuals, objective plans, atomic employment plans, OPLANS, and OPORDS from 1954 into the 1970s;

7. Secret/Restricted Data and below North American Air Defense Command/North American Aerospace Defense Command records, including but not limited to general orders, regulations, manuals, staff memos, policy memos, program documents, OPLANS, and OPORDS, from the 1960s and 1970s;

8. Top Secret and below Alaskan Command headquarters records, including but not limited to publications, general administrative files, regulations, OPLANS, and Capabilities Plans from 1961 into the 1970s;

9. Top Secret/Restricted Data and below U.S. Strike Command headquarters records, including but not limited to publications, regulations, conference files, exercise files, OPLANS, and OPORDS from 1961–1971;

10. Top Secret/Restricted Data and below U.S. Readiness Command head-
    quarters records, including but not limited to general administrative
    files, publications, regulations, OPLANS, and OPORDS from the
    1970s;

11. Top Secret U.S. Naval Military Representative, Supreme Headquarters
    Allied Powers Europe messages from 1962–1964;

12. Top Secret/Restricted Data/Single Integrated Operational Plan/Ex-
    tremely Sensitive Information U.S. Pacific Command headquarters
    OPLANS from 1951 into the 1970s;

13. Top Secret/Restricted Data and Top Secret U.S. Pacific Command
    headquarters briefing notes from 1965–1969 and serials from 1968–
    1971;

14. Secret/Restricted Data and below U.S. Pacific Command headquarters
    serials from the late 1950s into the 1970s;

15. Top Secret and below U.S. Army Air Defense Command headquarters
    general files, publications, manuals, and other records from 1971–
    1975; and Secret/Restricted Data and below annual historical summary
    files from 1965–1974, command reports from 1955–1963, and organ-
    ization history files from 1951–1963;

16. Secret and below Air Force Aeronautical Chart & Information Center
    files from 1955–1971;

17. Top Secret/Restricted Data Pacific Air Forces headquarters wartime
    planning records from 1974–1975.

As mentioned in the section on Air Force records, other records of the
North American Air Defense Command/North American Aerospace Defense Command, Alaskan Command, and Pacific Air Forces are in RG 342
at the Washington National Records Center and/or St. Louis Federal Records Center. As discussed in the section on Army records and in the section
on records of joint, specified, and unified commands, other records of General Headquarters, Far East Command and its subordinate commands are
in RG 338 and RG 349 at the College Park National Archives. Lastly, as
set forth in the section on records of joint, specified, and unified commands,
other records of the U.S. European Command and U.S. Strike Command
are in RG 349 at the College Park National Archives.

### Joint Chiefs of Staff (JCS) Records at the National Archives and Federal Records Centers

There are a large number of JCS records in RG 218 at the College Park
National Archives and Washington National Records Center. No other
National Archives or Federal records center has any RG 218 holdings.

With respect to declassification review under E.O. 12958, the JCS originally estimated that it had about 5 million pages of *permanent* pre-1975 classified records subject to the new order.[81] This initial figure was evidently low, as in early 1999 the White House granted the JCS an exemption from automatic declassification for 1.5 million pages (17%) of its subject records. This means, of course, that the JCS has about 9 million pages subject to the order. The FY 1996, FY 1997, FY 1998, and FY 1999 ISOO annual reports have not specifically listed the JCS as having declassified any records, although it is possible that its totals are listed under the "All Others" category in these reports.

There are more than 7.5 million pages of JCS records in RG 218 at the College Park National Archives. The *finding aids* list individual folder titles by box. Among the postwar records that have been reviewed for declassification and *processed* are:

1. Top Secret/Restricted Data and below Chairman's correspondence and message files, including Admiral Leahy (1942–1948), General Bradley (1949–1953), Admiral Radford (1953–1957), General Twining (1957–1960), General Lemnitzer (1960–1962), General Taylor (1962–1964), and General Wheeler (1964–1970);

2. Top Secret/Restricted Data and below Central Decimal and Geographic Files from 1945 to 1959;

3. a limited number of Top Secret/Restricted Data and below Central Files from 1959–1975;

4. JCS records relating to the Korean War, including an official history of the armistice negotiations, JCS reports prepared between May 1951 and July 1953 for the Senate Committee on Korean Operations, and messages concerning Far East operations from 1950–1953;

5. Top Secret and below subject files of the Joint Committee on New Weapons and Equipment from 1945–1946;

6. Top Secret and below records concerning U.S. combat operations in the Vietnam War, including Situation Report Army File from 1966–1973; Combat Naval Gunfire Support File from 1966–1973; Naval Surveillance Activities File from 1966–1972; Combat Air Summary File from 1962–1973; Combat Activities File from 1965–1970; RVN Incidents File from 1973–1975; and Southeast Asia Casualty File from 1973–1975.

There are a fairly large number of still-classified records, and they include the following:

1. Top Secret/Restricted Data and below indexes to the 1945–1959 Central Decimal and Geographic Files, 1959–1975 Central Files, and 1942–1970 Chairman's correspondence and message files;

2. Top Secret/Restricted Data and below Director for Strategic Plans and Policy (J-5) memos from 1962–1963 and PCPs from 1963;

3. Top Secret and below Joint Command and Control Requirements Group memos from 1964–1970;

4. Confidential and below Military Assistance Command Vietnam Ground OPREP-4 and OPREP-5 reports and messages from 1968–1969, and Southeast Asia Air OPREP-5 reports from 1970;

5. Secret and below files of Department of Defense representatives at the Panama Canal Treaty negotiations from 1975–1977.

Record Group 218 at the Washington National Records Center has approximately 1.6 million pages of mostly classified records as of 2000 (55% *permanent* and 45% *temporary*). As part of the P-2000 Project, about 300,000 pages of classified *permanent* records will be transferred to RG 218 at the College Park National Archives by the end of 2001. Even if they have been reviewed for declassification by the time of their transfer, they will not be available to the public until they are possibly re-reviewed by the DOE under the Kyl Plan and then *processed* by the National Archives. The records to be transferred include:

1. Top Secret/Restricted Data and below Lieutenant General Allison SALT files from 1964–1978 and the indices thereto, and Top Secret/Restricted Data and below Lieutenant General Rowny SALT files from 1970–1979;

2. Secret and below Worldwide Military Command & Communications System files from the late 1970s;

3. Secret and below files concerning negotiations and agreements for Philippine military bases from 1977–1979.

Records not eligible for transfer to RG 218 the College Park National Archives by 2001 include:

1. Top Secret/Restricted Data and below Director of Strategic Plans and Policy (J-5) files on SALT I, SALT II, INF, START, and the Comprehensive Test Ban Treaty from 1964–1989;

2. Secret/Restricted Data and below Joint Staff Exercise Files from 1960–1989;

3. Top Secret/Restricted Data and below transcripts of congressional testimony from the 1970s into the early 1990s;

4. Top Secret and below RPB minutes from 1970 into the 1990s;

5. Secret and below Military Communication Electronics Board records from 1959 into the 1990s;
6. Secret and below Joint Politico-Military Group files from 1983–1992;
7. Secret and below Historical Committee records on Somalia from 1992–1993;
8. Secret and below historical records from 1990–1991 on Gulf War operations, planning, and command and control.

### JCS Records at the JCS

Per the 1995 proposed implementation plan filed by the JCS with the ISOO, the post-1975 Central Files and the post-1970 Chairman's files are stored by the JCS at Ft. Ritchie, Maryland. There is no information available on the quantity or *appraisal* status of these holdings or of the holdings still at the JCS.

Requests under the FOIA and MDR for records at the Washington National Records Center, Ft. Ritchie, or at the JCS should be submitted to the Joint Chiefs of Staff, Information Management Division, Room 2B917, The Pentagon, Washington, D.C. 20318.

### Joint, Specified, and Unified Commands' Records at the National Archives and Federal Records Centers

There are currently nine unified combat commands and in recent years *record groups* have been established for each: U.S. Atlantic Command/U.S. Joint Forces Command (RG 528),[82] U.S. Central Command (RG 518), U.S. Pacific Command (RG 529), U.S. Southern Command (RG 530), U.S. European Command (RG 531), U.S. Space Command (RG 532), U.S. Special Operations Command (RG 533), U.S. Transportation Command (RG 534), U.S. Strategic Command (RG 535). However, only three of these *record groups* have any records in them at either the College Park National Archives or Washington National Records Center. No other National Archives or Federal records center has any records in any of the nine *record groups*.

Record Group 518 at the College Park National Archives has almost 1 million pages of U.S. Central Command records. The *finding aids* are good. Almost all the records are classified and they include:

1. Secret and below Joint Intelligence Center, USCENTCOM Forward, Riyadh, daily intelligence summaries from August 1990 into April 1991; requests for intelligence information from August 1990 into April 1991; intelligence publications reference file from August 1990 into April

1991; and intelligence planning, operations, and briefings files from August 1990 into April 1992;

2. Secret and below Joint Operations Center incoming and outgoing messages from August 1990 into April 1991; telephone conversation records files from August 1990 into January 1991; daily journals from January into March 1991; daily operations summaries from January into June 1991; command reports from January into March 1991; and air tasking orders from January into April 1991;

3. Secret and below C3IC Ground Operations Desk daily journals and command reports from August 1990 into April 1991, and Special Operations Desk daily journals and command reports from August 1990 into March 1991;

4. Secret and below Crisis Action Team incoming and outgoing messages from August 1990 into June 1991; situation reports from August 1990 into December 1991; telephone conversation records files from August 1990 into January 1991; and command orders from August 1990 into March 1991;

5. Secret and below Plans and Operations Branch operations planning files from August 1990 into June 1991; incoming and outgoing messages from December 1990 into September 1991; daily journals from December 1990 into June 1991; and general subject files from August 1990 into September 1991;

6. Secret and below Plans Division operations planning files from August 1990 into March 1991;

7. Secret and below Command Historian Office historical records files from August 1990 into May 1991; annual command histories from 1980–1989; records of USS Stark investigation from 1987; records of the investigation of the President Zia aircrash from 1988–1989; and records of the USS Vincennes investigation from 1988;

8. Secret and below Commander in Chief's file from August 1990 into August 1991.

Record Group 530 at the Washington National Records Center has about 38,000 pages of classified U.S. Southern Command records, including Secret Joint Operations Center Logs from 1993–1994; Secret Operations Reports, Situation Reports, and Intelligence Summaries from 1988 through January 1990; and Secret and below overseas base rights files from 1971–1998.

Record Group 531 at the Washington National Records Center has fewer than 125,000 pages of U.S. European Command records, including but not limited to the Secret and below records from the 1990s relating to

OPERATION PROVIDE COMFORT and OPERATION SUPPORT HOPE.

A large number of records of former joint, specified, and unified commands, as well as some older records of present unified combat commands, appear to be in several *record groups* at the College Park National Archives, Washington National Records Center, and St. Louis Federal Records Center. As discussed in the section on Air Force records, RG 342 at the College Park National Archives, Washington National Records Center, and St. Louis Federal Records Center has records of the Strategic Air Command. Record Group 338 at the College Park National Archives, as set forth in the section on Army records, contains General Headquarters, Far East Command, and subordinate command records. As mentioned in the section on interservice agency records, RG 334 at the Washington National Records Center has records of the U.S. Strike Command; U.S. European Command; U.S. Pacific Command; General Headquarters, Far East Command, and subordinate commands of General Headquarters, Far East Command. Lastly, joint command records are in RG 349 at the College Park National Archives.

Except for the Air Force's review of a small number of Strategic Air Command records and the U.S. European Command's and U.S. Pacific Command's review of their subject records at the Washington National Records Center, there apparently has been no declassification review under E.O. 12958 of any of the *permanent* pre-1975 classified records of the former joint, specified or unified commands or the current unified combat commands. In fact, it has not even been determined which organization has the responsibility to review the records of some former commands, such as the U.S. Strike Command.[83]

Record Group 349 contains records of joint commands. At the College Park National Archives, RG 349 has fewer than 1 million pages of records. No other National Archives or any Federal records center has any RG 349 holdings. The *finding aids* are good, but it is difficult to determine from them which records have been reviewed for declassification and *processed* and which records have not. The records include:

1. Top Secret and below Caribbean Command records, including but not limited to central decimal correspondence files from 1947–1963; J-2 weekly intelligence reports from 1955–1956 and annual intelligence reports on Latin American nations and leaders from 1956–1959; and J-3 correspondence relating to command defense planning from 1950–1960;

2. a small number of Top Secret/Restricted Data and below records of the U.S. Strike Command, including but not limited to general correspondence files from 1962–1964;

3. Top Secret/Restricted Data and below U.S. European Command records, including but not limited to central decimal correspondence files from 1952–1954; incoming and outgoing messages from 1952–1954; incoming and outgoing messages of the U.S. Military Representative, Supreme Headquarters Allied Powers Europe from 1951–1953; and historical reference files and operational and field exercise training files of the Support Operations Task Force, Europe from 1957–1964;

4. Top Secret/Restricted Data and below General Headquarters, Far East Command records, including but not limited to central decimal correspondence files from 1953–1954, Office of the Secretary of the Joint Staff decimal correspondence files from 1953–1954, command reports from 1953–1954, Korean armistice negotiation records from 1951–1953, organizational and emergency planning records from 1953–1954, and reports on OPERATION JIGSAW from 1955; J-2 decimal correspondence files and organizational planning records from 1953–1954; J-3 decimal correspondence files from 1954, correspondence files regarding operations in Korea from 1946–1953, and records relating to operational and emergency planning from 1953–1954; J-4 narrative histories from 1954; and J-5 narrative histories and operational planning records from 1953–1954;

5. Top Secret/Restricted Data and below records of various commands under General Headquarters, Far East Command, including but not limited to Combined Command for Reconnaissance Activities, Korea general correspondence files, intelligence reports, and combat reports from 1952–1953; Strategic Operations Force, Far East decimal correspondence files from 1954–1957 and staff studies from 1956–1957; Combined Command for Reconnaissance Activities, Far East general administrative files from 1953, intelligence reports and general decimal files from 1955–1956, R&D files from 1956, and intelligence project control files from 1954–1955; and Prisoner of War Command records from 1952–1953.

### Joint, Specified, and Unified Commands' Records at the Current Commands

At the headquarters of the U.S. Joint Forces Command (formerly the U.S. Atlantic Command), the Command Historian has a small archives with mostly post-1993 records on Haiti, counterdrug operations, and other topics. Although many of the records are classified, *finding aids* to a few of the collections are available to the public.[84] This office can be contacted at USACOM/JO2P4, Suite 200, Mitscher Avenue, Norfolk, VA 23551-2488 or at 757-836-6368. The quantity, nature, and *appraisal* status of holdings outside this archives are not known.

The Command Historian at the U.S. Transportation Command has a small archives with some operational files and the limited number of official histories that have been written, and a *finding aid* is available. Approximately one-third of the records are classified.[85] This office can be contacted USTRANSCOM/TRC, 508 Scott Drive, Scott Air Force Base, IL 62225–5357 or 618–256–6167. The quantity, nature, and *appraisal* status of holdings outside this archives are not known.

At the headquarters of the U.S. Special Operations Command there is an archives with about 1 million pages of records, but virtually all of them are classified, as are the *finding aids*.[86] The quantity, nature, and *appraisal* status of holdings outside this archives are not known.

The headquarters of the U.S. Space Command has an archives with an unknown quantity of records from the 1950s on, but all the records are classified, as are the *finding aids*.[87] The quantity, nature, and *appraisal* status of holdings outside this archives are not known.

The U.S. Pacific Command, U.S. Strategic Command, U.S. European Command, and U. S. Central Command report that they do not have any archives or central records storage facilities at their headquarters.[88] The quantity, nature, and *appraisal* status of the holdings at these commands and the U.S. Southern Command are not known.[89]

### Department of Justice (DOJ) Records at the National Archives and Federal Records Centers

A large number of DOJ records are in RG 60 at the College Park National Archives or the Washington National Records Center. A few regional National Archives and Federal records centers have extremely small RG 60 holdings.

With respect to declassification review under E.O. 12958, the DOJ estimated in 1995 that apart from the FBI it might have up to 25 million pages of *permanent* pre-1975 classified records.[90] The FY 1998 and FY 1999 ISOO annual reports list the DOJ as having declassified about 700,000 pages. It is not known exactly which records these are, but they are not any of the classification 146 ones described below.[91]

Virtually all DOJ records are filed by classification or subclassification number, and researchers must be familiar with these numbers. The classification number of greatest relevance here is 146 (World War II and Postwar Subversive Activities and Internal Security). Under classification 146, there are more than 50 subclasses of which the following are of particular interest: 146–1 (Communism), 146–7 (General Suspects), 146–14 (Consular or Diplomatic Activities), 146–29 (Subversive Activities of Non-Enemy Aliens), 146–41 (Disclosure of Official Secrets), 146–200 (Investigations of Government Employees Connected or Allegedly Connected with Subversive Organizations).[92]

Record Group 60 at the College Park National Archives has more than 62.5 million pages of records, but only two small classified collections (totaling about 250,000 pages) are of interest here. The first contains Secret 146–41 files, and the second Secret/Restricted Data 146–200 files. There are no *finding aids* to the two collections, although it is possible that the first box of each collection has some sort of folder list.

At the Washington National Records Center there are more than 680 million pages of records in RG 60 as of 2000 (60% *permanent*, 35% *temporary*, and 15% *unappraised*). It is not known whether any *permanent* records will be transferred to RG 60 at the College Park National Archives under the P-2000 Project, although some of them are now eligible for transfer. There are many millions of pages of records in the 146 class from World War II into the 1980s, many of which are either Secret or Top Secret. Unfortunately, most of the *SF-135s* for these *accessions* do not set forth the 146 subclassification numbers. The few *SF-135s* that do set forth subclassification numbers only list case numbers and not case names. In short, it is virtually impossible to determine whether a particular *accession* has records of interest. The only solution is to contact the DOJ and ask its assistance in identifying the exact contents of the *accessions*. Record Group 60 at the Washington National Records Center also contains the unclassified and classified Attorney General subject, project, and correspondence files from the mid-1970s into the 1990s and the unclassified and classified subject and correspondence files from the late 1970s into the 1990s of the Assistant Attorney Generals, Deputy Attorney Generals, and Associate Deputy Attorney Generals.[23]

### DOJ Records at the DOJ and Presidential Libraries

The quantity, nature, and *appraisal* status of records still held at the DOJ are not known.

Two presidential libraries have relevant holdings. The Kennedy Library has microfilm copies of the Deputy Attorney General's files and other headquarters office files from 1961–1963 in RG 60, but most are still closed. The library also has Attorney General Robert Kennedy's correspondence files, desk diaries, classified files, speeches, and telephone logs and messages from 1961–1964, but many portions are still closed. The Reagan Library has Attorney General Edwin Meese's files from 1985–1988 and Attorney General William French's files from 1981–1985, but very little of either collection is open.

Requests under the FOIA and MDR for records at the Washington National Records Center or at the DOJ should be submitted to the Freedom of Information/Privacy Act Unit, U. S. Department of Justice, Room 7100, 600 E Street, Washington, D.C. 20530.

## U.S. Marine Corps (USMC) Records at the National Archives and Federal Records Centers

A large number of USMC records are in RG 127 at the College Park National Archives and Washington National Records Center.

With respect to the number of *permanent* pre-1975 classified records subject to E.O. 12958, the 1995 Navy estimate of 500 million pages included USMC records. Similarly, the records declassified by the USMC in its declassification review program under the order have been reported in the ISOO annual reports under the Navy totals.

There are more than 8.75 million pages of USMC headquarters records in RG 127 at the College Park National Archives, most of which are from World War II and earlier. Most of the records have been reviewed for declassification and *processed*, and the *finding aids* are good. Postwar records include the Secret and below correspondence files of the Commandant through 1950, Secret and below Division of Plans and Policies correspondence files and war plans through 1947, and records of selected USMC units through 1949. A few regional National Archives have very small RG 127 holdings.

Record Group 127 at the Washington National Records Center contains more than 20 million pages of records as of 2000 (65% *permanent* and 35% *temporary*). Some regional Federal records centers have small RG 127 holdings. As part of the P-2000 Project, more than 3.3 million pages of unclassified *permanent* records and 2 million pages of classified *permanent* records will be transferred to RG 127 at the College Park National Archives by the end of 2001. Even if the classified records have been reviewed for declassification by the time of their transfer, none will be available to the public until they are possibly re-reviewed by the DOE under the Kyl Plan and then *processed* by the National Archives. The records to be transferred include:

1. Top Secret/Restricted Data and Top Secret Commandant correspondence files from the 1960s to 1973;

2. Secret/Restricted Data and below Commandant correspondence files from 1949–1974;

3. Secret and below indices to the 1941–1959 Commandant correspondence files;

4. Top Secret and below Commandant speeches, meeting files, and trip reports from 1961–1974;

5. Top Secret and below National Military Command Center Vietnam operational summaries from 1964–1968;

6. Secret and below CIA and DIA intelligence reports, summaries, and notices received by USMC headquarters from 1965–1970;

7. Secret and below Plans and Policies Division correspondence files from 1921–1942;

8. Secret and below 3rd Marine Amphibious Force journals and files from 1966–1970;

9. Secret and below 3rd Marine Division sitreps and messages from 1965–1969;

10. Secret and below 3rd and 4th Marine Regiment journals and sitreps from 1965–1967;

11. Top Secret/Restricted Data and below 1st, 2nd, 6th, 7th, Atlantic, and Pacific Fleet operations plans and orders, exercise reports, and related records from 1958–1979;

12. Secret/Restricted Data and below 1st Marine Division operations plans and orders, exercise orders and reports, and related records from 1952–1961;

13. Top Secret and below files of the U.S. Naval Mission Haiti, U.S. Military Group Haiti, and Military Assistance Advisory Group Haiti from 1959–1963.

Among the records not eligible for transfer to RG 127 at the College Park National Archives by 2001 are:

1. Commandant speeches, briefing files, trip files, notebooks, congressional testimony, flag officer correspondence files, and other records from the 1940s into the 1980s;

2. USMC headquarters incoming and outgoing messages and other records;

3. a wide range of records of various USMC units;

4. background materials used in writing various USMC histories.

### USMC Records at USMC Commands

The Marine Corps Historical Center at the Washington Navy Yard has the following important records in addition to a large amount of secondary literature:

1. combat operational reports, plans, unit diaries, and related records from Vietnam to the present (similar records from World War II to Vietnam are at the Washington National Records Center and can be recalled for the use of researchers);

2. more than 2,000 collections of personal papers;

3. more than 6,500 oral history interviews;

4. periodic and programmatic histories.

Researchers can contact the Center in writing at Bldg. 58, Washington Navy Yard, 901 M Street, S.E., Washington, D.C. 20374–5040 or by phone at 202–433–3239.

The quantity, nature, and *appraisal* status of holdings at other USMC commands are unknown.

Requests under the FOIA and MDR for records at Federal records centers or still at the USMC can be submitted to the commanding officer of the command holding the records. If headquarters records are sought, or if there is any doubt as to which command holds the records, the requests should be submitted to HQMC (ARAD), 2 Navy Annex, Washington, D.C. 20380–1775.

### National Aeronautics and Space Administration (NASA) / National Advisory Committee for Aeronautics (NACA) Records at the National Archives and Federal Records Centers

A large number of records of NASA (1958–present) and its predecessor, the NACA (1915–1958), are in RG 255 at the National Archives and Federal records centers.

It is not known how many *permanent* pre-1975 classified records NASA holds subject to E.O. 12958. The FY 1996, FY 1997, FY 1998, and FY 1999 ISOO annual reports list NASA as having declassified more than 1.7 million pages, but it is not known what these records are or where they are.

At the College Park National Archives there are approximately 12.5 million pages of records in RG 255. Most are NACA records, and all have been reviewed for declassification and *processed*. The *finding aid* to them is very good, listing all the folder titles by box. Important postwar collections include: (1) central correspondence files of the Director and Executive Secretary; (2) selected records of various research units; (3) agendas, minutes, reports, and related records of the Executive Committee and various individual committees and subcommittees. There is also a small number of NASA records from 1958 into the 1970s, most of which have been reviewed for declassification and *processed*. The *finding aid* to these records is also very good, listing all the folder titles by box. Among the records are: (1) correspondence files, chronological files, and speeches from 1965–1974 of Homer Newell, Associate Administrator; (2) correspondence files, subject files, technical reports, and reports from 1954–1966 of the Director, Goddard Space Flight Center; (3) Project VANGUARD files of the Goddard Space Flight Center; (4) Apollo 204 Review Board files.

A number of the regional National Archives have RG 255 holdings as well. The Philadelphia National Archives has about 875,000 pages of largely unclassified correspondence files, publications, and R&D reports of the Langley Research Center from 1918–1992. The Chicago National Archives has more than 500,000 pages of mostly unclassified records of the Lewis Flight Propulsion Laboratory from 1944–1972. The Laguna Niguel National Archives has fewer than 500,000 pages of largely unclassified records of the Dryden Flight Research Center from 1946–1959, Western Support Office from 1939–1967, and the Jet Propulsion Laboratory from 1971–1985. The Fort Worth National Archives has about 1.1 million pages of mostly unclassified Johnson Space Center records. These include: (1) correspondence files, technical reports, and weekly activity reports of the Director from the 1960s and 1970s; (2) technical reports of the Crew System Division from the 1960s; (3) reference files of the Public Affairs Office from 1962–1966; (4) contract administration files of the Director of Administration from the 1960s. The San Bruno National Archives has more than 2.5 million pages of largely unclassified central files of the Ames Research Center from 1939–1971. Lastly, the East Point National Archives has more than 4 million pages of mostly unclassified records. These include: (1) project files, technical reports, speech files, public affairs releases, and other material of the Marshall Space Flight Center from 1954–1998; (2) astronaut medical records, correspondence files, project files, technical reports, transcripts of speeches, and other material of the Kennedy Space Center from 1959–1997.

Record Group 255 at the Washington National Records Center contains more than 120 million pages of NASA records as of 2000 (60% *permanent* and 40% *temporary*). As part of the P-2000 Project, the National Archives has proposed that more than 16 million pages of unclassified *permanent* records, 4 million pages of classified *permanent* records, and a small quantity of unclassified *permanent* nontextual records be transferred to RG 255 at the College Park National Archives by the end of 2001 (NASA has not approved the transfer as of this writing). Even if the classified records have been reviewed for declassification by the time of their transfer, none will be available to the public until they are possibly re-reviewed by the DOE under the Kyl Plan and then *processed* by the National Archives. The records proposed for transfer include:

1. Confidential and below Administrator, Deputy Administrator, Associate Administrator, and Associate Deputy Administrator correspondence files, chronological files, speech files, and congressional files from 1959 into the late 1960s;

2. unclassified official files of James Webb, Dr. Robert Seamans, Dr. Thomas Paine, Dr. Homer Newell, Dr. Werhner von Braun, Dr. James Fletcher, and Willis Shapley from 1959–1972;

3. unclassified Office of the Administrator correspondence files and notes from the late 1960s to 1991;

4. Confidential and below Office of the Administrator Manned Space Flight Schedules from 1963–1968; Administrator's Progress Reports from 1959–1965; and Federal Council for Science and Technology agendas, meeting minutes, reports, and correspondence files from 1959–1966;

5. unclassified tape recordings, transcripts, and vugraphs of the 1966–1967 program review meetings attended by the Administrator and other top officials;

6. a large number of Secret and below Central Files from 1959–1966 concerning organization and management, personnel, physics, power plants, propellers, public relations, reports and statistics, research facilities, safety, scientific information, security, telcoms, travel, launch vehicles, aeronautics-astronautics, astronomy, budget and appropriations, committees, meetings, computers, contracts, foreign relations, fuels and lubricants, materials, legal issues, and other topics (the *SF-135s* for these files do not indicate which office maintained these files, but do state that the filing system was abolished in 1966);

7. Confidential and below Associate Administrator, Office of Manned Space Flight and predecessor correspondence files, technical reports, meeting files, and other records from 1959 into the 1970s;

8. Confidential and below Office of Manned Space Flight and predecessor Basic Large Launch Vehicle Planning Group records from 1957–1965;

9. a huge number of mostly unclassified Office of Manned Space Flight and predecessor records concerning the Mercury, Gemini, and Apollo programs, including but not limited to mission files, studies, technical reports, manuals, test reports, specifications, blueprints, quarterly program reviews, progress reports, program manager meeting files, general correspondence files, and budget files;

10. unclassified Office of Manned Space Flight studies, reports, and other records on Skylab from 1964 into the 1970s;

11. Secret and below Office of Manned Space Flight studies, reports, and other records on the Manned Orbiting Laboratory from the 1960s;

12. Secret and below Office of Manned Space Flight correspondence files, reports, briefing files, and other records concerning nuclear propulsion from the 1960s and early 1970s;

13. a wide range of unclassified Office of Manned Space Flight records relating to the Apollo/Soyuz Test Project from the 1970s;

14. unclassified Office of Manned Space Flight Space Station contractor studies from 1961–1966 and Space Station Task Force/Sortie Lab Task Force records from the late 1960s and early 1970s;

15. numerous unclassified Office of Manned Space Flight/Office of Space Flight records concerning the Space Shuttle from the 1960s into the 1980s;

16. mostly unclassified Associate Administrator, Office of Space Science & Applications files from the 1960s to 1982;

17. numerous Confidential and below Office of Space Science & Applications studies, specifications, technical reports, test reports, correspondence files and other records concerning the Scout, Delta, Atlas, Agena, Centaur, Thor, and other launch vehicles from the late 1950s into the early 1970s;

18. a large number of mostly unclassified Office of Space Science & Applications studies, technical reports, correspondence files, budget files, progress reports, program reports, data files, photographs, and other records on the Orbiting Solar Observatory, Orbiting Astronomical Observatory, Orbiting Geophysical Observatory, Explorer, Pioneer, Ranger, Surveyor, Voyager, Mariner, Telstar, Tiros, Relay, Echo, Nimbus, Lunar Orbiter, and other satellites and probes from the late 1950s into the 1970s;

19. Confidential and below minutes, correspondence, and other records of the 1961–1967 meetings between Homer Newell (Associate Administrator, Office of Space Science and Applications) and George Mueller (Associate Administrator, Office of Manned Space Flight);

20. unclassified Office of Advanced Research & Technology/Office of Aeronautics & Space Technology long range R&D planning studies, reports, and files from the 1960s and 1970s;

21. a large number of Confidential and below Office of Advanced Research & Technology/Office of Aeronautics & Space Technology studies, technical reports, correspondence files, budget files, progress reports, program reviews, and other records on the X-15, XB-70, VSTOL, lifting bodies, and other aircraft and aerospace vehicles from the 1960s and early 1970s;

22. a limited number of Secret and below Office of Advanced Research & Technology records concerning the SST from 1960–1965;

23. a huge number of Confidential and below Office of Advanced Research & Technology/Office of Aeronautics & Space Technology studies, technical reports, correspondence files, and other records on chemical, solar, and electrical propulsion systems and power systems from the 1960s and 1970s;

24. a limited number of Secret/Restricted Data and below Office of Advanced Research & Technology/Office of Aeronautics & Space Tech-

nology records pertaining to nuclear propulsion from the 1960s and early 1970s;

25. Confidential and below Office of Program Plans & Analysis speech and briefing files, aircraft files, general ships files, facilities files, budget files, and other records from the 1960s;

26. unclassified Office of Program Plans & Analysis Planning Review Panel records from 1963–1967;

27. Confidential and below Office of Tracking & Data Acquisition files on coordination and liaison with the DOD from the 1960s and 1970s;

28. unclassified Office of Tracking & Data Acquisition data system development plans, project development plans, budget files, and other records from the 1960s and 1970s;

29. Secret and below Office of DOD & Interagency Affairs background files, meeting minutes, reports, and other records concerning the DOD/NASA Aeronautics & Astronautics Coordinating Board from the 1960s;

30. unclassified Office of DOD & Interagency Affairs records relating to NATO's Advisory Group on Aeronautical Research & Development from the 1960s into the 1980s; interagency agreements from 1959–1988; and miscellaneous intergovernmental affairs program and correspondence files from the 1960s into the 1980s;

31. Secret and below Office of International Affairs and predecessor general country and subject files, United Nations files, Committee on Space Research files, U.S.S.R. files, U.S./U.S.S.R. files, disarmament files, congressional files, international exhibits files, foreign visitor files, and files concerning NASA personnel visiting other countries from 1959 into the 1970s; COCOM files, Department of Commerce Operating Committee files, Economic Defense Advisory Committee files, U.S. Military Information Control Committee/National Disclosure Policy Committee files, and files relating to Department of State munitions control cases from the 1960s; International Geophysical Year files from 1957–1961; and National Academy of Sciences/Space Science Board files from 1959 into the early 1960s;

32. mostly unclassified Office of Legislative Affairs correspondence files, briefing files, and other records from 1959 into the early 1980s;

33. unclassified Office of Public Affairs press releases, fact sheets, briefing files, correspondence files, and speeches, articles, and writings of the Administrator and other top officials from 1959 into the early 1980s;

34. a large number of unclassified Office of Public Affairs audiotapes, photographs, and films from 1959 into the 1980s (the audiotapes are of speeches, press conferences, radio and television appearances, and

communications with astronauts—the photographs and films cover the range of NASA activities and include many taken from manned and unmanned spacecraft);

35. unclassified Office of the Director, Goddard Space Flight Center program management reports, correspondence files, research proposal files, and other records from 1959 into the 1980s;

36. a wide range of unclassified Goddard Space Flight Center and predecessor records on satellites, orbiting observatories, launch vehicles, sounding rockets, and numerous scientific projects from the late 1940s into the 1980s;

37. unclassified Wallops Station project files on satellites, launch vehicles, and aircraft from 1959 into the 1960s;

38. unclassified Electronics Research Center chronological files, reading files, technical reports, project files, and other records from the 1960s and 1970s;

39. Confidential/Restricted Data and below Lewis Research Center studies, technical reports, and other records on nuclear propulsion from the 1960s and early 1970s;

40. Confidential and below Langley Research Center contract files, technical files, correspondence files, and other records on the Lunar Orbiter from the 1960s;

41. a wide range of unclassified Langley Research Center records, including aircraft company files from 1950–1960, project specification files from the late 1950s into the 1970s, and manned planetary mission studies from the 1960s.

Among the records not eligible for transfer to RG 255 at the College Park National Archives by 2001 are:

1. unclassified Office of the Administrator correspondence files and notes from 1991–1993;

2. unclassified Office of Policy & Planning files from 1977–1993;

3. a large number of unclassified records of the Office of International Affairs, Office of Space Science & Applications, Office of Aeronautics & Space Technology, Office of Legislative Affairs, Office of Public Affairs, and other headquarters offices from the 1970s into the 1990s;

4. numerous unclassified Goddard Space Flight Center records.

Several regional Federal records centers have important RG 255 holdings as well. The Laguna Niguel Federal Records Center has more than 21 million pages of largely unclassified Jet Propulsion Laboratory records from the 1960s on.[94] The Fort Worth Federal Records Center has more than 7.5 million pages of almost exclusively unclassified Johnson Space Center R&D project files, R&D drawing files, R&D technical reports, and other records from the 1960s to the present.[95]

Records of the President's National Aeronautics and Space Council from 1958 to 1973 are in RG 220 at the College Park National Archives. Most have been reviewed for declassification and *processed*, and the *finding aid* is good.

### NASA and NACA Records at NASA and Presidential Libraries

The History Office at NASA Headquarters in Washington, D.C., and the ten NASA centers around the country—Ames Research Center, Dryden Flight Research Center, Goddard Space Flight Center, Jet Propulsion Laboratory, Johnson Space Center, Kennedy Space Center, Langley Research Center, Lewis Research Center, Marshall Space Flight Center, and Stennis Space Center—all have historical record collections. They are described in detail in the 1997 NASA History Office publication, *Research in NASA History*, which is available online at www.hq.nasa.gov/office/pao/History. Any person planning to conduct research at a NASA facility should certainly first consult this work.

Three presidential libraries have relevant holdings. The personal papers of James Webb (Administrator of NASA from 1961–1968) are at the Truman Library. Microfilm copies of reports to the White House, correspondence with the White House, staff meeting notes, various headquarters files, and related materials from 1961–1963 are in RG 255 at the Kennedy Library. James Webb's chronological file from 1964–1967 is in his personal papers at the Johnson Library. All these records are open.

Requests under the FOIA and MDR for records still at NASA facilities or at Federal records centers should be submitted to the facility that has custody of the records. If headquarters records are sought, or if there is any doubt as to which facility has custody, the requests should be submitted to the FOIA Officer (Code PS), 300 E Street, S.W., Washington, D.C. 20546.

### National Defense University (NDU) / National War College (NWC) / Industrial College of the Armed Forces (ICAF) Records

The NDU, located at Ft. McNair in Washington, D.C., has a library that can be used by the public with the prior permission of the Library Director. The Library Director can be contacted at 202–685–3948 or in writing at the NDU Library, Ft. McNair, Washington, D.C. 20319–6000.

In addition to a large amount of secondary literature, the library has a number of diverse primary source materials. These include all the lectures given at the NWC and ICAF from 1945 to the 1970s (at which time lectures ceased being recorded and transcribed), as well as all the students' theses from 1945 to the present day. Many of the lectures are still classified. Although few of the theses are classified, even if they are not, they must be reviewed by the library before being made available to the public.

The library also has duplicates of many of the oral histories held by the Military History Institute at Carlisle Barracks. As discussed above in the section on Army records, a complete listing of this huge collection is in *Senior Officer Oral History Program Project Handlist* that is available from the Military History Institute. Additionally, the library has some duplicates of oral histories from the Kennedy and Johnson Presidential Libraries. A limited number of the oral histories from the Military History Institute and presidential libraries are classified or have other restrictions that limit public access.

There are also significant manuscript collections at the library, some of which remain classified. These include the Hudson Institute Archives and the personal papers of Herman Kahn, Bernard Baruch, General Maxwell Taylor, General Colin Powell, General Lyman Lemnitzer, General Andrew Goodpaster, General George Brown, General John Galvin, General Bernard Rogers, General James McCarthy, General Robert RisCassi, General Paul Adams, and Admiral David Jeremiah. A complete listing of all the manuscript collections can be found on the NDU's homepage at www.ndu.edu.

Lastly, there are many collections of records on microform, including the JCS records from 1947 to 1953 and transcripts and files of the Paris Peace Talks from 1968 to 1973. Many of these are still classified.

The NDU does accept FOIAs and MDRs for documents it holds, but it does not have any authority to declassify any documents. All such requests are forwarded to the originating agency (or its successor) for action.

### National Imagery and Mapping Agency (NIMA) / Central Imagery Office (CIO) / Defense Mapping Agency (DMA) and Predecessor Records at the National Archives and Federal Records Centers

There are only a small number of records of the NIMA (1996–present), CIO (1992–1996), DMA (1972–1996), and predecessor offices within the Defense Intelligence Agency and military departments at the College Park National Archives and Washington National Records Center. No other National Archives or Federal records center has any records of these agencies.

With respect to its declassification review program under E.O. 12958, the NIMA estimates that it has about 6.5 million pages of *permanent* pre-1975 classified textual records. All these records concern geo-spatial information. Through FY 1999, it had reviewed about 4 million pages but it is not known how many pages were actually declassified. No information is publicly available regarding which records have been reviewed or where they are located.[96] With respect to the presumably huge amount of imagery from space-based national intelligence reconnaissance systems the NIMA now has legal custody of due to its acquisition of the National Photographic Interpretation Center in 1996, E.O. 12951 is the controlling authority for its possible declassification and not E.O. 12958. As discussed in the previous chapter, E.O. 12951 provides in part that a comprehensive program be established "for the periodic review of imagery from systems other than Corona, Argon, and Lanyard, with the objective of making available to the public as much imagery as possible consistent with the interests of national defense and foreign policy." The order further mandates that this review concerning "imagery from obsolete broad-area film-return systems other than Corona, Argon, and Lanyard missions" be completed by February 2000 (as of this writing, studies and associated actions to make some post-CORONA imagery available are ongoing).

Record Group 537 was established for the records of the NIMA, but there are no records in this *record group* at any National Archives or Federal records center.

Record Group 456 contains records of the DMA and predecessor offices within the Defense Intelligence Agency (the Mapping, Charting, and Geodetic Directorate) and military departments (for example, the Air Force Aeronautical Chart & Information Center, Army Mapping Service/Army Topographic Command, and Navy Hydrographic Office/Navy Oceanographic Office). At the College Park National Archives, RG 456 has about 750,000 pages of textual records and a small quantity of nontextual records. All these records came to the College Park National Archives in 1996 under the P-1995 Project, and they include:

1. Secret and below Mapping, Charting & Geodesy project history files from 1958–1984 used in developing target information in the Soviet Union (these were formerly Top Secret but were downgraded to Secret by the NIMA);
2. a limited number of Secret and below Mapping, Charting, and Geodesy project history files, planning files, reporting files, conference files, program correspondence files, and study files from the 1960s;
3. Secret and below Navy Hydrographic Office/Navy Oceanographic Office correspondence files from before World War II into the 1960s.

All these collections have evidently been reviewed for declassification by the NIMA under E.O. 12958, but none have been re-reviewed by the DOE under the Kyl Plan (if needed) and then *processed* by the National Archives.

At the Washington National Records Center, RG 456 has about 20 million pages of textual records and a small quantity of nontextual records as of 2000 (90% *permanent* and 10% *temporary*). As part of the P-2000 Project, about 2.5 million pages of unclassified *permanent* records, 660,000 pages of classified *permanent* records, and a small quantity of unclassified and classified *permanent* nontextual records will be transferred to RG 456 at the College Park National Archives by the end of 2001. Even if the classified records have been reviewed for declassification by the time of their transfer, none will be available until they are possibly re-reviewed by the DOE under the Kyl Plan and then *processed* by the National Archives. The records to be transferred include:

1. Secret and below Navy Hydrographic Office/Navy Oceanographic Office bathymetric survey data from 1940 through the 1960s; bathymetric charts and sheets from the 1950s; fathograms, sounding journals, boat sheets, logs, and track charts from the 1950s and 1960s; CAP files and bulky enclosures to primary correspondence files from 1950–1961; primary correspondence files from 1962–1963; CAESER surveys from 1959–1961; and sailing directions for Pacific bases from 1944–1947;

2. Secret and below Air Force Aeronautical Chart & Information Center files from the 1960s and early 1970s on HIRAN/LORAN tests in Southeast Asia, the Space and Missiles Systems Organization, Safeguard antiballistic missile system, and other topics (as set forth in the section on interservice agency records, RG 334 at the Washington National Records Center has some Secret and below files of the Air Force Aeronautical Chart & Information Center from 1955–1971);

3. Secret and below aids to navigation files from 1959–1978 and navigation publications from the 1970s;

4. Top Secret aids to navigation charts from 1962–1977;

5. Secret and below Mapping, Charting & Geodesy program files, country files, international conference files, guidance and support files, project history files, development project files, reporting files, study files, and map distribution policy files from the 1950s into the 1970s;

6. Secret and below Mapping, Charting & Geodesy requirements, investigations, and validation files from 1947 into the 1970s.

Among the records not eligible for transfer to RG 456 at the College Park National Archives by 2001 are:

1. a large number of unclassified final geodetic control data files from 1945–1997;

2. a limited number of Secret and Confidential final geodetic control data files from the 1960s into the 1990s;

3. Secret and below Mapping, Charting & Geodesy requirements, investigations, and validation files; international conference files; program files; country files, guidance and support files; project history files; development project files; reporting files; and study files from the 1960s into the 1990s;

4. unclassified nautical/navigations source data files, chart records, and aids to navigation files from the 1960s into the 1990s;

5. unclassified hydrographic control data files from 1951–1989;

6. unclassified DOD Bathymetric Library files from the 1960s into the 1990s;

7. unclassified DOD foreign place names card files from 1945–1995;

8. unclassified publication record sets from 1918 into the 1990s.

### NIMA, DMA, and CIO Records at NIMA

The quantity, nature, and *appraisal* status of records still held at the NIMA is not known. Although in 1996, the agency took over the National Photographic Interpretation Center and its presumably massive overhead imagery holdings from both space-based and manned aircraft systems, according to the recent *Records Management in the Central Intelligence Agency, A NARA Evaluation*[97] these images and their master negatives are actually stored at the CIA's Agency Records Center. The report does not give the quantity of overhead imagery holdings, but does state that the master negatives for the overhead imagery are "scheduled for permanent retention in the National Archives," although no dates are given in the report for their eventual transfer.

Requests under the FOIA and MDR for records at the NIMA or at the Washington National Records Center should be submitted to the Office of the General Counsel, National Imagery and Mapping Agency, 4600 Sangamore Road (D-10), Bethesda, MD 20816. It should be noted that a provision in the FY 2000 Intelligence Authorization Act authorizes the Director of the NIMA (in coordination with the Director of Central Intelligence) to exempt certain operational files of the NIMA and the former National Photographic Interpretation Center from the FOIA. Whether a list of exempted files has been created is not known.

### National Reconnaissance Office (NRO) Records at the National Archives and Federal Records Centers

Record Group 525 has been created to hold the records of the NRO (1961–present), but there are no records in this *record group* at any National Archives or Federal records center (it is believed that the NRO has permission from NARA to store its inactive records at an internal facility instead of transferring them to Washington National Records Center).

The initial estimate of *permanent* pre-1975 classified records subject to E.O. 12958 was 6.5 million pages.[98] This was evidently high, as in early 1999 the White House granted the NRO an exemption from automatic declassification for 720,000 pages (63%). This of course means that the total of subject records is about 1.15 million pages. Progress in the declassification review program has been slow, with the ISOO annual reports since FY 1996 listing the NRO as having declassified only 38,000 pages. It is not known exactly what these records are or where they are.

### NRO Records at NRO

The NRO holds all of its records that still exist. However, there is no information publicly available regarding the quantity, nature, and *appraisal* status of the holdings.[99] The NRO *records schedule* that was available on its homepage (nro.odci.gov) did not specify when the *permanent* records are to be transferred to either the Washington National Records Center or the College Park National Archives. Consequently, even if some of the records have now been *appraised* as *permanent*, it is not known when they will be eligible for transfer to the College Park National Archives.

Requests under the FOIA and MDR should be submitted to the Director, External Relations, National Reconnaissance Office, 1040 Defense Pentagon, Washington, D.C. 20301–1040.

### National Security Agency (NSA) / Central Security Service (CSS) / Armed Forces Security Agency (AFSA) and Predecessor Agency Records at the National Archives and Federal Records Centers

The NSA (1952–present) and CSS (1971–present) hold virtually all of their records and the postwar records of their predecessors, the AFSA (1949–1952) and the many organizations and offices under the National Military Establishment, War Department, and Navy Department. There is only a very small number of records of the NSA and its predecessors in RG 457 at the College Park National Archives. No regional National Archives or any Federal records center has any RG 457 holdings (the NSA has permission from NARA to store inactive records at its Archives and at its Records Center instead of transferring them to the Washington National Records Center).

With respect to declassification review under E.O. 12958, originally it was estimated that the NSA had about 130 million pages of *permanent* pre-1975 classified records.[100] This initial figure was apparently high, as in early 1999 the White House granted the NSA an exemption from automatic declassification for 27 million pages (38%) of its subject records. This means that the NSA has a total of about only 67 million pages or so—the huge discrepancy between the figures has not been explained. The use of "pages" is somewhat erroneous, though. The NSA's *permanent* pre-1975 classified records include not only textual records but microfiche, microfilm, tapes, and other nontextual records as well.[101]

The FY 1996, FY 1997, FY 1998, and FY 1999 ISOO annual reports list the NSA as declassifying a total of approximately 27 million pages. The agency, however, states that during these fiscal years it declassified a total of 35 million pages of pre-World War I through World War II records. In 1996, approximately 14 million of these pages (of which the vast majority are Japanese and German intercepts from World War II formerly stored at a U.S. Navy facility in Crane, Indiana) were transferred to RG 38 and RG 457 at the College Park National Archives. The NSA states that subsequently it transferred the remaining 21 million pages to the College Park National Archives, but as of this writing the latter has no record of receiving them. In any event, the NSA states that it no longer has any World War II or pre-World War II records with the transfer of these 35 million pages.

In FY 1999, the agency began reviewing *accessions* of post-World War II *permanent* records stored at the NSA/CSS Archives, beginning with the first *accession* and working forward. It is important to note, though, that this does not mean that all the immediate postwar records the agency holds are being reviewed. Some individual offices, divisions, and directorates may still hold records from this period; such records may have been sent to the NSA/CSS Archives only in recent years; or such records may be in the NSA/CSS Records Center. Approximately 3 million pages from the earliest *accessions* in the NSA/CSS Archives have been reviewed as of this writing. Significantly, the NSA is *redacting*, which of course means that greater numbers of records are released but also means that the review process goes more slowly. It is not known when any of the reviewed records will be transferred to the College Park National Archives.[102]

Record Group 457 at the College Park National Archives now has many million of pages of records, but only a tiny number are from the postwar period. All the postwar records have been reviewed for declassification and *processed* and they include: (1) a small number of intelligence reports from the military services and other government agencies from 1941–1948, (2) a limited number of U.S. Army and U.S. Navy records relating to cryptology from the late 1940s and early 1950s, (3) a limited number of NSA studies on cryptology from the 1950s into the 1970s.

### NSA/CSS, AFSA, and Predecessor Agency Records at NSA/CSS

Virtually all the records of the NSA, CSS, AFSA, as well as all the postwar records of their predecessors, are at the NSA. The only information publicly available on the record holdings is that the NSA/CSS Archives holds more than 16 million pages of classified *permanent* records of the agency and its predecessors, and the NSA/CSS Records Center holds about 15,000 c.f. of classified *permanent* records awaiting transfer to the NSA/CSS Archives per the agency's *record schedules*.[103] The nature of these *permanent* records, as well as whether these two repositories hold any *unappraised* or *temporary* records, is not known. Furthermore, the quantity, nature, and *appraisal* status of records held outside these two repositories in individual offices, divisions, and directorates is not known. However, considering the mission of the agency, its long history, and the fact that it has transferred virtually no postwar records to the College Park National Archives or Washington National Records Center, it would be safe to assume that the total holdings of textual and nontextual records are huge. It is not known when any *permanent* records are eligible for transfer to the College Park National Archives under the NSA's *records schedules*.[104]

Requests under the FOIA and MDR should be submitted to the Freedom of Information/Privacy Act Branch, Office of Information Policy, National Security Agency, Fort George G. Meade, Maryland 20755.

### Navy Department Records at the National Archives

The records of the former Navy Department are in RG 80, and at the College Park National Archives, RG 80 contains more than 30 million pages of records dating from the late 1700s to 1947. The *finding aid* is good and, with few exceptions, all the records have been reviewed for declassification and *processed*. Postwar records include:

1. Top Secret and below Secretary of the Navy/Chief of Naval Operations correspondence and indices through 1947;

2. Top Secret and below Secretary of the Navy general correspondence files through 1947;

3. Top Secret and below meeting minutes and correspondence files of the Top Policy Group through 1947;

4. Top Secret and below Office of Budgets and Reports correspondence files, budget estimates, and budget presentations through 1947.

A few regional National Archives have small RG 80 holdings as well. There are no records in RG 80 at any Federal records center.

### Department of the Navy (Navy) Records at the National Archives and Federal Records Centers

A large number of Navy records are in several *record groups* at the National Archives and Federal records centers (records of the U.S. Marine Corps are discussed separately in preceding sections).

With respect to declassification under E.O. 12958, the Navy estimated in 1995 that it possibly had up to 500 million pages subject to the new order.[105] The FY 1996 through FY 1999 ISOO annual reports list the Navy as having declassified a little more than 144 million pages, but it is possible that this may be the total number of pages reviewed for declassification and not the total number of pages actually declassified. In either event, many of the these records are in RG 19 (Bureau of Ships), RG 74 (Bureau of Ordnance), RG 402 (Bureau of Naval Weapons), RG 346 (Naval Ordnance Command), RG 181 (naval shore commands), RG 313 (naval operating forces), and RG 344 (Naval Sea Systems Command) at various National Archives and Federal records centers. Although some of the records are in other *record groups* as well at these repositories, there is no detailed information available on exactly which records these are or where they are.[106]

Record Group 428 contains records of both the Office of the Secretary of the Navy and Office of the Chief of Naval Operations. At the College Park National Archives, RG 428 has more than 10 million pages of records. No other National Archives has any RG 428 holdings. The *finding aids* are good. Most of the records have been reviewed for declassification and *processed*, and they include the following:

1. Secret and below combined general correspondence files of the Chief of Naval Operations and the Secretary of the Navy from 1948–1951;

2. Formerly classified files of Secretary of the Navy John Sullivan from 1947–1949 and Secretary of the Navy Francis Matthews from 1949–1950;

3. Secret and below Deputy Chief of Naval Operations (Administration), Deputy Chief of Naval Operations (Operations), Deputy Chief of Naval Operations (Logistics), and Deputy Chief of Naval Operations (Air) correspondence files from 1949–1950;

4. Secret and below OP-20 (Communications) correspondence files from 1948–1951;

5. Secret and below Commander in Chief, U.S. Pacific Fleet Korean War Interim Evaluation Reports from June to November 1950;

6. Secret and below records relating to naval history and organization from 1923–1954;

7. Secret and below records relating to unification of the armed forces from 1945–1949.

At the Washington National Records Center, RG 428 has about 50 million pages of mostly classified records as of 2000 (55% *permanent*, 10% *temporary*, and 35% *unappraised*). No other Federal records center has any RG 428 holdings. As part of the P-2000 Project, about 7 million pages of unclassified *permanent* records and 1.6 million pages of classified *permanent* records will be transferred to RG 428 at the College Park National Archives by the end of 2001. Even if the classified records have been reviewed for declassification by the time of their transfer, they will not be available to the public until they are possibly re-reviewed by the DOE under the Kyl Plan and then *processed* by the National Archives. The records to be transferred include:

1. Secret and below Secretary of the Navy general correspondence files from 1942–1949, aeronautics files from 1940–1949, and War Department correspondence files from 1943–1945;

2. Secret and below files of Admiral King from 1942–1949;

3. Secret and below files of OP-01 (Personnel), OP-02 (Intelligence), OP-03 (Operations), OP-04 (Logistics), and OP-20 (Communications) from 1941–1945;

4. Top Secret and below Office of the Navy Comptroller/Assistant Secretary of the Navy (Financial Management) budget estimates from the 1940s into the 1960s; and Secret and below general correspondence files from 1948 into the 1960s and files concerning the Japanese Peace Treaty and financial support to Korea from 1947–1953;

5. Secret/Restricted Data and below Assistant Secretary of the Navy (Research & Development)/Assistant Secretary of the Navy (Research, Engineering & Systems) correspondence files and subject files from 1962–1976 (it is not known whether these duplicate what is in RG 298 at the Washington National Records Center); and Secret and below navigation files from 1962–1976;

6. Secret and below Cruise Missiles Project/Joint Cruise Missiles Program Office files from 1973–1978;

7. Secret and below Office of Public Relations correspondence and publications regarding action reports, conferences, Fuehrer Conferences, and other topics from 1940–1948;

8. unclassified Secretary of the Navy speeches and press conference files from 1941–1948;

9. unclassified Secretary of the Navy logs from 1944–1951.

Among the records not eligible for transfer to RG 428 at the College Park National Archives by 2001 are:

1. Top Secret and below miscellaneous Secretary of the Navy project files, personal files, and subject files from 1940–1954;

2. Top Secret/Restricted Data and Top Secret Secretary of the Navy official files from 1945–1954;

3. Top Secret and below Secretary of the Navy diaries and miscellaneous papers from 1945–1949;

4. Top Secret/Restricted Data and below Secretary of the Navy names files, invitation files, project files, subject files, general correspondence files, logs, and appointment books from 1954–1974;

5. Secret/Restricted Data and below Secretary of the Navy administrative files, program files, and personnel files from 1975 into the 1990s;

6. Top Secret and below Secretary of the Navy speeches and Friday Book files from the late 1960s;

7. Secret and below SECNAV Notices and Instructions from the 1940s into the 1990s;

8. Top Secret/Restricted Data and below Under Secretary of the Navy general files from 1947–1954;

9. Secret/Restricted Data and below Under Secretary of the Navy general files from 1955 into the 1960s;

10. Top Secret/Restricted Data and Top Secret Assistant Secretary of the Navy (Research & Development)/Assistant Secretary of the Navy (Research, Engineering & Systems) correspondence files and subject files from 1964 into the 1970s (it is not known whether these duplicate what is in RG 298 at the Washington National Records Center);

11. Confidential and below Assistant Secretary of the Navy (Research, Development & Acquisition) files from the 1970s and 1980s;

12. Top Secret/Restricted Data and below Office of Special Counsel to the Secretary of the Navy files on a wide range of topics, including but not limited to Guantanamo/Cuba (1961–1965), Lee H. Oswald (1959–1966), congressional hearings on tactical air (1967–1968), USS Scorpion (1968–1969), and the Tonkin Gulf incident (1964–1968);

13. Top Secret Assistant Secretary of the Navy (Air) official files from 1944–1952;

14. Secret and below Assistant Secretary of the Navy (Air) official files from 1953 into the 1960s;

15. Secret and below Office of the Navy Comptroller/Assistant Secretary of Navy (Financial Management) general correspondence files, budget files, and submissions from the 1960s into the 1990s;

16. Secret and below Office of General Counsel files from the 1950s into the 1980s;

17. Secret and below Office of Legislative Liaison/Office of Legislative Affairs files from the 1950s into the 1990s;

18. Top Secret and below Navy Management Office studies, reports, organization charts and manuals, and related records from the 1940s into the 1980s;

19. Secret and below Cruise Missiles Project/Joint Cruise Missiles Project Office files from the late 1970s into the 1990s;

20. Secret and below Unmanned Aerial Vehicles Joint Project files from the 1980s and 1990s;

21. Secret and below Navy Office of Technology Transfer and Security Assistance COCOM export case files from 1985 into the 1990s; State Department munitions export license files from the mid-1980s into the 1990s; CCL export subject files from 1982 into the 1990s; nuclear submarine visits and atomic log records from 1965–1988; and foreign military case files from 1980 into the 1990s.

Record Group 38 at the College Park National Archives contains more than 21 million pages of records of the Office of the Chief of Naval Operations, the vast majority of which are from World War II and earlier. No other National Archives has any RG 38 holdings. The *finding aids* are very good, in many cases listing folder titles by box. Postwar records that have been reviewed for declassification and *processed* include:

1. Secret and below Director of Naval Intelligence and Assistant Director of Naval Intelligence day files, *Daily Information Memorandums*, and *DNI Summaries* from 1946–1950;

2. Secret and below Administration Branch, Office of Naval Intelligence administrative correspondence files from 1945–1948;

3. Secret and below Foreign Intelligence Branch, Office of Naval Intelligence correspondence with naval attaches, observers, and liaison officers from 1945–1948;

4. Secret and below correspondence and reports of several sections under the Foreign Intelligence Branch, including the Eastern European Section from 1945–1952, Collection & Dissemination Section from 1949–1953, and Planning Section from 1945–1952;

5. Secret and below Domestic Intelligence Branch, Office of Naval Intelligence files through 1948;

6. Secret and below Office of Naval Intelligence naval attaché office files from the 1940s and 1950s;

7. Secret and below Office of Naval Intelligence publications from 1945–1954 and foreign publications from 1945–1950;

8. Secret and below Office of Naval Intelligence case files on U.S. POWs during the Korean War from 1952–1956.

Still-classified records include: (1) Top Secret/Restricted Data and below Navy Logistics Plans, Navy Objectives Plans, and Nuclear Warfare Operations Plans from the 1950s and 1960s; (2) Top Secret and below Estimates Section, Foreign Intelligence Branch files on *National Intelligence Estimates* and *Special National Intelligence Estimates* from 1952–1954.

Record Group 38 at the Washington National Records Center has more than 45 million pages of mostly classified records as of 2000 (60% *permanent* and 40% *unappraised*). No other Federal records center has any RG 38 holdings. As part of the P-2000 Project, about 2.6 million pages of unclassified *permanent* records and 2.6 million pages of classified *permanent* records will be transferred to RG 38 the College Park National Archives by the end of 2001. Even if the classified records have been reviewed for declassification by the time of their transfer, they will not be available to the public until they are possibly re-reviewed by the DOE under the Kyl Plan and then *processed* by the National Archives. The records to be transferred include:

1. Top Secret and below incoming and outgoing Chief of Naval Operations messages from 1969–1977 and message records from 1978–1980;

2. Secret and below incoming and outgoing Chief of Naval Operations messages from 1963–1968;

3. Secret and below OPNAV Notices and Instructions from 1951–1976;

4. Top Secret/Restricted Data and below Strategic Submarine Division site negotiation/development records from 1963–1976, R&D records from 1961–1979, and Strategic Ballistic Missile Committee meeting minutes and reports from 1957–1964;

5. Top Secret and below Air Board minutes from 1948–1953;

6. Top Secret and below Deputy Chief of Naval Operations (Air) program records from 1951–1954;

7. Secret and below Deputy Chief of Naval Operations (Air) World War II reports;

8. a wide range of records from the Operational Archives Branch of the Division of Naval History/Naval Historical Center, including but not limited to Secret/Restricted Data and below historical records of the Atomic Energy Branch/Atomic Energy Division and the Guided Missiles Division from the late 1940s and 1950s; Secret and below World War II records, including action reports, air action reports, war diaries, naval command war diaries, Commander in Chief, Atlantic Fleet messages, and captured German naval records; unclassified personal papers of Rear Admiral Byrd and several other naval officers; Secret and below post-World War II command files; Secret and below records

from the 1960s and 1970s relating to Vietnam; Secret and below Task Force files from 1967–1974; Secret and below records relating to the history of Naval Special Warfare Group, Pacific from 1946–1970; and Secret and below *Office of Naval Intelligence Reviews* from 1942–1963;

9. Top Secret/Restricted Data and below Deputy Chief of Naval Operations (Plans, Policies & Operations) and predecessor files on arms control negotiations and agreements from 1959–1979;

10. Top Secret and below Inspector General reports and investigative files from 1942 into the 1970s.

Among the records not eligible for transfer to RG 38 at the College Park National Archives by 2001 are:

1. Top Secret/Restricted Data and Top Secret Chief of Naval Operations files, route sheets, and related materials from 1950–1954 (as noted in the following section, the post-1954 Top Secret/Restricted Data and Top Secret Chief of Naval Operations files are at the Naval Historical Center); and Secret/Restricted Data and below files, route sheets, and related materials from 1952–1999;

2. Top Secret and below incoming and outgoing Chief of Naval Operations messages from 1980–1995;

3. Secret and below Chief of Naval Operations reports from 1950–1955;

4. Secret and below speeches of the Chief of Naval Operations and other flag officers from the 1950s;

5. Secret and below Chief of Naval Operations Executive Board briefing files from 1977–1988;

6. Secret and below Chief of Naval Operations Executive Panel files and reports from 1970 into the 1990s;

7. Secret and below OPNAV Notices and Instructions and SECNAV Notices and Instructions from the mid-1970s into the 1990s;

8. Secret and below Deputy Chief of Naval Operations (Development) files from the late 1950s;

9. Top Secret Director of Naval Communications/Assistant Chief of Naval Operations (Communications) files from 1952–1964, Top Secret Southeast Asia files from 1959–1962, and Secret and below files from the 1950s and 1960s;

10. Secret and below Assistant Chief of Naval Operations (Intelligence)/ Director of Naval Intelligence foreign visitor, foreign training, and foreign liaison files from 1958 into the 1970s; Secret/Restricted Data and below day, country, intelligence, correspondence, and atomic program files from the late 1950s into the 1960s; Secret and below TEMPEST

and TELEWISP files from 1963–1973; Secret and below security policy and security planning files from 1952–1969; and unclassified ship technical files from 1900–1985;

11. classified and unclassified deck logs from the late 1960s into the 1990s;

12. Top Secret and below Fleet Operations Division general files from 1947–1955;

13. Secret and below Undersea Warfare Division general and serial files from 1948 into the 1950s, and publications from 1955–1958;

14. Top Secret Submarine Warfare Division SSBN Patrol Reports from the 1960s;

15. Secret/Restricted Data and below Strike Warfare Division intelligence surveys, studies, reports, and other records from World War II into the 1950s;

16. Secret and below Special Assistant for Countermeasures reports, charts, illustrations, correspondence files, and other records from 1944–1972;

17. Secret and below military urgency monthly status reports from the late 1950s;

18. Secret and below Foreign Military Assistance Branch country files, reports, and messages from the 1950s and 1960s;

19. Secret and below Military Sales Branch files from the 1960s;

20. Secret and below Grant Aid Branch Military Assistance Program documents from the 1950s, and messages, subject files, and country files from the 1960s;

21. Secret and below Undersea Surveillance Branch Technical Cooperation Program Subgroup G meeting minutes, reports, and correspondence files from 1968–1982;

22. Secret and below Mine Warfare & Harbor Defense Branch files from the 1950s;

23. Secret and below Research & Special Studies Section reports, correspondence files, and serial files from the 1950s;

24. Secret and below Munitions Control Branch/Technology Transfer Control Branch State Department munitions control case files from 1954 into the 1990s;

25. Secret and below Satellite Surveillance Branch records from 1961–1962 on a wide range of subjects, including but not limited to the Mercury, Gemini, and Apollo manned spaceflight programs; Tiros; Vanguard; Dynasoar; Grab; Hugo; Albatross; Hydra; Aurora; Discoverer; Samos; Early Spring; Big Dish; space surveillance orbital elements, satellite summaries, ephemeris, progress reports, and messages; ballistic

missile defense; anti-satellite defense; anti-submarine warfare; geodesy; reconnaissance; probes; liaison with other government agencies; inter-agency boards and committees; budgets; meetings and briefings; and ONR *Program Highlights*;

26. Secret and below Ship Characteristics Board files from the 1950s and 1960s;

27. Secret and below Program Objectives Memorandums from the 1970s into the 1990s;

28. Secret and below Naval Research Advisory Committee meeting minutes, technical board files, and committee files from 1946–1986;

29. Secret and below Center for Naval Analysis studies and reports from the 1940s into the 1990s;

30. Secret and below Command, Control, Communications & Electronic Warfare Branch subject files, memo files, and serial files from 1964 into the 1990s;

31. Secret and below historical files from the 1950s to 1993 relating to the U.S./U.S.S.R. Incidents at Sea Agreement.

Record Group 289 contains records of the Office of Naval Intelligence (1882–present) and Naval Intelligence Command (1967–present). There are no records in RG 289 at the College Park National Archives or any regional National Archives. At the Washington National Records Center, RG 289 has several million pages of mostly classified textual records and a large quantity of classified aerial film, photographs, telemetry tapes, and acoustic tapes as of 2000 (60% *permanent* and 40% *unappraised*). No regional Federal records center has any RG 289 holdings. It is not known whether under the P-2000 Project any *permanent* records will be transferred to RG 289 at the College Park National Archives, although some *permanent* records are eligible for transfer now. Records that are both eligible and not eligible for transfer by 2001 include:

1. Secret and below Assistant Chief of Naval Operations (Intelligence) country files, day files, message files, foreign visitor request files, foreign requests for classified information files, and foreign training files from 1951–1967;

2. Top Secret and below Director of Naval Intelligence material files from 1965–1974, serial files from 1969–1974, and message files from 1973–1974;

3. Secret and below Director of Naval Intelligence office day files from 1971–1982;

4. Top Secret and below Office of Naval Intelligence headquarters administrative files from 1940–1967, general correspondence files from 1956–1959, project files from 1956–1959, and fleet support files from 1955–1956;

5. Secret and below Office of Naval Intelligence headquarters subject files from 1952–1960, serial files from 1960–1963, and country files from 1957–1965;

6. Top Secret/Restricted Data and below Office of Naval Intelligence headquarters files on the Intelligence Advisory Committee from 1949–1958; *National Intelligence Estimate/Special National Intelligence Estimate* working papers from 1959–1960 and 1965–1966; United States Intelligence Board files from 1960; CIA/United States Intelligence Board memos from 1961–1962; JCS briefing memos from 1957–1961; unnumbered NSC memos from 1958–1961; OPERATION ALERT files from 1955–1959; National Intelligence Survey Committee minutes, monthly progress reports, and serial files from the early 1960s; monthly progress reports on defectors from 1957–1958; SES bi-weekly reports and panel minutes from 1959–1960; and CSDB reports on IRONBARK, CHICKADEE, and COUPLETS (these are unknown cryptonyms);

7. Secret and below Office of Naval Intelligence/Naval Intelligence Command headquarters files on censorship from 1933–1973, including but not limited to Office of Censorship official histories and post-World War II U.S. and U.S./foreign telecommunication censorship plans, instructions, and manuals; and miscellaneous defector records from 1950–1973 including Interagency Defector Committee minutes and reports;

8. Secret and below Naval Intelligence Command headquarters administrative files from 1967 into the mid-1970s;

9. Top Secret and below *Naval Intelligence Estimates* from 1953–1954;

10. Secret and below *Naval Attache Information Reports/Naval Attache Intelligence Reports* from 1952–1964; *ONI Weekly*, *ONI Review*, and *ONI Study* from 1942–1964; *ONI Bulletin* from 1956–1961; and *DOD Information Reports* from 1961–1964;

11. Top Secret and below Commander, Task Force 168 (Germany) files from 1949–1971;

12. Secret and below Naval Photographic Interpretation Center/Naval Reconnaissance & Technical Support Center photographs, films, and reports from the 1960s and early 1970s;

13. Top Secret Naval Scientific & Technical Intelligence Center/Naval Intelligence Support Center intelligence correspondence files from 1970–1976;

14. Secret and below Naval Scientific & Technical Intelligence Center/Naval Intelligence Support Center general correspondence files from 1968–1980; command history records from 1967–1975; serial files from the mid-1970s; foreign documents from the 1960s; author and subject index to the 1945–1964 foreign documents; and ship characteristic reports from the 1960s;

15. Top Secret and below acoustic intelligence recording magnetic tapes from the 1960s into the 1970s;

16. Secret and below radar data tapes, telemetry tapes, and missile digital telemetry plots from the 1960s into the 1980s;

17. Secret and below naval attaché (Dominican Republic) files from 1955–1956; naval attaché (Japan) general administrative files from 1955–1958; naval attaché (Yugoslavia) files from 1945–1955; naval liaison officer (Hong Kong) chronological files from 1955–1956; naval attaché (Cuba) administrative files from 1960; and naval attaché (South Vietnam) general files from 1962–1964;

18. Confidential and below naval attaché (Finland) serial files from 1945–1951 and naval attaché (Argentina) correspondence files from 1950–1958;

19. Secret and below captured French naval records from World War II; intelligence reports on German, Japanese, and Soviet aircraft from 1945–1949; records on air operations in the Far East from 1941–1946; technical intelligence documents from 1940–1947; reports from the 1945 Navy Technical Mission in Europe; reports on German science from 1936–1949; World War II ship tonnages and losses records; ship, aviation, and personnel tables from 1914–1940; summaries and ships data of the principal navies from 1931–1947; and records on worldwide navy budgets from 1926–1950.

Record Group 72 contains the records of the Bureau of Aeronautics (1921–1959). At the College Park National Archives, RG 72 has more than 80 million pages of records, many of which are from World War II and earlier. A few regional National Archives have very small RG 72 holdings. With the exception of a limited number of technical reports, all the postwar records have been reviewed for declassification and *processed*. The *finding aids* are very good, in many cases listing folder titles by box. Postwar records include:

1. unclassified general correspondence and central correspondence files from 1945–1959;

2. Aeronautical Engine Laboratory technical reports from 1922–1965;

3. technical reports prepared by universities, colleges, and research institutions from 1940–1947;

4. technical reports prepared by other Navy components and government agencies from 1940–1947;

5. Board of Inspection and Survey reports from 1943–1948;

6. Patuxent test reports and Aeronautical Radio and Radar Laboratory reports from 1944–1947;

7. Naval Air Experimental Station reports and Naval Research Laboratory technical reports from 1945–1946;

8. aircraft mock-up reports from 1946–1956;

9. aircraft specifications and drawings from 1919–1961;

10. formerly classified handbooks for the operation and maintenance of avionics equipment;

11. a wide range of records of the Ships' Installation Division, including but not limited to catapult, launcher, and missile project records from 1941–1953; aircraft carrier drawings from 1942–1952; files on arresting gears, barriers, and brakes from 1942–1959; and contract files and reports relating to missiles from 1947–1954;

12. a number of records of the Power Plant Division, including but not limited to engine test reports from 1923–1946, research project files from 1946–1954, and records relating to propellers from 1946–1955;

13. Production Division aircraft production program monthly reports from 1942–1949;

14. Plans Coordination Division division and office progress reports from 1944–1956;

15. Airborne Equipment Division records relating to metal and other aircraft materials from 1941–1959;

16. Airframe Design Division/Design Elements Division airframe reports from 1947–1958, correspondence files from 1943–1956, and administrative summary reports from 1946–1959;

17. historical summaries, periodic histories, management studies, organization charts, and other historical records from 1921–1959;

18. reports on the quantity, type, and location of naval aircraft from 1939–1957;

19. notes of division directors' meetings from 1947–1959;

20. background materials used by Rear Admiral D.S. Fahrney in writing *History of Pilotless Aircraft and Guided Missiles*;

21. Inter-Bureau Technical Committee meeting minutes and other records from 1945–1957;

22. records of the Board Convened to Study and Report upon the Adequacy of Naval Aviation Support (Arnold Board) from 1953–1958;

23. Committee on the Integrated Aeronautic Program meeting minutes from 1954–1957;

24. National Advisory Committee for Aeronautics technical memos and notes from 1921–1958;

25. files on classified contracts awarded from 1951–1958.

There are no records in RG 72 at the Washington National Records Center.

Record Group 74 contains records of the Bureau of Ordnance (1862–1959). At the College Park National Archives, RG 74 has more than 35 million pages of records, the vast majority of which are from World War II and earlier. The *finding aid* is good. Postwar records that have been reviewed for declassification and *processed* are the Secret and below contract files from 1945–1962. Among the postwar records that have been reviewed for declassification but still await a possible re-review by the DOE under the Kyl Plan and *processing* before they will be available to the public include the Secret and below general correspondence files of various headquarters offices from 1945–1959 and the Secret and below scientific and technical reports from 1945–1961. A few regional National Archives have small RG 74 holdings, but most date from World War II and earlier. There are no postwar records in RG 74 at any Federal records center.

Record Group 402 contains records of the Bureau of Naval Weapons (1959–1966). It also has records of the Bureau of Aeronautics, Bureau of Ordnance, and Naval Air Systems Command. At the College Park National Archives, RG 402 has about 1.25 million pages of records. No other National Archives has any RG 402 holdings. All the records have been reviewed for declassification, but they still require a possible re-review by the DOE under the Kyl Plan and *processing* before they will be available to the public. The records include:

1. Confidential and below contract files of the Bureau of Aeronautics, Bureau of Ordnance, Bureau of Naval Weapons, and the Naval Air Systems Command from the 1950s and 1960s;

2. Secret and below Bureau of Aeronautics, Bureau of Ordnance, Bureau of Naval Weapons, and Naval Air Systems Command technical reports from World War II into the 1960s;

3. Secret and below Bureau of Naval Weapons correspondence files from 1959–1966.

Record Group 402 at the Washington National Records Center has about 1.5 million pages of largely classified records as of 2000 (almost all *temporary*). No other Federal records center has any RG 402 holdings. The records include: (1) Secret and below Bureau of Ordnance Directives and technical instructions from World War II to 1960, (2) Secret and below

Bureau of Naval Weapons and predecessor foreign military sales files, foreign military assistance files, Notices, and Directives from the 1950s to 1966. As part of the P-2000 Project, fewer than 13,000 pages of *permanent* records are scheduled to be transferred to RG 402 at the College Park National Archives.

Record Group 346 contains records of the Naval Ordnance Systems Command (1966–1974). It also has some records of the Bureau of Naval Weapons. There are no records in RG 346 at the College Park National Archives or any regional National Archives. At the Washington National Records Center, RG 346 has almost 4.5 million pages of records as of 2000 (95% *permanent* and 5% *temporary*). No regional Federal records center has any RG 346 holdings. As part of the P-2000 Project, about 40,000 pages of unclassified *permanent* records and 2.2 million pages of classified *permanent* records will be transferred to RG 346 at the College Park National Archives by the end of 2001. Even though these classified records have already been reviewed for declassification, they will not be available to the public until they are possibly re-reviewed by the DOE under the Kyl Plan and then *processed* by the National Archives. The records to be transferred include:

1. Secret and below Commander, Naval Ordnance Systems Command correspondence files from 1966 into the early 1970s;

2. Confidential and below Instructions, Notices and Directives from 1966 into the early 1970s;

3. Confidential and below Anti-Submarine Warfare Systems Project Office files from the 1960s;

4. Confidential and below Special Navy Task Force correspondence files from 1962–1965;

5. Confidential and below Surface Missile Systems Project Office correspondence files from 1966–1971;

6. Confidential and below studies and reports on various weapons systems from the 1960s;

7. Confidential and below Bureau of Naval Weapons histories and the background materials used in writing them.

Records that are not eligible for transfer to RG 346 at the College Park National Archives by 2001 include Confidential and below foreign military sales files from the 1960s and early 1970s.

Record Group 343 contains records of the Naval Air Systems Command (1966–present). It also has records of the Bureau of Aeronautics and Bureau of Naval Weapons. There are no records in RG 343 at the College Park National Archives or any regional National Archives. At the Washington

National Records Center, RG 343 has about 55 million pages of mostly classified records as of 2000 (45% *permanent* and 55% *temporary*). No regional Federal records center has any RG 343 holdings. As part of the P-2000 Project, about 800,000 pages of unclassified *permanent* records and 17 million pages of classified *permanent* records will be transferred to RG 343 at the College Park National Archives by the end of 2001. Even if the classified records have been reviewed for declassification by the time of their transfer, they will not be available to the public until they have possibly been re-reviewed by the DOE under the Kyl Plan and then *processed* by the National Archives. The records to be transferred include:

1. Secret and below Commander, Bureau of Naval Weapons subject files from 1964–1966;

2. Secret and below Commander, Naval Air Systems Command incoming and outgoing correspondence files from 1966–1976;

3. Secret and below administration and management files from the 1960s and 1970s;

4. Confidential and below incoming and outgoing messages from 1967–1969;

5. Confidential and below Bureau of Naval Weapons/Naval Air Systems Command Instructions, Notices, and Directives from 1959–1976;

6. Secret and below Bureau of Aeronautics, Bureau of Naval Weapons, and Naval Air Systems Command Technical Library research memos, technical reports, and technical report files from the 1940s into the 1970s,

7. Confidential and below records of the commanders meetings of the Air Material Command/Naval Material Command/Air Force Logistics Command/Air Force Systems Command from the 1960s;

8. Confidential and below data on historical aircraft and miscellaneous aerodynamic historical data (the *SF-135s* do not provide any further information);

9. Confidential and below records relating to model designations for aircraft from 1923 into the 1960s and for rockets and missiles from the 1960s;

10. Confidential and below ACCB/CCCB/MCCB masters, indexes, and notes from the 1960s and 1970s;

11. Confidential and below Navy Aeroballistic Advisory Committee annual reports from 1952–1979;

12. Confidential and below Airframe Division correspondence folders on helicopters and aircraft from 1957–1965; government and contractor windtunnel data reports, technical reports flight test reports, and other

records from the 1930s into the early 1970s; and specifications from 1923 into the 1960s;

13. Secret and below historical records on the OV (X) from 1967–1968;

14. a large number of Confidential and below feasibility studies, competition files, development reports, progress reports, program files, project directives, mock up files, flight test reports, technical reports, technical manuals, and other records on aircraft and helicopters from the 1950s into the 1970s, including but not limited to the A-4E, A-4F, A-4M, A-4N, A-5, A-6C, A-6E, EA-6B, A-7E, AV-8A, AV-16A, E-2C, EC-130, F-4J, F-14A, F-14B, F-111A, F-111B, KC-130R, P-3A, P-3B, P-3C, P-3D, OV-1, OV-10A, OV-12, T-2B, T-2C, T-33, T-37, T-39, VFX, VSTOL, VSX, Advanced Harrier, CH-46, CH-53E, LAMPS, QH-50, RH-53D, SH-3A, UH-1N, and UH-2;

15. Confidential and below aircraft engine specifications from 1955–1968;

16. a large number of Confidential and below feasibility studies, development reports, progress reports, program files, program directives, flight test reports, technical reports, technical manuals, and other records on air-launched missiles from the 1950s into the early 1970s, including but not limited to aerial targets, Agile, Bullpup, Condor, cruise missiles, Harm, Harpoon, Hellfire, Maverick, Phoenix, Shrike, Sidewinder, Sparrow, Standard ARM, and Walleye;

17. Secret project files on the Harm from the 1970s;

18. Confidential and below Advance Planning Office files from 1967–1969;

19. Confidential and below IGLOO-WHITE correspondence files, reports, and contracts from 1967–1969;

20. Confidential and below records on the TACAMO and other communications systems and equipment from the 1950s and 1960s;

21. Confidential and below records on launching, landing, and arresting systems and equipment from the 1950s and 1960s;

22. Confidential and below records on radar systems and equipment from the 1950s and 1960s;

23. Confidential and below records on submarine detection systems and equipment from the 1960s;

24. Confidential and below NATOPS manuals, including flight manuals, pocket check lists, weapons check lists, and guided missile manuals from the 1950s into the early 1970s;

25. Confidential and below Airship Test Facility correspondence with NASA from 1960–1966, records relating to field activities from 1958–1967, and division directors memos from the 1960s;

26. Confidential and below correspondence files, reports, and other records on the Manufacturing Technology Program from 1976–1977 and on the Advanced Technology Program from 1975–1978;

27. Confidential and below chemical warfare and biological warfare weapons files, history project files, safety files, testing files, and other records from 1924–1973;

28. Confidential and below historian's files, including Deputy Chief of Naval Operations (Air) records from 1943–1945; OPNAV organization records from 1946–1956; Naval Aviation Field Organization records from 1941–1945; miscellaneous World War II reports from 1942–1945; records on the Carson Board, McClure Board, Hopwood Board, Welsh Board, and Eckstrom Board; Bureau of Aeronautics organization records from 1919–1959; records on post–World War II towed targets; data processing records from World War II into the 1960s; F-111 records from 1962–1968; VSTOL records from 1959–1965; miscellaneous aircraft history records from 1945 into the 1960s; records on important contracts during the postwar period; records on the Condor from the 1960s; and records on de-icing, ordnance, electronics, maintenance, and procurement from 1930–1965.

Among the records not eligible for transfer to RG 343 at the College Park National Archives by 2001 are:

1. Secret and below Commander, Naval Air Systems Command incoming and outgoing correspondence files from 1977 into the 1990s;

2. Confidential and below Instructions, Notices, and Directives from 1977 into the 1990s;

3. Secret and below Technical Library technical reports and technical report files from the 1970s and 1980s;

4. a wide range of Confidential and below files on aircraft, helicopters, and missiles from the 1970s into the 1990s;

5. Confidential and below foreign military sales files from the 1950s into the 1980s.

Record Group 19 contains records of the Bureau of Ships (1940–1966). At the College Park National Archives, RG 19 has more than 85 million pages of records, most of which are from World War II and earlier. No other National Archives has any RG 19 holdings. The *finding aids* are good. All the records have been reviewed for declassification in recent years, although many still await a possible re-review by the DOE under the Kyl Plan and *processing* before the public can access them. The postwar records include:

1. Secret and below general correspondence and central correspondence files through 1949;
2. unclassified general correspondence and central correspondence files from 1950–1966;
3. a large number of Secret and below technical reports and technical manuals from before World War II to 1966;
4. Secret and below ship preliminary design and data files from before World War II to 1966;
5. Secret and below ship hull design history and data files from before World War II to 1966;
6. Secret and below ship weight reports from before World War II to 1967;
7. Secret and below ship machinery design history files from before World War II to 1966;
8. Secret and below ship inclining data and load line reports to the mid-1960s;
9. Secret and below specification files to the mid-1960s;
10. Secret and below contract and preliminary design files from before World War II to the mid-1960s.

Record Group 19 at the Washington National Records Center has about 11 million pages of records as of 2000 (80% *permanent* and 20% *unappraised*). As part of the P-2000 Project, about 300,000 pages of unclassified *permanent* records and 600,000 pages of classified *permanent* records will be transferred to RG 19 at the College Park National Archives by the end of 2001. Even though all these classified records have already been reviewed for declassification, they will not be available to the public until they are possibly re-reviewed by the DOE under the Kyl Plan and then *processed* by the National Archives. The records to be transferred include:

1. Confidential and below in-house and contractor technical reports from 1931–1949;
2. Confidential and below R&D Division Silencing Branch surveys and reports from the 1950s and 1960s;
3. Confidential and below Supervisor of Salvage general correspondence files, contract case files, salvage case files, and related materials from 1935 into the 1960s;
4. Confidential and below technical manuals for ships' equipment from 1945–1970.

Among the records not eligible for transfer to RG 19 at the College Park National Archives by 2001 are:

1. a limited number of Secret and below ships plans from the 1950s and 1960s;
2. Confidential/Restricted Data and below files of the Nuclear Propulsion Directorate from 1947 into the 1960s.

Record Group 344 contains records of the Naval Ship Systems Command (1966–1974). It also has many records of the Bureau of Ships, Naval Sea Systems Command, Bureau of Ordnance, and Naval Ordnance Systems Command. There are no records in RG 344 at the College Park National Archives or any regional National Archives. At the Washington National Records Center, RG 344 has more than 155 million pages of records as of 2000 (45% *permanent* and 55% *temporary*). No regional Federal records center has any RG 344 holdings. As part of the P-2000 Project, about 500,000 pages of unclassified *permanent* records and 13 million pages of classified *permanent* records will be transferred to RG 344 at the College Park National Archives by the end of 2001. Even though these classified records have already been reviewed for declassification, they will not be available to the public until they have been possibly re-reviewed by the DOE under the Kyl Plan and then *processed* by the National Archives. The records to be transferred include:

1. Secret and below Commander, Naval Ship Systems Command subject files from 1966–1970;
2. Secret and below Commander, Naval Sea Systems Command general files from 1974;
3. Confidential and below Naval Ship Systems Command Instructions, Notices, and Directives from 1966–1968; Bureau of Ordnance Instructions from 1952–1959; and Bureau of Ships Instructions from 1952–1966;
4. Confidential and below Naval Sea Systems Command organization files from the 1970s;
5. Secret and below Commander, Naval Ordnance Systems Command general correspondence files from 1974;
6. Secret/Restricted Data and below Special Projects Office/Strategic Systems Office files on the Polaris, Poseidon, and Trident missiles from 1956–1980; naval messages and TWXs on the Polaris from 1958–1967; general files from 1958–1966; weekly staff meeting reports and notes from 1965–1967; and Chief Scientist chronological reading files, travel files, and speech files from 1957–1969;

7. Secret and below Naval Ship Engineering Center official files from 1956–1969;

8. Confidential and below Naval Ship Engineering Center library copies of technical manuals from 1941 into the 1970s and preliminary ship design files from 1956–1968;

9. a number of Confidential and below files of the many offices under the Naval Ship Engineering Center, including Tactical Data Systems Branch Navy Tactical Data System files from the 1950s into the 1970s; Ship Protection & Safety Office files from the 1960s; Assistant for Propulsion Systems general files from 1950–1974; Propulsion Systems Branch reports, test data, and mathematical analyses from 1959–1972; Advance Technology Branch feasibility studies from the 1970s; Radar Systems Branch correspondence files and reports from the 1960s and 1970s; Ship Design Division project files, reports, and drawings from the late 1960s and early 1970s; Assistant for Structures studies and project files on submarines from 1951–1974 and test and evaluation reports on other warships from 1967–1970; Assistant for Mine Countermeasures correspondence files, reports, and studies from 1968–1973; Project Coordinating Office project files and design studies from 1957–1971; Surface Ship Structure Branch files on flight deck construction from 1942–1967; Assistant for Naval Architecture ship project files from 1970–1973; and Systems Engineering & Analyses Branch sea control ships project files from 1971–1975;

10. Confidential and below Deep Submergence Systems Project Office general files and reports from the 1960s;

11. Confidential and below Sonar Directorate general files from the 1960s;

12. Confidential and below R&D Directorate Silencing Division general files from the 1960s and Acoustics Branch files from the 1960s and 1970s;

13. Confidential and below High Energy Laser Project Office general files from the 1970s;

14. Confidential and below Weapons System & Engineering Directorate general files from the 1960s and 1970s, files on the Phalanx from 1969–1976, and files on torpedoes from 1964–1978;

15. Confidential and below Surveillance Systems Group general files from the 1970s;

16. Confidential and below Ship Systems Directorate files on diesel and gas turbine engines from 1944–1977;

17. Confidential and below Aircraft Carrier Program Office ships case files from 1942–1968.

Records not eligible for transfer to RG 344 at the College Park National Archives by 2001 include:

1. Secret and below Commander, Naval Sea Systems Command general files from 1975 into the 1990s;

2. Confidential and below Naval Sea Systems Command Instructions, Notices, and Directives from the 1970s into the 1990s;

3. Confidential and below foreign military assistance files and foreign military sales files from the 1950s into the 1990s;

4. Secret/Restricted Data and below Strategic Systems Programs Office files on submarine-launched ballistic missiles from the 1980s and 1990s;

5. Confidential/Restricted Data and below records of the Nuclear Propulsion Directorate from the 1950s into the 1990s;

6. Confidential and below records of the many other Naval Sea Systems Command offices, branches, and directorates from the 1970s into the 1990s.

Record Group 345 contains records of the Naval Electronics Systems Command (1966–1985). It also has some records of predecessor commands and the Space and Naval Warfare Systems Command (1985–present). There are no records in RG 345 at the College Park National Archives or any regional National Archives. At the Washington National Records Center, RG 345 has about 5 million pages of mostly classified records as of 2000 (50% *permanent* and 50% *temporary*). No regional Federal records center has any RG 345 holdings. As part of the P 2000 Project, about 450,000 pages of unclassified *permanent* records and 700,000 pages of classified *permanent* records will be transferred to RG 345 at the College Park National Archives by the end of 2001. Even if these classified records have been reviewed for declassification by the time of their transfer, they will not be available to the public until they are possibly re-reviewed by the DOE under the Kyl Plan and then *processed* by the National Archives. The records to be transferred include:

1. Secret and below Naval Electronic Systems Command and predecessor headquarters incoming and outgoing correspondence files from 1957–1973;

2. Confidential and below R&D files from the 1950s and 1960s;

3. Confidential and below field activity histories from 1966–1969.

Among the records not eligible for transfer to the College Park National Archives by 2001 are:

1. Secret and below Naval Electronics Systems Command/Space and Naval Warfare Systems Command and predecessor contract files, technical reports, program files, project files, and foreign military sales files from the 1940s into the 1980s;

2. Secret and below Naval Electronics Systems Command/Space and Naval Warfare Systems Command headquarters incoming and outgoing correspondence files from 1974 into the 1980s.

Record Group 313 contains records of naval operating forces. At the College Park National Archives, RG 313 has almost 50 million pages of records, the vast majority of which are from World War II and earlier. Some of the regional National Archives have small RG 313 holdings. Most of the *finding aids* are not particularly useful. Postwar records that have been reviewed for declassification and *processed* include the following:

1. Commander in Chief, U.S. Pacific Fleet records, including but not limited to Top Secret and below general administrative files and subject files from 1944–1948 and Top Secret flag files from 1943–1959;

2. Commander Submarine Forces, Pacific records, including but not limited to Secret and below serial files from 1931–1952 and Confidential and below general administrative files from 1944–1948;

3. Commander Amphibious Forces, Pacific records, including but not limited to Secret and below incoming/outgoing correspondence files from 1946–1950;

4. Commander Mine Forces, Pacific records, including but not limited to Top Secret and below general administrative files from 1941–1947 and unclassified general administrative files from the 1950s;

5. Commander Naval Air Forces, Pacific records, including but not limited to Top Secret flag files from 1946–1952;

6. Commander U.S. Naval Forces, Japan records, including but not limited to Top Secret flag files from 1950–1960;

7. Commander in Chief, U.S. Atlantic Fleet records, including but not limited to Top Secret and below correspondence files from 1948–1956, Top Secret and below publications correspondence files from 1943–1951, Top Secret flag files from 1947–1960, and Secret and below administrative files from 1941–1949;

8. Commander U.S. Naval Forces, Europe records, including but not limited to Top Secret and below subject files from 1938–1947;

9. Commander Naval Forces Eastern Atlantic and Mediterranean records, including but not limited to Top Secret flag files from 1942–

1958 and Top Secret and below intelligence files and general administrative files from 1946–1950;

10. Secret and below Commander Operational Development Force files from 1945–1956;

11. unclassified U.S. Naval Support Force Antarctica reports, orders, and other records from 1955–1994.

Record Group 313 at the Washington National Records Center has almost 15 million pages of mostly classified records as of 2000 (30% *permanent* and 70% *temporary*). As part of the P-2000 Project, about 350,000 pages of unclassified *permanent* records and 2 million pages of classified *permanent* records will be transferred to RG 313 at the College Park National Archives by the end of 2001. Even though all these classified records have already been reviewed for declassification, none will be available to the public until they are possibly re-reviewed by the DOE under the Kyl Plan and then *processed* by the National Archives. The records to be transferred include:

1. Commander in Chief, U.S. Pacific Fleet records, including Top Secret chronological serial files from 1961–1968; Secret and below chronological serial files from 1962–1970; Confidential and below general files from 1962–1968; Secret personal decoration serial files from 1966–1969; and Confidential and below general and financial files for the administration of the Bonnin/Volcano Islands from 1950–1968;

2. Top Secret/Restricted Data and Top Secret Commander Naval Air Forces, Pacific serial files from 1952–1956;

3. Secret and below Commander Barrier Forces, Pacific staff studies from 1964–1965;

4. Commander Mine Forces, Pacific records, including Secret and below studies from the late 1950s and early 1960s; Secret and below OPLANS and OPORDS from 1966–1967; and Confidential and below general files from 1959;

5. Secret and below Commander U.S. Naval Forces, Japan subject files from 1946–1961;

6. Secret and below Commander Service Force, Pacific general files from 1964;

7. Confidential and below Commander Naval Forces Marianas command's file from 1964;

8. Confidential and below Commander Amphibious Forces, Pacific general files from 1967–1970, serial files from 1968–1974, and Instructions from 1958–1974;

9. Confidential and below Commander Cruiser Destroyer Force, Pacific serial files from 1969–1974;

10. Commander in Chief, U.S. Atlantic Fleet records, including Top Secret/ Restricted Data and Secret/Restricted Data Reference Library documents from 1954–1970; Top Secret messages and sitsums regarding Cuba from October and November 1962; Secret through Top Secret/ Restricted Data general files from 1962–1963; Confidential and below general files from 1962–1964 and serial files from 1965–1973; and Secret and below chronological route slips from 1959–1967;

11. Top Secret Commanding General Fleet Marine Force, Atlantic correspondence files from 1951–1957;

12. Confidential and below Commander Antisubmarine Warfare Force, Atlantic serial files from 1962–1964;

13. Confidential and below Deputy Commander Submarine Forces, Atlantic general files and serial files from 1961–1963;

14. Commander Amphibious Forces, Atlantic records, including Top Secret serial files from 1948–1962 and Confidential and below general files from 1963–1965;

15. Commander U.S. Naval Forces, Europe records, including Top Secret/ Restricted Data and Top Secret correspondence and OPLANS from 1954–1959; Top Secret serial files from 1952–1964; and Secret and below general files and history files from 1962;

16. Secret and below Caribbean Sea Frontier & Antilles Defense Command headquarters administration and operations files from 1961– 1969;

17. Secret and below Commander Eastern Sea Frontier general files from 1962 and serial files from 1965;

18. a large number of Commander Operational Development Force/Commander Operational Test & Evaluation Force records, including Top Secret serial files from 1956–1968; Secret and below serial files from 1946–1958; Confidential and below serial files from 1964–1966; Secret/Restricted Data and below aircraft weapons systems handbooks from 1959; Secret and below Surface Warfare & Space Division project folders from 1962–1964; Confidential and below Undersea Warfare Division project folders from 1956–1961; and Secret and below project folders, project files, project case files, and project reports of other unknown divisions from 1955–1975;

19. numerous records of the Naval Transportation Service/Commander Military Sea Transportation Service/Commander Military Sealift Command, including Secret and Confidential headquarters subject/central files from 1949–1972; Secret and below histories, logistics plans, and

mobilization requirements files from 1939–1952; Secret and below historical diaries from 1956–1965 and command histories from the 1960s; Secret and below files on activities and requirements by geographical area, postwar plans, and inventories and employment studies and tables from 1942–1946; Confidential and below directives on arming merchant vessels from 1942–1946; and Secret and below files on the Army/Military Sealift Command merger from 1971;

20. Secret and below VW-2, Naval Air Station Patuxent River historical files from 1956–1962.

Among the records not eligible for transfer to RG 313 at the College Park National Archives by 2001 are:

1. Commander in Chief, U.S. Pacific Fleet records, including Secret and below command policy files from 1971–1978;

2. Confidential and below Commander Submarine Forces, Pacific Directives from 1968–1976;

3. Secret and below Commander U.S. Naval Forces, Philippines military base negotiation files and Mutual Defense Board files from 1946–1992;

4. Top Secret Deputy Commander Submarine Forces, Atlantic serial files from 1961–1964;

5. Confidential and below Fleet Operations (OP-33) ships movement records from 1946–1957;

6. Commander in Chief, U.S. Fleet master dispatch files from 1942–1945 (it is unclear from the *SF-135* what the classification level is);

7. Commander Operational Test & Evaluation Force records, including Secret and below project folders, project files, project case files and project reports from the 1960s and 1970s;

8. Secret and below Air Development Squadron One project files from the 1960s.

Record Group 313 at the San Bruno Federal Records Center has about 2.25 million pages of records as of 2000 (30% *permanent*, 20% *temporary*, and 50% *unappraised*). Most are unclassified administrative records, but there are a limited number of classified subject and serial files of Commander in Chief, U.S. Pacific Fleet and various subordinate commands from the late 1950s and early 1960s. Even though these have already been reviewed for declassification, they not will be available to the public until they are transferred to the San Bruno National Archives, possibly re-reviewed by the the DOE under the Kyl Plan, and then *processed* by the National Archives. Some other regional Federal records centers have small RG 313 holdings that are almost entirely unclassified.

Record Group 181 has the records of naval districts and shore establishments. At the College Park National Archives RG 181 has only about 2.5 million pages of records, almost all of which are from World War II and earlier. A number of regional National Archives have RG 181 holdings as well. The Seattle National Archives has about 4.5 million pages of records in RG 181, many of which are from World War II and earlier. Postwar records include a limited number of files of the Puget Sound Naval Shipyard and the 13th Naval District headquarters. The Philadelphia National Archives has almost 6.5 million pages of records in RG 181, most of which are from World War II and earlier. Postwar records include files of the Commandant, 4th Naval District; Commandant, 5th Naval District; Washington Naval District headquarters; Naval Ship Research & Development Center; Norfolk Naval Air Base; and Norfolk Naval Base. The New York National Archives has about 11.25 million pages of records in RG 181, many of which are from World War II and earlier. Postwar records include files of the Naval Air Rocket Test Station from 1950–1960, Naval Submarine Base in New London from 1953–1959, and Naval Training Device Center from 1942–1961. The Boston National Archives has approximately 5.25 million pages of records in RG 181, the majority of which are from World War II and earlier. Postwar records include files of U.S. Navy Submarine Base in New London from 1940–1952 and 1956–1971 and Commandant, 1st Naval District from 1903–1961. The Chicago National Archives has almost 3.5 million pages of records in RG 181, most of which are from World War II and earlier. Postwar records include files of the Commandant, 9th Naval District from the 1930s to 1953. The Laguna Niguel National Archives has about 4.25 million pages of records in RG 181, the majority of which are from World War II and earlier. Postwar records include files of the Pacific Missile Test Center from 1946–1959 and Commandant, 11th Naval District from 1923–1959. The San Bruno National Archives has over 17.5 million pages of records in RG 181, many of which are from World War II and earlier. Postwar records include files of the 12th Naval District from 1903–1975, 14th Naval District from 1912–1960, and Naval Radiological Defense Laboratory from 1946–1969. The East Point National Archives has almost 6.25 million pages of records in RG 181, most of which are from World War II and earlier. Postwar records include files of the 7th Naval District from 1921–1961 and 6th Naval District from 1903–1961.

Record Group 181 at the Washington National Records Center has approximately 110 million pages of textual records and a small quantity of nontextual records as of 2000 (25% *permanent*, 65% *temporary*, and 10% *unappraised*). As part of the P-2000 Project, about 4.5 million pages of unclassified and classified *permanent* textual records and a limited number of unclassified and classified *permanent* nontextual records will be transferred to the College Park National Archives by the end of 2001. Even though all the classified records have already been reviewed for declassification, they will not be available to the public until they are possibly re-reviewed by the DOE under the Kyl Plan and then *processed* by the National Archives. The records to be transferred include:

1. Secret/Restricted Data and below Commandant, 5th Naval District/Commander Naval Base, Norfolk general correspondence files, Instructions, Directives, and other records from the 1940s into the early 1970s;

2. Secret and below Naval Weather Service Command central correspondence files from 1946 into the early 1970s and Technical Division memorandums and other records from 1947–1957;

3. Confidential and below Board of Inspection & Survey ships case files from before World War II into the 1970s;

4. Naval Photographic Center/Naval Photographic Interpretation Center records, including but not limited to Secret and below general correspondence files of the Commander from 1941–1957; Confidential and below serial files from 1950–1954; Confidential and below production files from 1942–1950; and Secret and below OPERATION CROSSROADS photographs from 1946;

5. Secret and below Commander, Naval Communications Command subject files from the 1960s.

Among the records not eligible for transfer to RG 181 at the College Park National Archives by 2001 are:

1. a number of Naval Research Laboratory records, including but not limited to unclassified personal papers and office files of Louis Gebhard from 1914–1953; unclassified records on underwater sound detection from 1917–1919; Confidential and below central technical and administrative records from 1918–1945; Confidential and below general correspondence files from 1922–1950; Confidential and below records relating to the National Advisory Committee on Aeronautics from 1943–1951; Secret and below Director of Naval Research correspondence files from 1967–1978; Secret and below SPB agendas and minutes from 1946–1965; Secret and below Research Program Office files from 1945–1965; Secret and below Director of Research Management division and branch reviews from 1967–1982; Secret and below Sound Division files from 1952–1965; Secret and below Acoustics Division files from 1942–1968; Secret and below Chemistry Division files from 1962–1970; Secret and below Systems Analysis Staff, Radar Division files from 1948–1969; Secret and below Radio-Physics Branch files on various electronic intelligence projects from 1954–1974; Secret and below personal papers and office files of Louis Gebhard from

1948–1970; Secret and below correspondence files of Dr. Newell from 1956–1958; Secret and below R&D files and correspondence files of Dr. Berman from 1953–1976; Secret and below Louis Drummeter (Optics Division) files from 1946–1976; Secret and below files of Charles Johnson on upper atmospheric research from 1946–1958; Secret/Restricted Data and below files on OPERATION GREENHOUSE from 1950–1951; Secret and below R&D records from 1954–1979; Secret and below R&D project files from 1957 into the early 1980s; Secret and below laboratory notebooks from 1937 into the 1970s; Secret and below Project ARTEMIS records from 1958–1966; Secret and below records on ballistic missile submarines from 1956–1964; Secret and below files on various missile systems from 1957–1970; R&D test data files from 1956–1973; Secret and below NRL work problem files from 1954–1976; and Secret and below Navy laboratory program summary reports from 1967–1978. (As discussed in Chapter 2, approximately 2.25 million pages of *temporary* Naval Research Laboratory records in RG 181 at the Washington National Records Center were routinely destroyed in 1996 and 1997. After a NARA investigation determined that many of these records should have been *permanent*, all the remaining records are being *re-appraised*. In all likelihood, a number of the records identified here will be *appraised* as *permanent* and will be transferred to the College Park National Archives.);

2. a wide range of Naval Ordnance Laboratory, White Oak records, including but not limited to Secret and below central general correspondence files from 1918 to the early 1970s (the files for a few years during the 1950s and 1960s are Secret/Restricted Data and below); Secret and below project and committee files from the 1960s; Secret and below library records from 1942–1954; Secret and below technical reports from 1949–1953; Secret/Restricted Data and below Associate Technical Director/Head Air & Surface Weapons Development project files from 1957–1966; Secret/Restricted Data and below Advanced Planning & Analysis Staff files from 1957–1966; Secret and below Task Planning & Progress Division task records from 1957–1970; Secret/Restricted Data and below Systems Analysis Group files on anti-submarine warfare from 1959–1965; Secret and below Undersea Warfare R&D Planning Council records from 1960–1964; Confidential and below Subroc manuals development files (photographs, films, progress reports, field test reports, and correspondence) from 1959–1964; Secret and below records of the command's representative in London from 1946–1951; Secret/Restricted Data and below files on OPERATIONS GREENHOUSE and IVY from 1949–1951; Secret/Restricted Data and below OPERATION HARDTACK films, photo-

graphs, and correspondence files from 1959–1967; Secret and below files on mine control from 1945–1953; Confidential and below films and oscillograph records of tests of missiles and other ordnance from 1948–1953; Confidential and below HASP correspondence files and test data from 1959–1966; Confidential and below test records on the Talos, Terrier, and Tartar from the 1960s; and Secret and below Vietnam Laboratory Assistance Program files from the 1960s and early 1970s. (Many of the early records were *unappraised* or *temporary* and are being *re-appraised*. Undoubtedly, some will be *appraised* as *permanent* and will be transferred to the College Park National Archives.);

3. Naval Proving Ground, Dahlgren/Naval Weapons Laboratory, Dahlgren records, including but not limited to Confidential and below general correspondence files of the Commander from 1911–1946; Secret/Restricted Data and below reports from 1949–1955; Confidential and below technical reports from 1933–1944; Confidential and below missile and other ordnance test directives, firing data, ballistic test data, drawings, and other records from 1935–1963; and Confidential and below Chemical & Biological Sciences Division files from the 1960s. (Many of the early records were *unappraised* or *temporary*, and are being *re-appraised*. In all likelihood, some will be *appraised* as *permanent* and will be transferred to the College Park National Archives.);

4. Naval Surface Weapons Center, Dahlgren/Naval Surface Weapons Center, White Oak and predecessor records, including but not limited to Secret and below historical records from 1940–1978 (these include photographs, organization charts and manuals, Technical Directors' files, Senior Scientists Council records, and Undersea Warfare R&D Council records); Secret/Restricted Data and below Associate Technical Director/Head Air & Surface Weapons Development files on the Polaris from 1962–1971; Secret and below Advanced Weapons Department project files from 1959–1970; Confidential and below Mechanical Systems Division files on mines from 1931–1971; Secret and below laboratory notebooks from the 1950s into the 1980s; and Confidential and below outgoing/incoming correspondence R&D data bank files from 1888–1980. (Many of the early records were *unappraised* or *temporary*, and are being *re-appraised*. Undoubtedly, some will be *appraised* as *permanent* and will be transferred to the College Park National Archives.);

5. Naval Gun Factory records, including but not limited to Confidential and below central general correspondence files from 1925–1950; and Confidential and below files on the manufacture, testing, and proofs of ordnance from 1925–1948;

6. Naval Ordnance Test Station, China Lake/Naval Weapons Station, China Lake records, including but not limited to Confidential and be-

low central general correspondence files from 1944 into the 1960s; Secret and below Project Engineering Division chronological files from 1960–1964; Confidential and below R&D development files, tech reports, and contract files from 1952–1967; Confidential and below ordnance testing records from the 1950s; Confidential and below Asroc, Redeye, Shrike, Trap, Mauler, Arcas, Terrier, Caleb, and Hihoe project files from 1958–1964; Confidential and below SARAH firing reports from 1957–1963; and Confidential and below correspondence files on the Sidewinder from 1951–1967;

7. Confidential and below Naval Missile Center, Pt. Mugu testing records from 1956–1958;

8. Confidential and below Naval Ordnance Laboratory, Corona project files from 1959–1963, CORVUS files from 1952–1962, and R&D primary program correspondence files from 1953–1960;

9. Confidential and below Naval Weapons Plant central correspondence files from the 1950s;

10. Naval Air Test Center, Naval Air Station Patuxent River records, including but not limited to Secret and below Technical Director instrumentation and aircraft files from the 1960s; Secret and below Program Manager's Office aircraft files from the 1960s; Confidential and below Flight Test Division project and airplane files from 1946–1972; Confidential and below Weapons Systems Test Division project files from the 1960s; Secret and below Strike Aircraft Test Directorate project files from 1972–1973; and unclassified Force Warfare Aircraft Test Directorate and Rotary Wing Aircraft Test Directorate project files from the 1970s and early 1980s;

11. Naval Ship R&D Center/David Taylor Naval Ship R&D Center records, including but not limited to Confidential and below central general correspondence files from the 1950s and 1960s; Secret and below Ship Acoustics Department acoustic noise trial tapes from the 1960s into the 1980s; Confidential and below Aviation & Surface Effects Department files from the 1960s; Secret and below completed assignments files from the 1960s; Confidential and below wind tunnel reports from 1941–1970; Confidential and below aeronautical reports and data folders from 1945–1969; Confidential and below films from 1944–1975; Confidential and below Project SURPASS files from 1968–1973; and Confidential and below data folders from 1958–1967;

12. Confidential and below Naval Electronics Laboratory R&D files from 1946–1956 and unclassified drawing and specification files from 1946–1955;

13. Secret and below Deputy Commander Operational Test & Evaluation Force, Pacific serial files from 1951–1964;

14. Confidential and below Naval Ordnance Station, Indian Head correspondence files, monthly progress reports, test reports, technical reports, and other records from the 1940s into the 1960s;

15. Secret/Restricted Data and below Naval Weapons Evaluation Facility, Kirtland correspondence files, technical reports, and progress reports from 1957–1966;

16. Top Secret and below Naval Air Facility, Warminster files on Project GREAT CIRCLE and submarine operations;

17. Secret and below Commander U.S. Taiwan Defense Command files from 1960–1979;

18. Confidential and below naval attaché (Stockholm) general correspondence files from 1947–1950 and naval attaché (Rome) general correspondence files from 1957;

19. Secret and below Naval Advisory Group Korea reader files from 1955–1963;

20. Secret and below Navy Tactical Doctrine Activity files from the late 1960s;

21. Secret and below Court of Inquiry records on the USS Thresher from 1963.

Record Group 181 at the San Bruno Federal Records Center has about 62.5 million pages of records as of 2000 (4% *permanent*, 92% *temporary*, and 4% *unappraised*). The vast majority are unclassified administrative records, but there are also the following records of interest: (1) Secret/Restricted Data and below Naval Weapons Station, China Lake test reports from the 1960s on regarding a wide range of weapons systems; (2) Top Secret/Restricted Data records relating to the 1958 Pacific Command Commanders' Conference. Even though these have already been reviewed for declassification, they will not be available to the public until they are transferred to the San Bruno National Archives, possibly re-reviewed by the DOE under the Kyl Plan, and then *processed* by the National Archives.

Record Group 181 at the Seattle Federal Records Center has about 75 million pages of almost entirely unclassified records of various naval bases, shipyards, stations, and other facilities in that region dating from the early 1950s to the present.[107] The Laguna Niguel Federal Records Center has more than 32.5 million pages of exclusively unclassified records of assorted naval bases, shipyards, stations, and other facilities in that region from the 1950s to the present.[108] The Boston Federal Records Center has about 29 million pages of records as of 2000 (25% *permanent* and 75% *temporary*). It appears that the majority of records are from the U.S. Navy Submarine Base in New London. The records include: (1) unclassified torpedo R&D records from 1911–1957; (2) Secret and below submarine detection records from the 1950s and 1960s; (3) Confidential and below records of the Court of Inquiry on the USS Thresher; (4) Secret and below Technical Library R&D reports from the 1940s into the 1970s.[109]

Record Group 298 contains records of the Office of Naval Research (1946–present). There are fewer than 250,000 pages of records in RG 298 at the College Park National Archives, almost all of which are World War II records of its predecessors. No regional National Archives has any RG 298 holdings.

At the Washington National Records Center, RG 298 has more than 12.5 million pages of records as of 2000 (20% *permanent* and 80% *temporary*). No other Federal records center has any RG 298 holdings. Under the P-2000 Project, about 750,000 pages of unclassified *permanent* records and 1.5 million pages of classified *permanent* records will be transferred to RG 298 at the College Park National Archives by the end of 2001. Even if the classified records have been reviewed for declassification by the time of their transfer, they will not be available to the public until they are possibly re-reviewed by the DOE under the Kyl Plan and then *processed* by the National Archives. The records to be transferred include:

1. Top Secret/Restricted Data and below Assistant Secretary of the Navy (Research & Development) correspondence files from 1952–1970 (it is not known whether these duplicate what is in RG 428 at the Washington National Records Center);

2. Secret and below Assistant Secretary of the Navy (Research & Development) records on 1966–1967 meetings with the Secretary of Defense regarding the F-111;

3. Secret/Restricted Data and below Office of the Chief of Naval Research general correspondence files from 1946–1963;

4. unclassified Office of Naval Research records of daily events;

5. Secret/Restricted Data and below Assistant Chief for Research/Director of Research correspondence files from 1958–1968 and program records from 1962–1964;

6. Confidential and below Development Coordinator general correspondence files from 1956–1963;

7. Secret and below Office of the Director, Naval Analysis Group files from 1947–1964;

8. Secret and below Advanced Planning Branch, Naval Analysis Group files from 1962;

9. Secret/Restricted Data and below Air Programs Branch, Naval Applications Group files from 1959–1967;

10. Secret and below Surface & Amphibious Branch, Naval Applications Group files from 1960–1961;

11. Secret and below Acoustics Branch, Naval Applications Group files from 1963–1966;

12. Secret and below Undersea Programs Branch, Naval Applications Group files from 1963–1966;

13. Secret and below Naval Analysis Programs Branch, Naval Applications & Analysis Division correspondence files and reports from 1966–1999;

14. unclassified Research Division general subject files and project files from 1947–1956;

15. unclassified Biological Sciences Division correspondence files from the 1960s;

16. unclassified Ocean Science & Technology Division general correspondence files from 1952–1976 and miscellaneous geophysics correspondence files from 1957–1965;

17. unclassified Geophysics Branch, Earth Sciences Division correspondence files and reports from the 1960s;

18. unclassified Geography Branch, Earth Sciences Division correspondence files from the 1960s;

19. Secret/Restricted Data and below Power Branch, Material Sciences Division files from 1960–1962;

20. unclassified Chemistry Branch, Material Sciences Division project files from the late 1940s and technical reference files from the 1960s and 1970s;

21. Confidential and below Engineering Services Branch, Materials Division and predecessor records from 1944–1947;

22. Confidential and below Nuclear Physics Branch, Physical Sciences Division files from 1961–1963;

23. Confidential and below Engineering Psychology Branch, Psychological Science Division files from 1965;

24. unclassified Mathematical Sciences Division project files from 1946–1950;

25. Confidential and below Information Systems Branch, Mathematical & Information Sciences Division and predecessor records on R&D in computational procedures and techniques from 1944–1949, and correspondence files and reports from the 1960s;

26. Secret and below records relating to the National Development & Research Committee from 1942–1947;

27. Secret and below correspondence with other agencies and Navy offices regarding research projects from 1945–1946;

28. Confidential and below foreign scientists file jackets from 1945–1953.

Records not eligible for transfer to the College Park National Archives by 2001 include:

1. unclassified Office of Naval Research Directives from 1946–1987;
2. unclassified Naval Research Advisory Committee records from 1946–1986;
3. unclassified Physical Science Administrator records relating to technical boards and committees from 1959–1972;
4. a large number of unclassified contract files;
5. a huge number of Secret and below technical reports from the 1940s into the 1970s (most of these were *unappraised* or *temporary*, but they are being *re-appraised* to determine whether they should be *permanent*).

Record Group 52 has the records of the Bureau of Medicine and Surgery. At the College Park National Archives, RG 52 has about 3.75 million pages of records, most of which are from World War II and earlier. No regional National Archives has any RG 52 holdings. The *finding aid* is good. The only postwar records are the almost completely unclassified or declassified and *processed* general correspondence files of various headquarters offices from 1945 to the mid-1960s. At the Washington National Records Center, RG 52 has approximately 3 million pages of completely unclassified records. The primary records of interest are the headquarters general correspondence files from the 1960s on.

### Navy Records at Navy Commands, Presidential Libraries, and Other Repositories

There are numerous Navy commands around the world, and some have significant record holdings with which researchers should be familiar. It should be noted, however, that the following list is not comprehensive as there is no information available on the holdings at some commands.

The Naval Historical Center (phone: 202–433–4131 / fax: 202–433–2833) at the Washington Navy Yard in Washington, D.C., holds a number of significant postwar primary source materials in its Operational Archives Branch, and these can be reviewed by researchers with a prior appointment. The Branch contains Navy periodic and programmatic histories, manuscripts, oral histories, biographies, personal papers, and operational records. A list of unclassified and declassified and *processed* collections is available on the Center's homepage (http://www.history.navy.mil). Significant collections in this category include Strategic Plans/War Plans files from 1919–1955, Politico-Military Policy Division files from 1945–1950, periodic and programmatic histories from 1946–1953 in the Post 1 Jan 1946 Command File, Director of Naval History files from 1942–1994, and oral histories from 1940 to the present. There are also numerous completely classified collections, including the Top Secret/Restricted Data and Top Secret Chief of Naval Operations files from 1955 into the 1980s. Many of the classified collections are in RG 38 at the Washington National Records Center.

The Naval Historical Foundation (phone: 202–433–2005) at the Washington Navy Yard has some relevant personal paper collections that can be examined by researchers with a prior appointment. A few of the collections have classified material in them. To obtain information on the collections, the Naval Historical Foundation can be contacted directly or one of their two publications can be consulted. *Naval Historical Foundation— Manuscript Collection—A Catalog* describes the collections acquired through 1974 and *Naval Historical Foundation—Manuscript Collection— 1975–1994* describes the collections acquired during these years.

Commands that report that they do not have any archives or central records storage facility include the Naval Sea Systems Command;[110] Naval Space Command;[111] Office of Naval Intelligence;[112] Commander in Chief, Atlantic Fleet;[113] and Commander in Chief, Pacific Fleet.[114] The quantity, nature, and *appraisal* status of the record holdings at these and other major commands, such as the Naval Air Systems Command and Space and Naval Warfare Systems Command, are unknown.

Two presidential libraries have relevant holdings. At the Truman Library there are the personal papers of Dan Kimball (Under Secretary of the Navy from 1949–1951 and Secretary of the Navy from 1951–1953), Francis Matthews (Secretary of the Navy from 1949–1951), and John Sullivan (Under Secretary of the Navy from 1946–1947 and Secretary of the Navy from 1947–1949). The personal papers of Robert Anderson (Secretary of the Navy from 1953–1954) are at the Eisenhower Library. All of these personal paper collections are open.

Requests under the FOIA and MDR for records at a Federal records center or at a Navy command can be submitted to the commanding officer of the command holding the records. If headquarters records are sought, or if there is any doubt as to which command holds the records, the requests should be submitted to Chief of Naval Operations, Code OP-09B30, Room 5E521, Pentagon, Washington, D.C. 20350–2000.

## Office of Scientific Research and Development (OSRD) Records at the National Archives

Record Group 227 contains the records of OSRD (1941–1947). Two National Archives have RG 227 holdings, but no Federal records center has RG 227 holdings.

At the College Park National Archives, there are about 11.25 million pages of records in RG 227. The *finding aids* are good, in many cases listing folder titles by box. Most of the records have been reviewed for declassification and *processed*, and they include:

1. subject and correspondence files of OSRD's Director and Executive Secretary;
2. records of the Office of the Historian;
3. records of various officials at OSRD and other agencies engaged in atomic energy research from 1940–1950;
4. contract files;
5. subject and correspondence files of the chairman of the National Defense Research Committee;
6. correspondence files, project files, reports, and related records of the various research divisions under the National Defense Research Committee.

Record Group 227 at the Boston National Archives has more than 4.25 million pages of records, most of which are from MIT's Radiation Laboratory.

### On-Site Inspection Agency (OSIA) Records at the National Archives and Federal Records Centers

Record Group 505 was established for records of the OSIA (1988–1998),[115] but there are no records in this *record group* at any National Archives or Federal records center. For unknown reasons, there is a small quantity of unclassified OSIA inspection reports, handbooks, site books, and other materials from 1985–1993 in RG 338 at the Washington National Records Center.

### OSIA Records at the Defense Threat Reduction Agency

With the one exception noted above, all of the OSIA's records that still exist are at the Defense Threat Reduction Agency. However, there is no information available on the quantity, nature, and *appraisal* status.[116]

Requests under the FOIA and MDR for records should be submitted to the Freedom of Information Act Officer, Defense Threat Reduction Agency, FOIA Division, 45045 Aviation Drive, Dulles, VA 20166–7517.

### Department of State (State) Records at the National Archives and Federal Records Centers

A large number of State records are in one of several *record groups* at either the College Park National Archives or the Washington National Records Center.

State is one of the few agencies that nearly completed its declassification review under E.O. 12958 of all of its *permanent* pre-1975 classified records by 2000. (One of the notable exceptions is the approximately 1.5 million pages of Bureau of Intelligence and Research records exempted by the White House from automatic declassification in early 1999.) The following numbers show the magnitude of State's efforts in this area. Of the approximately 45 million pages of subject records either at the Washington National Records Center or at the State's internal records storage facility (the Records Service Center), more than 40 million pages had been reviewed by the end of 1999. Of the roughly 28 million pages of subject records at the National Archives, presidential libraries, other agencies, and the Library of Congress, more than 22 million pages had been reviewed by the end of 1999.[117]

Record Group 59 contains the general records of the Department of State. At the College Park National Archives, RG 59 has more than 87.5 million pages of records from the late 1700s into the 1980s. No regional National Archives has any RG 59 holdings.

All RG 59 records are in one of two filing systems. The first is the Central Files, a filing system used from the late 1700s to the present. Copies of all permanently valuable records are directed to be included in the Central Files, although for any number of reasons this has not always been done (especially since World War II). Since 1910, the Central Files have utilized a series of decimal filing systems, and the Civil Branch at the College Park National Archives has publications explaining these systems. All the Central Files through 1973 are at the College Park National Archives and they have been declassified and *processed*. The 1973–1975 Central Files are in electronic form and will apparently be available to the public in 2002.[118]

The second filing system is Office or Lot Files. These are generally the files of a particular office, bureau, individual or committee. Lot Files are supposed to include only reference copies of correspondence, memoranda, minutes of meetings, studies, and other types of documents; however, in many instances they also contain originals and copies that should have been sent to the Central Files but were not. The *finding aids* to the Lot Files are very good, in many cases listing folder titles by box. It should be noted that the other *record groups* discussed in this section contain Lot Files as well.

The following are among the more important Lot Files containing Executive Secretariat records in RG 59 at the College Park National Archives that have been reviewed for declassification and *processed*:

1. Top Secret/Restricted Data and below files of Dean Acheson during his tenure as Assistant Secretary of State, Under Secretary of State, and Secretary of State;

2. Top Secret/Restricted Data and below files of Dean Rusk from 1961–1969;

3. Top Secret/Restricted Data and below records of Ambassador-at-Large Llewellyn Thompson from 1961–1970;

4. Top Secret and below files of Ambassador Averell Harriman from 1967–1968;

5. Top Secret and below records of Ambassador-at-Large Ellsworth Bunker from 1962–1967;

6. Top Secret and below chronological files of Deputy Under Secretary for Political Affairs Foy Kohler from 1966–1967;

7. Secret and below records of Ambassador Joseph Satterthwaite from 1953–1972;

8. Top Secret and below records of Under Secretary of State George Ball from 1961–1966;

9. Top Secret and below records of Robert Komer from 1948–1968;

10. Top Secret and below records of Ambassador Charles Bohlen from 1942–1963;

11. Secret and below chronological files of the Special Assistant to the Secretary for MLF from 1963–1965;

12. Top Secret/Restricted Data and below files of Deputy Secretary of State Charles Robinson from 1976–1977;

13. Top Secret/Restricted Data and below SALT files of Under Secretary of State John Irwin from 1969–1973;

14. Top Secret/Restricted Data and below Deputy Under Secretary for Political Affairs memorandums relating to allied force objectives from 1950–1958 and memorandums relating to contingency defense planning for West Berlin from 1961–1963;

15. Top Secret/Restricted Data and below files of the Special Assistant to the Under Secretary for Political Affairs from 1958–1966;

16. Top Secret and below memorandums from the Secretary and Under Secretary to the President from 1947 and 1948;

17. Top Secret and below memorandums of conversations with the President from 1949–1952 and 1956–1964;

18. Top Secret and below *President's Evening Reading Reports* from 1964–1974;

19. Top Secret and below Presidential and Secretary of State official exchanges of correspondence from 1961–1966;

20. Top Secret and below agendas for the Secretary's luncheon meetings with the President from 1964–1969;

21. Top Secret/Restricted Data and below Bureau of Intelligence and Research *Morning Briefs* for the Secretary from 1959–1971;

22. Top Secret and below correspondence of President Nixon with U.S. ambassadors;

23. Top Secret and below Secretary's staff meeting minutes from 1952–1966;

24. Top Secret and below congratulatory and condolence messages sent by foreign governments to the Secretary from 1952–1966;

25. Top Secret/Restricted Data and below briefing books, country fact sheets, and planning and contingency reports used by the Secretary and other top officials from 1952–1976;

26. Top Secret/Restricted Data and below summaries of Under Secretary's meetings with the National Security Advisor from 1970–1972;

27. Top Secret/Restricted Data and below briefing books for the secretary-designate from 1968;

28. Top Secret/Restricted Data and below *Weekly Focus Reports* from 1966–1971;

29. Top Secret and below country files from 1961–1966 and policy and history files from 1950–1966;

30. Top Secret/Restricted Data and below Committee of the Principals records from 1964–1966;

31. Top Secret and below *Morning Summary of Significant Reports* from 1971–1974;

32. Top Secret and below Berlin Crisis files from 1961–1962, Middle East Crisis files from 1967, Cyprus Crisis files from 1967, Pueblo Crisis files from 1968, and Czechoslovak Crisis files from 1968;

33. Top Secret and below records of the Special Group (Counter Insurgency) from 1962–1966;

34. Secret/Restricted Data and below *Daily Activity Reports* from principals from 1973–1975;

35. Secret/Restricted Data and below Multilateral Force documents from 1960–1965;

36. Secret and below Operations Center watch logs from 1961–1969 and 1975;

37. Secret and below *Daily Secret Summaries* and *Daily Staff Officers Summaries* from 1945–1961;

38. Secret and below *White House Daily Summaries* from 1944–1964;

39. Top Secret and below minutes and related papers of the Under Sec-

retary meetings from 1949 to 1952 and of the Secretary's staff meetings from 1952–1961 and 1973–1977;

40. Top Secret and below Secretary and Under Secretary memorandums of conversation from 1953–1964;

41. Top Secret and below Presidential and Secretary of State correspondence with foreign heads of state from 1953–1971;

42. Top Secret and below telegrams, memos, biographical material, reports, briefing books, and other records from 1949–1976 used by the President, Vice-President, and senior officials concerning foreign dignitaries visiting the United States and international conferences attended by these U.S. officials;

43. Top Secret and below records relating to Cabinet meetings from 1953–1965;

44. Top Secret/Restricted Data and below records of the Operations Coordinator from 1953–1961 and State participation in the Operations Coordinating Board and the National Security Council from 1947–1963;

45. Top Secret/Restricted Data and below National Security Council meeting files and project report files from 1959–1970, National Security Council general files from 1969–1972, National Security Council politico-military contingency planning files from 1963–1966, and National Security Action memo files from 1961–1968;

46. Secret and below White House and agency files from 1963–1967;

47. Secret and below transcripts of the Paris meetings on Vietnam from 1968–1972 and telegrams regarding these meetings from 1969;

48. Secret and below *Daily Staff Summaries* from 1944–1971 and *Afternoon Summaries* from 1959–1971;

49. Top Secret and below secretariat memorandums from 1964–1976;

50. Top Secret and below historical reports relating to China and Sri Lanka from 1949–1969;

51. Top Secret and below historical reports relating to diplomacy during President Johnson's tenure;

52. Top Secret and below Psychological Strategy Board working files from 1951–1953;

53. Top Secret/Restricted Data and below Presidential transition files from 1959–1977.

The following are some of the Lot Files containing non-Executive Secretariat records in RG 59 at the College Park National Archives that have been reviewed for declassification and *processed* or should be *processed* shortly:

1. Top Secret and below subject files of the International Security Affairs Committee from 1951–1952;

2. Top Secret/Restricted Data and below Policy Planning Staff/Policy Planning Council reports, subject files, country files, and related materials from 1947–1970;

3. Top Secret/Restricted Data and below files of Winston Lord, Director of the Planning Coordination Staff/Policy Planning Staff, from 1969–1977;

4. Top Secret/Restricted Data and below files, reports, and studies of the Special Assistant to the Secretary of State for Atomic Energy/Special Assistant to the Secretary of State for Atomic Energy and Aerospace from 1944–1962;

5. Secret and below Office of Science Advisor files relating to international conferences and the International Geophysical Year from 1949–1958;

6. Top Secret/Restricted Data and below central files of the Bureau of International Scientific and Technological Affairs from 1964–1966;

7. Top Secret and below miscellaneous files of the Office of International Scientific Affairs/Bureau of International Scientific and Technological Affairs from 1962–1966;

8. Top Secret/Restricted Data and below files relating to atomic energy of the Office of International Scientific Affairs/Bureau of International Scientific and Technological Affairs from 1962–1966;

9. Top Secret and below files, reports, and studies relating to the Mutual Defense Assistance Program from 1947–1952;

10. Top Secret and below records of the Special Assistant for Mutual Security Coordination from 1952–1959;

11. Top Secret/Restricted Data and below Deputy Assistant Secretary for Politico-Military Affairs records concerning the military aid program and the Draper Committee from 1957–1962, subject files from 1961–1968, and files regarding military forces and NATO from 1961–1968;

12. Top Secret/Restricted Data and below subject files of the Office of Politico-Military Affairs' Office of Operations and the Combined Policy Office from 1961–1966, and subject files of its Office of International Security Policy and Planning from 1969–1971;

13. Top Secret/Restricted Data and below Office of Politico-Military Affairs records relating to disarmament and arms control from 1961–1966;

14. Top Secret/Restricted Data and below Under Secretary for Political Affairs subject files from 1961–1963;

15. Top Secret/Restricted Data and below Deputy Under Secretary for Political Affairs memorandums relating to allied force objectives from 1950–1958, memorandums on contingency defense planning for West Berlin from 1961–1963, correspondence concerning overseas military bases from 1957–1963, memorandums regarding foreign military assistance programs from 1959–1963, and minutes of meetings from 1959–1963 with the Joint Chiefs of Staff on overseas internal security measures;

16. Top Secret/Restricted Data and below Multilateral Force records, including records of the negotiating team from 1961–1965 and Paris Working Group and Sub-Group files from 1963–1965;

17. Top Secret/Restricted Data and below Office of Intelligence Research/ Bureau of Intelligence and Research political, military, economic, cultural, and social reports from the 1940s and 1950s; *National Intelligence Estimates, Special Estimates,* and *Special National Intelligence Estimates* from 1950 to 1954; intelligence research reports from 1955– 1967; program files from 1944–1975; research reports from 1942– 1978; subject files from 1959–1965; and individual defector files from 1949–1963;

18. Top Secret/Restricted Data and below Director of the Office of Intelligence Research/Bureau of Intelligence and Research miscellaneous files from 1949–1959 and Special Assistant to the Director subject files from 1957–1960;

19. Top Secret/Restricted Data and below Senior Interdepartmental Group (State, CIA, DOD, JCS) files from 1968–1969;

20. Secret and below Office of Munitions Control subject files, technical assistance agreements, and security screening files from the 1940s to the 1960s, and COCOM program files from 1962–1975;

21. Top Secret and below Vietnam POW/MIA files from 1966–1979;

22. Top Secret and below Deputy Assistant Secretary for Budget and Finance annual budget files from 1948–1977;

23. Top Secret and below records of the Division of Foreign Activity Correlation, including memorandums and reports furnished by the FBI from 1947 to 1953 and name files from 1941 to 1951;

24. Top Secret and below research papers of the Historian's Office from 1969–1974;

25. Top Secret and below Bureau of Administration files on interagency relations from 1948–1961;

26. Top Secret and below Assistant Secretary for Public Affairs subject files from 1947–1969;

27. Top Secret and below Bureau of Public Affairs research files relating to the Palestine problem from 1948–1970;

28. Top Secret/Restricted Data and below Office of Legal Advisor records, including but not limited to country and subject files of the Legal Advisor from 1939–1958; subject files of the Deputy Legal Advisor from 1953–1959; Japanese and German war crimes files from 1942–1960; aircraft incidents files from 1944–1962; files from 1922–1957 on bilateral agreements between countries in which the United States is not a signatory; files from 1945–1959 on legislation on un-American activities; Assistant Legal Advisor for Inter-American Affairs country files from 1958–1965; Assistant Legal Advisor for Far Eastern Affairs country files from 1951–1965; Assistant Legal Advisor for Near Eastern and South Asian Affairs country files from 1948–1966; and Assistant Legal Advisor for Economic Affairs subject files from 1945–1966 and files on U.S. foreign aid programs from 1947–1966;

29. Secret/Restricted Data and below Bureau of European Affairs files, including but not limited to Multilateral Force documents from 1962–1966, country director files from the 1950s and 1960s, NATO and Atlantic politico-military affairs files from 1957 into the 1960s, records relating to atomic energy from 1956–1963, U.S./U.S.S.R. bilateral political relations files from 1921–1973, Berlin Task Force files from 1944–1988, and Four Power Talks files from 1969–1971;

30. Top Secret and below Assistant Secretary for Near Eastern and South Asian affairs subject files from 1958–1973;

31. Top Secret and below Bureau of Near Eastern and South Asian Affairs files, including but not limited to country director files from the 1950s and 1960s, Central Treaty Organization records from 1956–1964, and military assistance files from 1954–1966;

32. Top Secret and below Assistant Secretary for Far East Affairs subject files from the 1950s and 1960s;

33. Top Secret and below Bureau of Far Eastern Affairs/Bureau of East Asian and Pacific Affairs files, including but not limited to Vietnam Working Group files from 1963–1966, Vietnam subject files from 1955–1962, country director files from the 1950s and 1960s, Central Treaty Organization records from 1956–1964, and Southeast Asia Treaty Organization records from 1954–1977;

34. Top Secret and below files of the other two geographic bureaus, the Bureau of Inter-American Affairs and Bureau of African Affairs, from the 1940s into the early 1970s;

35. Top Secret and below files of the Bureau of United Nations Affairs/Bureau of International Organization Affairs and predecessor offices, including but not limited to subject files from 1903–1964, international

conference files from 1914–1964, COCOM program files from 1962–1975, GATT trade negotiation files from 1947–1979, and United Nations position papers from 1953–1965;

36. Secret and below Office of Refugee and Migration Affairs refugee relief program subject files from 1946–1971.

Record Group 59 at the Washington National Records Center has more than 510 million pages of records as of 2000 (10% *permanent*, 35% *temporary*, and 55% *unappraised*). No regional Federal records center has any RG 59 holdings. As part of the P-2000 Project, only 55,000 pages of unclassified *permanent* records and 105,000 pages of classified *permanent* records will be transferred to RG 59 at the College Park National Archives by the end of 2001. All the records in RG 59 at the Washington National Records Center are Lot Files and the vast majority are classified. Among the records are:

1. numerous Executive Secretariat records, including but not limited to Secret and below briefing books used by the President, Secretary of State, and other officials for trips, congressional testimony, foreign visitors, meetings, and conferences from the mid-1970s to 1988; Secret/Restricted Data and below INF negotiation files from 1981–1987; Secret and below memoranda files from the 1980s; Secret and below daily briefing books from the late 1970s and early 1980s; Top Secret/Restricted Data and below reports regarding Henry Kissinger's nomination as Secretary of State; and Top Secret and below Secretary's *Morning Intelligence Summaries* from 1992–1995;

2. subject files, country files, correspondence files, and personal files of many Secretaries, Special Advisors, Under Secretaries, Assistant Secretaries, Deputy Assistant Secretaries, Ambassadors, and Ambassadors-at-Large from the 1940s into the 1980s, including but not limited to those of Paul Nitze (1953 and 1972–1989), Lawrence Eagleburger (1967–1984 and 1989–1993), Gerard Smith (1977–1980), Philip Habib (1979–1980), Marshall Shulman (1974–1981), Richard Kennedy (1981–1992), Henry Cooper and Max Kampelman (1981–1992), Raymond Garthoff (1960–1980), Alfred Atherton, Jr. (1965–1979), Seymour Weiss (1960–1976), David Anderson (1968–1981), Jonathan Dean (1966–1981), Martin Hillenbrand (1959–1978), James Robbins (1982–1984), W. Tapley Bennett, Jr. (1947–1973), Robert Sayre (1965–1984), Alvin Adams (1949–1981), David Popper (1968–1979), Richard Fairbanks (1979–1985), William Clark (1981), James Baker (1972–1978), John Whitehead (1982–1989), Walter Stoessel (1959–1982), Edmund Muskie (1963–1980), Richard Moose (1976–1980), Elliott Abrams (1981–1989), George McGhee (1961–1963), Elliot

Richardson (1977–1980), Brian Atwood (1977–1980), Carlyle Maw (1974–1976), Patricia Derian (1977–1981), and H. Allen Homes (1985–1989);

3. Top Secret/Restricted Data/Sensitive Compartmented Information and below records of the Office of Intelligence Research/Bureau of Intelligence and Research, including chronological files of the Assistant Secretary for Intelligence and Research from 1961 into the 1990s, miscellaneous files from 1945–1981, and Office of Politico-Military Analysis & Warning program files from 1968–1986;

4. Secret/Restricted Data and below Office of Intelligence Research/Bureau of Intelligence and Research general office subject files from 1944–1985; POW/MIA office files from 1968–1992; Soviet general subject files from 1945–1992; Soviet office subject files from 1922–1991; Soviet research studies from 1946–1971; East & West Division office subject files from 1943–1988; East & West Division subject files from 1947–1989; weekly activity reports on the Soviet economy from 1973–1985; Soviet/Middle East relations subject files from 1945–1983; Soviet foreign policy and U.S./Soviet relations program files from 1946–1985; Soviet/Asia relations program files from 1960–1981; Soviet/European relations program files from 1960–1987; Soviet/African relations program files from the 1960s to 1979; intelligence exchange files regarding Latin American terrorism from 1977–1992; South Africa subject files from 1983–1987; East European subject files from 1959–1985; DESERT SHIELD/DESERT STORM Task Force records from 1990–1991; contract studies from 1955–1989; Poland subject files from 1960–1990; weekly activity reports on Eastern European affairs from the 1960s to 1988; historical files on *National Intelligence Estimates* and *Special National Intelligence Estimates* from 1950–1987; historical files on the Tiananmen crisis from 1989; program files on individual countries in Southeast Asia from the 1970s and 1980s; arms control program files from 1976–1985; Latin American program files from 1940–1985; China program files from 1985–1993; Central American and Caribbean program/subject files from 1962–1986; Cuba and Grenada program files from 1983–1986; and program/subject files on Laos, Vietnam and Cambodia from the 1960s and 1970s;

5. Secret/Restricted Data and below meeting and plenary records of the U.S. delegation to SALT from 1973–1976;

6. Secret and below papers, studies, cables, and other records regarding the Paris Peace Talks from 1968–1972;

7. Secret/Restricted Data and below Bureau of Politico-Military Affairs program files, subject files, and country files regarding nonproliferation and the Chemical Weapons Convention from 1972–1993; Nuclear

Risk Reduction Center notification country files, watch officer logs, incoming and outgoing messages, and reports from the mid-1980s to 1994; subject files, country files, and country briefing book files regarding nuclear energy and nuclear weapons from 1964–1992; program files, policy files, and country files on security assistance programs from 1980–1992; Conference on Confidence and Security Building Measures and Disarmament in Europe files from 1984–1985; Falklands Crisis subject files from 1982–1983; Mutual Balanced Forces Reduction negotiations and INF arms control files from 1979–1985; Indian Ocean and nuclear warships files from 1972–1984; El Salvador files regarding security assistance, arms transfers, and human rights from 1977–1992; subject files on the NPT, SALT, INF, START, and Mutual Balanced Forces Reduction negotiations and treaties from the 1960s into the 1990s; missile country files and chemical subject files from the 1990s; general correspondence files on the NPT, SALT, and Comprehensive Test Ban Treaty negotiations from 1970–1981; and subject files on space topics from the 1980s to the early 1990s;

8. Secret and below correspondence files of the Director of the Policy Planning Staff from 1989–1993;

9. Secret and below Bureau of Inter-American Affairs internal memos regarding individual countries from 1978–1989; security assistance program files, project files, and country issue files from 1983–1989; Nicaraguan conflict files from the 1980s, and working files on El Salvador and Nicaragua of the Assistant Secretary for Inter-American Affairs from 1978–1981;

10. Secret and below Bureau of European & Canadian Affairs/Bureau of European Affairs political director's meetings subject files from 1977–1989; NATO files from the 1980s; Soviet economic subject files from 1949–1984; files on NATO's approach to arms control and security issues from 1987–1989; Soviet human rights documents from 1971–1986; U.S./Soviet airplane incident files from 1946–1960; U.S./Soviet exchange agreements and negotiation files from 1958–1980; Soviet subject files from 1944–1988; political subject files from 1970–1991; Soviet dissident and political prisoner subject files from 1974–1988; defense and conventional forces subject files from 1980–1987; Soviet/European affairs general subject files from 1950–1988; and Conference on Security & Cooperation of Europe files from 1973–1989;

11. Secret and below Bureau of African Affairs special collection files from 1947–1988; Somalia special collection files from 1966–1985; South Africa special collection files from 1954–1990; Horn of Africa, Kenya, and Uganda special collection files from 1961–1989; Angola briefing books from 1982–1988; and Namibia special collection files from 1981–1988;

12. Secret and below Bureau of Oceans and International Environmental & Scientific Affairs subject files and country files on a wide range of issues from the 1970s into the 1990s; subject files and country files on nuclear export policy from the 1950s into the 1990s; space and advanced technology files from the 1960s into the 1980s; and policy files, meeting files, subject files, and other records on Law of the Sea from 1966 into the 1980s;

13. Secret and below Bureau of Near Eastern and South Asian Affairs Israeli historical files from 1978–1995; briefing books from 1961–1993; program files on individual countries from the 1970s to 1994; Saudi historical files from the 1970s to 1990; hostage crisis historical files from 1982–1989; and Kuwait Task Force briefing books and coordinator data books;

14. Secret and below Bureau of Public Affairs office chronological files and subject files from the 1970s to 1989 and Madrid Conference subject files from 1991;

15. Secret and below Bureau of Economic Affairs/Bureau of Economic and Business Affairs Gulf War subject files and Iraq/Kuwait crisis country files from 1990–1991, COCOM program files and case files from the 1950s into the 1990s, and general country files and subject files from the 1970s into the 1990s;

16. Secret and below Bureau of International Organization Affairs position papers for the U.S. delegation to the United Nations from 1955–1981; United Nations organization and conference files from the 1960s to 1988; general subject files regarding host country issues from 1949–1990; a wide range of files from the 1950s into the 1990s regarding the Food and Agriculture Organization, World Health Organization, United Nations Education, Scientific & Cultural Organization, and other multilateral bodies; and general subject files regarding South Africa issues from 1970–1987;

17. Secret and below subject files, export application files, intelligence reports, and related materials from the 1960s into the 1990s of the Office of Munitions Control and its successors;

18. Secret and below Office of Legal Adviser texts and background information of terminated, perfected, and unperfected treaties from the 1940s into the 1980s; and bilateral agreement files between countries in which the U.S. is not a party from 1810–1986;

19. Secret/Restricted Data and below Office of Legal Adviser records, including but not limited to the subject and country files of the Legal Adviser from the 1970s into the 1990s; subject and country files regarding politico-military affairs from the 1950s into the 1990s; Egypt/Israel peace treaty files from 1978–1995; U.S./Canadian subject files

from 1951–1983; SALT and ABM Treaty subject files from 1972–
1992; atomic energy subject files from 1959–1980; terrorism subject
files from 1974–1981; security assistance subject files from 1969–1988;
arms control and chemical warfare subject files from the 1970s and
1980s; Organization of American States subject files from the 1950s
into the 1980s; European country files from the 1940s into the 1980s;
and Asian nations subject files from the 1970s and 1980s;

20. Secret and below Office of Refugee and Migration Affairs/Bureau for
Refugee Programs general files, subject files, country files, individual
files, and reports from the 1950s into the 1990s;

21. Secret and below central subject files, policy files, and procedural files
of the Deputy Assistant Secretary for Refugee Programs from the
1980s into the 1990s; and various files of the Special Assistant to the
Secretary for Refugee Programs from 1979–1981;

22. Secret and below Office of Humanitarian Affairs/Bureau of Human
Rights and Humanitarian Affairs general files, subject files, country
files, individual files, human rights country files, human rights subject
files, multilateral organization human rights subject files, and reports
from the 1970s into the 1990s;

23. Secret and below subject files, country files, and chronological files of
the Under Secretary for Security Assistance, Science & Technology
from the 1970s and 1980s;

24. Historian Program files from 1967–1996;

25. Secret and below files from 1945–1980 of the adviser on records policy
in the Office of the Historian;

26. Secret and below Visa Office files regarding the Intergovernmental
Committee for Internal Security from 1949–1974;

27. Secret and below Iran/Contra files from 1983–1989.


Record Group 84 contains the records of embassies, consulates, and legations. At the College Park National Archives, RG 84 has more than 95
million pages of records, the majority of which are from World War II and
earlier. No regional National Archives has any RG 84 holdings. Most of
the records have been reviewed for declassification and *processed*, and the
*finding aids* are good. The records include:


1. Secret and below U.S. Mission to the Organization of American States
central subject files from 1960–1969;

2. Secret and below U.S. Mission to the United Nations central subject files
from 1950–1963, telegram and airgram files from 1950–1963, back-

ground books and position books from 1946–1959, and memoranda of conversation from 1951–1961;

3. Top Secret correspondence and incoming and outgoing messages of the U.S. Mission to the United Nations from 1950–1978;

4. a huge number of Top Secret and below record books, subject files, general records, and other files of embassies, consulates, and legations from the end of World War II into the 1970s.

Record Group 84 at the Washington National Records Center has more than 35 million pages of mostly classified records as of 2000 (90% *permanent* and 10% *temporary*). No regional Federal records center has any RG 84 holdings. As part of the P-2000 Project, only 2,500 pages of unclassified *permanent* records will be transferred to RG 84 at the College Park National Archives by the end of 2001. Among the records not eligible for transfer to the College Park National Archives by 2001 are:

1. Secret and below U.S. Embassy Office Berlin political files, subjective files, and political-military files from the 1950s into the 1980s; basic historical documents from 1962–1980; communications records from the 1950s; and Allied/Soviet protest books from 1961–1990;

2. Secret and below U.S. Embassy, Bonn files from 1957–1990 relating to issues and activities in Berlin;

3. Secret and below personal files of various Ambassadors, including but not limited to Harlan Cleveland (1965–1969), Robert Ellsworth (1969–1971), Ellsworth Bunker (1968–1972), Graham Martin (1972–1974), David Bolen (1972–1980), Malcolm Toon (1969–1979), and Armin Meyer (1962–1972);

4. Top Secret and below political, economic, chronological, and other files of numerous embassies, consulates, and legations from the mid-1970s into the 1990s.

Record Group 43 contains records of international conferences, commissions, and expositions. At the College Park National Archives, RG 43 has more than 3.75 million pages of records, including those of several key early postwar meetings and councils. No regional National Archives has any RG 43 holdings. Almost all the records have been reviewed for declassification and *processed*, and the *finding aids* are good. Postwar records include those of the Far Eastern Commission (1945–1951), 1946 Paris Peace Conference, Allied Council for Japan (1946–1952), the six meetings of the Council of Foreign Ministers (1945–1950), other meetings of the foreign ministers and deputy foreign ministers (1945–1953), meetings of the North Atlantic Treaty Organization and North Atlantic Council (1949–

1954), meetings between President Truman and foreign heads of state (1950–1952), 1954 Four Power Conference, U.S./U.S.S.R. Joint Commission on Korea (1946–1948), and various international conference files from the 1940s into the 1970s. There are no records in RG 43 at any Federal records center.

Record Group 353 has records of State interdepartmental and intradepartmental committees. At the College Park National Archives, RG 353 contains fewer than 750,000 pages of records. No regional National Archives has any RG 353 holdings. Most of the records have been reviewed for declassification and *processed*, and the *finding aids* are good. Among the records are:

1. summary minutes, action and decision summaries, document files, and subcommittee records from 1944–1947 of the State-War-Navy Coordinating Committee and from 1947–1949 of its successor, the State-Army-Navy-Air Force Coordinating Committee;

2. agendas, summary minutes, and related materials from the mid-1940s into the early 1950s of the numerous intradepartmental Area and Country Committees;

3. country files, subject files, and general records from 1945–1949 of the intradepartmental Policy Committee on Arms and Armaments;

4. a limited number of directives, documents, and project status reports from 1946–1947 of the Central Intelligence Group, as well as the agendas, summary minutes, and memoranda from 1946–1947 of the Intelligence Advisory Board;

5. agendas, summary minutes, and memoranda from 1948–1961 of the intradepartmental National Intelligence Survey Coordinating Committee and from 1948–1965 of the interdepartmental National Intelligence Survey Permanent Committee;

6. miscellaneous records of 1948–1951 Army attaché conferences;

7. miscellaneous NATO-related records, including verbatim minutes of the 1948–1949 Ambassador's Committee on the Washington Security Talks, summary minutes and files from 1948–1949 of the International Working Group on the Washington Security Talks, and summary minutes and files from 1949–1950 of the American and International Working Groups on Pact Organization.

At the Washington National Records Center, RG 353 has about 250,000 pages of largely classified records as of 2000 (all *permanent*). No regional Federal records center has any RG 353 holdings. It is not known whether under the P-2000 Project any *permanent* records will be transferred to RG 353 at the College Park National Archives by the end of 2001. Records not eligible for transfer to the College Park National Archives by 2001 include:

1. Secret Grenada Rescue Mission and Task Force subject files from 1979–1984;
2. Secret Grenada Rescue Mission and Task Force operations files from 1983;
3. Secret Iran Working Group subject files from 1978–1981.

As mentioned in Chapter 5, RG 220 at the College Park National Archives contains the files and papers of the Commission on Organization of the Government for the Conduct of Foreign Policy from 1972–1975, which have been reviewed for declassification and *processed*.

### State Records at State, Presidential Libraries, Library of Congress, and Other Repositories

State does have a central records storage facility, the Records Service Center, but there is no information publicly available on the quantity, nature, and *appraisal* status of its holdings or the holdings at individual offices and bureaus.[119]

Important papers of some high-level State officials from the postwar era are at presidential libraries. The personal papers of Dean Acheson (Under Secretary of State from 1945–1947 and Secretary of State from 1949–1953) and James Webb (Under Secretary of State from 1949–1952) are at the Truman Library, and they are open. At the Eisenhower Library there are the personal papers of John Foster Dulles (Secretary of State from 1953–1959) and Christian Herter (Under Secretary of State from 1957–1959 and Secretary of State from 1959–1961), and they are open. The personal papers of Harlan Cleveland (Assistant Secretary of State for International Organizations from 1961–1965 and NATO Ambassador from 1965–1969) and Roger Hilsman (Director of the Bureau of Intelligence and Research from 1961–1963 and Assistant Under Secretary of State for Far Eastern Affairs from 1963–1964) are at the Kennedy Library, and both are open. At the Johnson Library are the personal papers of George Ball (Under Secretary of State from 1963–1966) and U. Alexis Johnson (Deputy Under Secretary and Under Secretary of State for Political Affairs), but neither is open. The personal papers of Warren Christopher (Deputy Secretary of State from 1977–1981) are at the Carter Library, but they are not open.

The personal papers of George Schultz (Secretary of State from 1982–1989) are at the Hoover Institution at Stanford University, but they are closed. The Manuscript Division in the Library of Congress has the personal papers of W. Averell Harriman (Ambassador, Ambassador-at-Large,

Assistant Secretary of State for Far Eastern Affairs, and Under Secretary of State for Political Affairs), and State has recently completed its declassification review of them. The personal papers of Henry Kissinger (National Security Affairs Adviser from 1969–1973 and Secretary of State from 1973–1977) are also at the Manuscript Division, but they are closed due to their classification and restrictions imposed by Dr. Kissinger. A large number of John Foster Dulles's papers are at Princeton University, and State has recently completed its declassification review of them as well.

Requests under the FOIA and MDR for records at the Washington National Records Center or still held at State should be submitted to the Director, Office of Freedom of Information, Privacy, and Classification Review, Department of State, 2201 C Street, N.W., Washington, D.C. 20520. This office also has an excellent reading room that can be used by appointment. There is an index to all documents declassified since 1984 pursuant to FOIAs and MDRs submitted directly to State (in contrast, for example, to those submitted to the National Archives for records there). All these declassified documents are on microfiche, and the microfiche is available for review or purchase.

### U.S. Information Agency (USIA) / International Communication Agency (ICA) / International Information Administration (IIA) Records at the National Archives and Federal Records Centers

A large number of records of the USIA (1953–1977 and 1982–1999),[120] ICA (1978–1982), and IIA (1945–1953) are in RG 306 at the National Archives or the Washington National Records Center.

With respect to its declassification review program under E.O. 12958, the USIA is one of the few agencies that reviewed all of its records subject to the order by 2000. The FY 1996, FY 1997, FY 1998, and FY 1999 ISOO annual reports list the USIA as having declassified a total of more than 19 million pages.

At the College Park National Archives, RG 306 has more than 12,000 c.f. of records, most of which are photographs, motion pictures, and other nontextual records. Textual records that have been reviewed for declassification and *processed* include:

1. Top Secret and below Director's chronological files from 1953–1964 and subject files from 1959–1967;

2. Top Secret and below Office of Research reports and related studies from 1948–1953; research reports from 1953–1987; special reports from 1953–1982; special studies from 1955–1959; R reports from 1960–1982; subject files from 1953–1963; country project files from 1951–1973; area project files from 1952–1963; intelligence bulletins,

memos, and summaries from 1954–1956; briefing papers from 1979–1982; current briefs from 1963–1966; research notes from 1958–1962; world project files from 1952–1963; estimates and evaluations from 1966–1978; and research memos from 1963–1982;

3. Secret and below master budget files from 1948–1954;

4. Voice of America daily content reports and script translations from 1950–1955;

5. Top Secret and below Office of Coordinator for Psychological Intelligence special papers from 1952–1954;

6. Secret and below records from 1948–1957 of the U.S. Advisory Commission on Information.

The only regional National Archives that has any RG 306 holdings is in New York, and it has 148 c.f. of Voice of America scripts and related materials from 1948–1954.

Record Group 306 at the Washington National Records Center has almost 10,000 c.f. of records as of 2000 (50% *permanent*, 40% *temporary*, and 10% *unappraised*). A large percentage of these records are also photographs, motion pictures, and other nontextual records. No regional Federal records center has any RG 306 holdings. As part of the P-2000 Project, about 2,200 c.f. of unclassified and classified *permanent* records will be transferred to the College Park National Archives by the end of 2001. Even though the classified records have already been reviewed for declassification, they will not be available to the public until they are possibly re-reviewed by the DOE under the Kyl Plan and then *processed* by the National Archives. Textual records to be transferred include:

1. Secret and below Director's chronological files from 1964 to the mid-1970s, and subject files from 1952–1959 and from the late 1960s to the mid-1970s;

2. Top Secret and below Office of East Asian & Pacific Affairs Vietnam political analysis reports from 1964–1975;

3. Secret and below Office of Policy & Plans policy files from the mid-1950s into the 1970s;

4. Top Secret and below Office of Policy & Plans National Security Council files from 1953–1964 and Korean biological warfare allegation files from 1951–1954;

5. Secret and below Office of Policy & Plans Atomic Energy Commission, Department of Defense, and Operations Coordinating Board liaison files from 1951–1962;

6. Secret and below Vietnam Working Group subject files from 1964–1967.

Among the textual records not eligible for transfer to the College Park National Archives by 2001 are:

1. Secret and below Director's chronological files and subject files from the 1970s into the 1990s;
2. Secret and below Operations Center watch logs from the mid-1970s into the 1990s;
3. Secret and below Office of Policy & Plans/Office of Programs & Policy subject files, policy files, liaison files, reports, studies, evaluations, and other records from the 1950s into the 1990s;
4. a wide range of other Secret and below other headquarters records from the mid-1970s into the 1990s;
5. Secret and below field office reports from the mid-1970s to the early 1990s;
6. numerous mostly unclassified publications, motion pictures, motion picture scripts, and related materials from this period.

### USIA, ICA, and IIA Records at the Department of State and Presidential Libraries

The quantity, nature, and *appraisal* status of USIA records still at the Department of State are unknown.

At the Reagan Library there are the personal papers of Charles Wick (Director of the USIA from 1981–1989). Microfilm copies of Edward R. Murrow's chronological file and other USIA headquarters files from 1961–1963 are in RG 306 at the Kennedy Library. Both are open.

Requests under the FOIA and MDR for records at the Washington National Records Center or still at the Department of State should be submitted to the Director, Office of Freedom of Information, Privacy, and Classification Review, Department of State, 2201 C Street, N.W., Washington, D.C. 20520.

### War Department Records at the National Archives

War Department records from the post–World War II period can be found in two *record groups* at the College Park National Archives. No regional National Archives or any Federal records center has any postwar records.

Record Group 107 has records of the Office of the Secretary of War. At the College Park National Archives RG 107 contains more than 6.25 million pages of records, most of which are from World War II and earlier. All the records have been reviewed for declassification and *processed*, and the *finding aids* are good. Postwar records include the Top Secret and below subject files and decimal files of the Secretary, Under Secretary of War, Assistant Secretary of War, Assistant Secretary of War for Air, and their subordinate offices through 1947; and various Top Secret and below records of the special assistants and expert consultants to the Secretary through 1947.

Record Group 165 has the records of the War Department General and Special Staffs. At the College Park National Archives, RG 165 has more than 27.5 million pages of records, most of which are from World War II and earlier. Most of the records have been reviewed for declassification and *processed,* and the *finding aids* are very good. Postwar records include:

1. Top Secret and below files of the Chief of Staff to 1947;
2. Top Secret and below files of the Personnel Division (G-1) through 1947;
3. a limited number of Top Secret and below files of the Military Intelligence Division (G-2) through 1948;
4. Top Secret and below files of the Organization and Training Division (G-3) through 1947;
5. Top Secret and below files of the Supply Division (G-4) through 1947;
6. a limited number of Top Secret and below files of the Operations Division through 1947.

As mentioned in the section on Office of the Secretary of Defense records, there are also some War Department records in RG 330 at the College Park National Archives and Washington National Records Center.

## NOTES

1. For an excellent discussion of the practice and propriety of officials taking office records when their employment ends, see *Federal Records: Removal of Agency Documents by Senior Officials Upon Leaving Office* (General Accounting Office/GGD-89–91, July 25, 1989) and *Federal Records: Removal of Agency Documents by Senior Officials Upon Leaving Office* (General Accounting Office/GGD-91–117, August 30, 1991).

2. *See,* 44 U.S.C. 2107 for the general authority of the National Archives. 36 C.F.R. 1228.180, et seq. set forth in detail the responsibilities of the National Archives and the federal agencies in this area.

3. 44 U.S.C. 2107(b) and 36 C.F.R. 1228.183.

4. *Records Management in the Central Intelligence Agency, A NARA Evalu-*

*ation* (Washington, D.C.: National Archives and Records Administration), p. 27. The report is on the FAS homepage at www.fas.org and is also available in hard copy at the National Archives.

5. 36 C.F.R. 1228.182.

6. 36 C.F.R. 1260.20 and 1260.40.

7. 36 C.F.R. 1254.42 and 1260.50.

8. In November 1999, the DOE submitted its first report to Congress detailing the inadvertent releases it discovered in re-reviewing records initially reviewed by other agencies under E.O. 12958 prior to October 17, 1998, and *processed* by the National Archives before that date. The report states that the DOE reviewed 948,000 pages in this category and discovered eight file series containing about 14,980 pages of inadvertently released Restricted Data or Formerly Restricted Data (two of the file series had been reviewed under President Reagan's executive order but had been *processed* under E.O. 12958). In early 2000, the DOE submitted a second report that states it re-reviewed about 52 million pages initially reviewed by other agencies under E.O. 12958 and *processed* by the National Archives. The DOE found twenty-five documents totaling about 560 pages containing inadvertently released Restricted Data or Formerly Restricted Data. The unclassified Executive Summaries of these reports are available on the FAS homepage at www.fas.org.

9. 36 C.F.R. 1228.150.

10. 36 C.F.R. 1228.162.

11. 36 C.F.R. 1228.150.

12. 36 C.F.R. 1228.152.

13. Ibid.

14. The author's personal experience in getting permission from agencies to examine completely unclassified *accessions* varies widely. In most cases, the agencies have quickly granted permission. However, in a few instances, the agencies have taken many months to act on the request and/or have imposed restrictions such as not allowing the copying of any records.

15. See the NTIS home page at www.ntis.gov/tools for further information on the CD-ROM.

16. The size of the *record groups* in cubic feet at the various National Archives is set forth in *List of Record Groups of the National Archives and Records Administration* (Washington D.C.: National Archives and Records Administration, January 1999). This publication is available in hard copy at the National Archives and also on NARA's home page at www.nara.gov/research/findaids. To determine the number of pages, simply multiply the number of cubic feet by 2,500 (the number of pages in a cubic foot of records).

17. The size of this and the other *record groups* at the Washington National Records Center, as well as the *appraisal* information, are from the *0–1 lists.*

18. The original estimate was in the Air Force's proposed E.O. 12958 implementation plan filed with the ISOO in October 1995. The revised figure was given by Air Force representatives at the March 1999 meeting of the DOD Historical Records Declassification Advisory Panel.

19. Air Force presentation at the March 1999 meeting of the DOD Historical Records Declassification Advisory Panel.

20. This information about the records solely comes from a review of the *O–1 list* and not a review of the *SF-135s*.

21. Author's conversation with staff at the Boston Federal Records Center, January 2000.

22. Letter from the Office of the Command Historian to author, dated 21 April 1999.

23. Letter from the History Office to author, dated 28 April 1999.

24. For a more detailed description of the archives, see Rick Sturdevant's "Headquarters Air Force Space Command History Office (HQ AFSPC/HO) Archives" in the July 1998 issue of *Quest: The History of Spaceflight Quarterly*.

25. Author's conversation with Alaskan Command History Office, August 1999.

26. Author's conversation with Air Force Material Command History Office, August 1999.

27. Author's conversation with Air Combat Command History Office, April 1999; Letter from AFTAC's History Office to author, dated March 18, 1999.

28. In early 1999, ACDA was disestablished and became part of the Department of State.

29. Frederick Smith, Jr., Office of the General Counsel, to Dr. Ethel Theis, Information Security Oversight Office, dated January 23, 1996. This is on file at the ISOO.

30. Author's conversation with ACDA, August 5, 1999.

31. Togo D. West, Jr., Secretary of the Army, to Steven Garfinkel, Director of the Information Security Oversight Office, dated 30 October 1995. This is on file at the ISOO.

32. Presentation of Army representative at DOD's Historical Records Declassification Advisory Panel meeting in March 1999.

33. This information about the records solely comes from a review of the *O-1 list* and not a review of the *SF-135s*.

34. Author's conversation with staff at the Boston Federal Records Center, January 2000.

35. Letter from the Directorate of Information Management to author, dated April 22, 1999.

36. "IRR's Initial Statement of Compliance"; Box #87; Entry #4; Records of the JFK Assassination Records Review Board, RG 541; National Archives, College Park, MD.

37. Author's conversation with Redstone Scientific Information Center, August 1999.

38. Author's conversations with the Command Historians at the U.S. Army Space and Missile Defense Command and the Army Intelligence and Security Command, August 1999.

39. *Report of the Commission on Reducing and Protecting Government Secrecy* (Washington, D.C.: Government Printing Office, 1997), p. 74. This report is available in hard copy from the Government Printing Office or on its home page at www.access.gpo.gov/int.

40. *1998 Report to the President* (Washington, D.C.: Information Security Oversight Office, 1999), p. 5. This publication is available on the FAS homepage at www.fas.org.

41. CIA press releases of 6 October 1999 and 2 October 2000, which are available on the CIA's homepage at www.cia.gov and the FAS homepage at www.fas.org.

42. This report is available in hard copy at the National Archives or on the FAS homepage at www.fas.org.

43. The headquarters and field stations 1968 total of almost 251,500 c.f. is contained in the *Records Administration Program—Third Quarter Report—1 October 1968*; Box no. 26; CIA Declassified Reference Material; Records of the Central Intelligence Agency, RG 263; National Archieves, College Park, Maryland. The Agency Records Center 1969 total of more than 100,000 c.f. and its breakdown are contained in the *CIA Archives & Records Center Statistical Report—1 July 1969* in Box no. 211 of the same collection in RG 263. Before these documents were available to the public, the author wrote the CIA in March 1999 asking for the quantity of records still held by the agency. The agency's May 1999 reply did not disclose it. In May 2000, the author forwarded a copy of the second document to the CIA asking for the total quantity of records held today in the Agency Records Center, as well as how many are *permanent, temporary* or *unappraised*, but no reply was received.

44. As mentioned in footnote no. 22 in Chapter 3, the author has unsuccessfully tried to learn from the CIA the number or percentage of exempted files.

45. The letter from the CIA to the chair of the Senate Select Committee on Intelligence on the decennial review can be found on the FAS homepage at www.fas.org.

46. Author's conversation with the OSD's Declassification Branch, July 1999. This office has an internal database of records reviewed under E.O. 12958, but the public does not have any access to it.

47. *1998 Report to the President* (Washington, D.C.: Information Security Oversight Office, 1999), p. 5.

48. Author's conversation with the OSD's records management office, March 1999.

49. Author's conversation with the DISA's records manager, March 1999.

50. Defense Intelligence Agency Declassification Plan, undated. This is on file at the ISOO.

51. Author's conversation with the declassification office, September 1999.

52. The report is available at the National Archives.

53. In October 1998, the DSWA and several other DOD agencies were combined to form the new Defense Threat Reduction Agency.

54. Richard A. Brushwood, Director for Intelligence and Security, Defense Nuclear Agency, to Steven Garfinkel, Director, Information Security Oversight Office, dated November 9, 1995.

55. The histories are also available at many public and private libraries around the nation.

56. *Human Radiation Experiments: The Department of Energy Roadmap to the Story and Records* (U.S. Department of Energy, February 1995), p. 7. The work is also available through the DOE homepage at tis.eh.doe.gov/ohre/roadmap.

57. *Report of the Commission on Protecting and Reducing Government Secrecy* (Washington, D.C.: Government Printing Office, 1997), p. 7. This report is

available from the Government Printing Office and is also on its homepage at www.access.gpo.gov/int.

58. In this regard, for FY 2001 the DOE requested a 25% increase in Office of Nuclear and National Security Information funding in order to conduct the re-reviews of other agency records. *See*, the 28 March 2000 testimony of General Eugene Habiger (Ret.), Director of the Office of Security and Emergency Operations, before the Senate Appropriations Committee's Energy and Water Development Subcommittee. This is available on the FAS homepage at www.fas.org.

59. Record Group 77 contains the records of the Army Corps of Engineers. The only reason this small group of MED records was placed in RG 77 was that the MED was part of the Army Corps of Engineers.

60. *A Guide to Archival Collections Relating to Radioactive Fallout from Nuclear Weapon Testing*, prepared by History Associates under contract for the DOE. The work is undated, but it is clear from the text that it was prepared sometime in the late 1980s. This work is available through the DOE's homepage at raleigh.dis.anl.gov/new/findingaids.

61. This information is derived solely from the review of the *0–1 lists* and not the *SF-135s*.

62. This information is derived solely from the review of the *0–1 lists* and not the *SF-135s*.

63. This information is derived solely from a review of the *0–1 lists* and not the *SF-135s*.

64. *Evaluation of the Records Management Program of the Department of Energy* (Washington, D.C.: National Archives and Records Administration, December 1988). This is available at the National Archives.

65. *DOE Management—Better Planning Needed to Correct Records Management Problems* (GAO/RCED 92 88, May 1992).

66. In late 1998, the author contacted all the operations offices asking about the quantity and type of their record holdings, as well as the existence and public availability of *finding aids*. No operations office responded.

67. *Human Radiation Experiments: The Department of Energy Roadmap to the Story and the Records*, p. 197.

68. The author's October 1998 inquiry as to the nature and quantity of ANL record holdings went unanswered.

69. Author's communications with LANL Information and Records Management Office, October 1998.

70. *Human Radiation Experiments: The Department of Energy Roadmap to the Story and the Records*, pp. 179–190.

71. *A Guide to Archival Collections Relating to Radioactive Fallout from Nuclear Weapon Testing*.

72. Ibid.

73. *Appraisal Report and Background Information for DOE R&D Records Schedule*, December 30, 1997, p. 6. The author's October 1998 inquiry as to the nature and quantity of records, as well as the existence and public availability of any *finding aids*, went unanswered.

74. The author's October 1998 inquiry as to the nature and quantity of records held, as well as the existence and public availability of any *finding aids*, went unanswered.

75. Ibid.

76. The Memorandum of Understanding and related papers are on file at the ISOO.

77. This report is available at the National Archives.

78. On page 2-2 of *Appraisal of the Records of the Federal Bureau of Investigation, A Report to Hon. Harold H. Green, United States District Court for the District of Columbia*, it is stated that abstracts of individual documents were made on 3 × 5 slips from 1921–1979. One set was arranged alphabetically by the source or originator of the document and a second set was arranged by file number. A third set was prepared for foreign material relating to the FBI's Special Intelligence Program from 1940–1948.

79. Author's conversation with the FBI records management office, June 1997.

80. On several occasions the author has recommended to the National Archives that it accession all the FBI's declassified files. This would mean that the public could learn quickly what files are available and then have only a wait of several hours before examining them (versus waiting years for the FBI to respond to a FOIA or MDR request). However, this recommendation has not been adopted.

81. *Report of the Commission on Protecting and Reducing Government Secrecy*, p. 74.

82. In October 1999, the U.S. Atlantic Command was renamed the Joint Forces Command.

83. Responses to author's inquiry at the March 1999 meeting of the DOD Historical Records Declassification Advisory Panel.

84. Author's conversation with Command Historian, U.S. Atlantic Command, August 1999.

85. Author's conversation with Command Historian's office, August 1999.

86. Author's conversation with Command Historian's office, August 1999.

87. Author's conversation with Command Historian's office, August 1999.

88. Author's conversation with the Public Affairs Office, U.S. Strategic Command, March 1999; Letter from U.S. Pacific Command to author, dated 1 June 1999; Author's conversation with the Command Historian, U.S. Central Command, August 1999; Author's conversation with the Command Historian, U.S. European Command, March 2000.

89. The author's inquiry to the U.S. Southern Command went unanswered.

90. Department of Justice Executive Order 12958 Declassification Plan, dated September 26, 1995. This is on file at the ISOO.

91. Author's conversation with the DOJ's systematic declassification review office, October 1999.

92. For a complete listing of all the DOJ classification numbers (but not subclassification numbers), see Appendix IX in Gerald K. Haines and David A. Langbart, *Unlocking the Files of the FBI: A Guide to its Records and Classification System* (Wilmington: Scholarly Resources, Inc., 1993). For the subclassification numbers, the researcher must review the DOJ's *records schedule*.

93. Prior to 1975, the files of the Attorney Generals and Deputy Attorney Generals were not maintained in a distinct file system. Their records were forwarded to the DOJ component having jurisdiction over the materials. Melanie Ann Pustay, Senior Counsel, Office of Information and Privacy, Department of Justice, to David Marwell, Executive Director, Assassination Records Review Board, August 6, 1998;

Box no. 99; Entry no. 4; Records of the JFK Assassination Records Review Board, RG 541; National Archives, College Park, Maryland.

94. Author's conversation with staff at the Laguna Niguel Federal Records Center, January 2000.

95. This information is derived solely from a review of the *O-1 list* and not from a review of the *SF-135s*.

96. Author's conversation with the NIMA's systematic declassification review office, March 2000. Both the DMA and CIO filed proposed implementation plans with the ISOO in 1995, but neither contains any estimate of the quantity of subject records.

97. This report is available on the FAS homepage at www.fas.org.

98. *Report of the Commission on Protecting and Reducing Government Secrecy*, p. 74.

99. In March 1999, the author wrote the NRO asking about the quantity of records held by it and the existence and availability of any *finding aids*. The NRO's reply did not address these issues.

100. *Report of the Commission on Protecting and Reducing Government Secrecy*, p. 74.

101. Author's conversation with Public Affairs Office, July 1997.

102. Author's conversation with the FOIA/Privacy Act Office, March 2000.

103. Letter from the NSA to author, dated 13 July 1999.

104. In August 2000, the author wrote the NSA asking what the retention period or periods were in the agency's *records schedules* for *permanent* records. The NSA's reply did not address the question.

105. M.F. Brown, Assistant for Information and Personnel Security, to Director, Information Security Oversight Office, dated 30 November 1995. This document is on file at the ISOO.

106. Author's conversations with the Navy's systematic declassification review office, October 1999.

107. Author's conversation with staff at the Seattle Federal Records Center.

108. Author's conversation with staff at the Laguna Niguel Federal Records Center.

109. This information is derived solely from a review of the *O-1 list* and not the *SF-135s*.

110. Letter from Records Officer to author, dated 22 March 1999.

111. Author's conversation with Naval Space Command, March 1999.

112. Author's conversation with the Office of Naval Intelligence, March 1999.

113. Letter from Assistant Flag Secretary to author, dated 30 April 1999.

114. Author's conversation with the Public Affairs Office, September 1999.

115. In October 1998 the On-Site Inspection Agency and several other Department of Defense agencies were combined to form the new Defense Threat Reduction Agency.

116. The author's written inquiry to the OSIA in March 1999 was not answered.

117. These figures are from the March 27, 2000, report of the State Department's Advisory Committee on Historical Diplomatic Documentation. This report is available on the FAS homepage at www.fas.org.

118. The minutes of the Advisory Committee on Historical Diplomatic Documentation document the efforts of both the State Department and the National

Archives to make electronic records accessible. The minutes are available on the FAS homepage at www.fas.org.

119. Letter from the IRM Programs and Services office to author, dated June 16, 1999.

120. In October 1999, the USIA was disestablished and many of its functions transferred to the Department of State.

# 5

# Where White House Records Are Located

Almost all the postwar White House records that have not been destroyed or lost are in the presidential libraries. Only a few have ended up in the National Archives or Federal records centers. Although the Roosevelt Library was the first to open in 1946, it was not until 1955 that legislation was passed that formally established the system of presidential libraries and facilitated the construction of others. There are now eleven presidential libraries (funds are currently being raised for the building of the Clinton Library). However, due to a 1974 law, the Nixon White House records are not in the Nixon Library but are at the College Park National Archives in what is called the Nixon Presidential Materials.

The holdings in the ten libraries and the Nixon Presidential Materials pale in size with the holdings at either the National Archives, Federal records centers, or the agencies. Along these lines, NARA estimates that the total of textual records in the ten libraries and Nixon Presidential Materials is only 250 million pages. In comparison, there are more than 7 *billion* pages of textual records at the Washington National Records Center, which is just one of eleven Federal records centers.

All the presidential libraries have several different types of records and the laws and regulations governing access to them differ. As mentioned above in Chapter 1, the records of the Presidents, Vice-Presidents, and their advisors through the Carter Administration were considered the private property of those individuals (the one exception being the records of the Nixon White House). When given to a presidential library, they are called *donated historical materials*. Access to them is not only a question of classification but also of any restrictions the individual donor may impose. Furthermore, they are subject only to the MDR procedure and not the FOIA. In contrast, the records of the President, Vice-President, and their advisors from the Reagan Administration on are the property of the federal government and are denominated *Presidential records*. These records are subject to both FOIA and MDR requests beginning five years after the President has left office (and in some cases the President can exempt records from any declassification review for up to twelve years after leaving office).

Every presidential library also has personal paper collections donated by various individuals and oral history interviews conducted by presidential library staff or others. Access to these items is governed not only by questions of classification but also by any restrictions the individual donor or interviewee may impose. Lastly, the presidential libraries have small quantities of *federal records* organized by *record group*. These are usually duplicates of what can be found in the identical *record group* at the National Archives or a Federal records center. Access to these *federal records* is by either FOIA or MDR requests if they are not already open.

Set forth in the following sections are the *record groups* at the National Archives and Federal records centers with White House records, followed by brief descriptions of the holdings at the presidential libraries and in the Nixon Presidential Materials.

## NATIONAL SECURITY COUNCIL (NSC) RECORDS AT THE NATIONAL ARCHIVES

The vast majority of NSC records are at the presidential libraries. There is only a small quantity of NSC records in RG 273 at the College Park National Archives, and it is not known whether they duplicate what is in the presidential libraries. No regional National Archives or any Federal records center has any RG 273 holdings.

The NSC has about 450,000 pages of *permanent* pre-1975 classified records subject to E.O. 12958. This is figured on the basis that in early 1999 the White House granted the NSC an exemption from automatic declassification for 65,000 pages (15%) of its subject records. Progress apparently has been slow, and only the FY 1999 ISOO annual report lists the NSC as declassifying any records (55,300 pages). It is not known what these records are or where they are.

At the College Park National Archives, RG 273 has approximately 250,000 pages of records. The *finding aids* to them are very good, listing in some cases individual documents and in other cases folder titles by box. Records that have been reviewed for declassification and *processed* include:

1. Top Secret/Restricted Data and below NSC Policy Papers from 1947–1960, NSC P Papers from 1947–1956, NSC Mill Papers from 1948–1960, and NSC Intelligence Directives from 1947–1972;

2. a limited number of Top Secret/Restricted Data and below National Security Action Memorandums from the Kennedy and Johnson Administrations; National Security Study Memorandums and National Security Decision Memos from the Nixon and Ford Administrations; National Security Presidential Directives and Presidential Review Memos from the Carter Administration; and National Security Study Directives and National Security Decision Directives from the Reagan and Bush Administrations;

3. Top Secret/Restricted Data and below minutes of NSC meetings from 1947–1960;

4. Top Secret/Restricted Data and below records of the Under Secretaries Committee and records of the Operations Coordinating Board from 1957–1961;

5. Top Secret/Restricted Data and below records of NSC actions from 1947–1964;

6. Top Secret and below NSC staff directories from 1950–1964; attendance lists from 1961–1964; records relating to reorganization from 1953–1960; official statements from 1947–1960; annotated lists of serially numbered NSC documents from 1947–1961; and records concerning the Subversive Activities Control Board from 1950–1958;

7. Top Secret/Restricted Data and below senior staff files from 1947–1961.

A number of records are still awaiting declassification review, and among them are the following:

1. Top Secret/Restricted Data and below records of Dr. Edward Lilly from 1957–1961, Joseph Russell from 1957–1961, and Robert Blum from 1948–1949;

2. Top Secret/Restricted Data and below miscellaneous records from 1948–1971;

3. Top Secret and below records of the NSC representative on the Interdepartmental Committee on Internal Security from 1947–1969;

4. Top Secret and below records of the Subcommittee on Communications from 1962–1963;

5. Top Secret and below administrative history files from 1947–1961 and administrative budget files from 1947–1958;

6. Top Secret/Restricted Data and below agency information files from 1947–1961;

7. Top Secret/Restricted Data and below Joint Study Group's Intelligence Survey records from 1959–1960;

8. Top Secret/Restricted Data and below general correspondence files from 1948–1960;

9. Top Secret and below records relating to NSC Problem 17 from 1950–1961.

## NSC RECORDS AT THE NSC

The NSC retains about 1.5 million pages of historical records, but beginning in 2001, all of these should be transferred to the appropriate presidential library and thereafter the NSC will have only records relating to the current administration.[1]

## OFFICE OF MANAGEMENT AND BUDGET (OMB)/BUREAU OF THE BUDGET (BOB) RECORDS AT THE NATIONAL ARCHIVES AND FEDERAL RECORDS CENTERS

A large number of records of the OMB (1970–present) and its predecessor, the BOB (1921–1970), are in RG 51 at the College Park National Archives and the Washington National Records Center. No other National Archives or Federal records center has any RG 51 holdings.

The number of records the OMB has subject to E.O. 12958, as well as its progress in its declassification review program, are unknown. The ISOO annual reports since 1995 have not listed the OMB as declassifying any records.

At the College Park National Archives, there are about 15 million pages of records in RG 51. The *finding aids* are not particularly useful. Among the records that have been reviewed for declassification and *processed* are:

1. Top Secret and below subject files, office files, and program records of the Director, Assistant Director (BOB), and Deputy Director (OMB) from the 1940s into the 1970s;

2. Top Secret and below Military Division subject files and annual budget estimates for the War Department, National Military Establishment, and Department of Defense from the 1940s into the early 1970s;

3. Top Secret and below Military Division subject files on independent agencies assigned to this division from the 1940s into the early 1970s;

4. Top Secret and below classified legislative history files from the 1940s into the 1960s.

Record Group 51 at the Washington National Records Center contains about 14.75 million pages of records as of 2000 (85% *permanent*, 12% *temporary*, and 3% *unappraised*). It is not known whether under the P-2000 Project any *permanent* records will be transferred to RG 51 at the

College Park National Archives, although a number are now eligible for transfer. Records that are both eligible and not eligible for transfer by 2001 include:

1. Top Secret and below files of the National Security Division from the 1970s and 1980s;
2. Secret and below files of the International Affairs Division from the 1970s and 1980s;
3. Secret and below files of the Director and immediate subordinates from the 1970s into the 1990s;
4. Secret and below files of the Energy and Sciences Division from the 1970s into the 1990s.

## OMB AND BOB RECORDS AT THE OMB AND PRESIDENTIAL LIBRARIES

There is no information available on the quantity, nature, and *appraisal* status of records still held by the OMB.

At the Truman Library are the personal papers of James Webb (Director of BOB from 1946–1949) and the personal papers of Frank Pace, Jr. (Director of BOB from 1949–1950). Microfilm copies of the Director's files and other BOB headquarters files from 1961–1965 are in RG 51 at the Kennedy Library. The Ford Library has the personal papers of Paul O'Neill (Deputy Director of OMB from 1975–1977). The Carter Library has the personal papers of James McIntyre (Deputy Director and then Director of OMB from 1976–1981). All these records are open.

Requests under the FOIA and MDR for records at the Washington National Records Center or still held by OMB should be submitted to the Office of General Counsel, Office of Management and Budget, 464 Old Executive Office Building, Washington, D.C. 20503.

## PRESIDENTIAL COMMITTEES, COMMISSIONS, BOARDS, AND ADVISORY GROUPS' RECORDS AT THE NATIONAL ARCHIVES AND FEDERAL RECORDS CENTERS

The majority of records of these bodies are at the presidential libraries. However, there are two *record groups* at the National Archives and Federal records centers that have some. It is not known whether these records duplicate what is in the presidential libraries.

Record Group 359 contains the records of the Special Assistant to the President for Science and Technology (1957–1962), and its successors, the Office of Science and Technology (1962–1973), and the Office of Science and Technology Policy (1973–present). At the College Park National Archives, RG 359 has more than 1.5 million pages of records. No other National Archives has any RG 359 holdings. The *finding aid* is excellent and gives the folder titles for each box. Most of the records are classified, although a limited number of folders have been declassified and *processed*. The records include the subject files of the Office of the Special Assistant to the President for Science and Technology from 1957–1962 and the subject files of the Office of Science and Technology from 1962–1973.

Record Group 359 at the Washington National Records Center contains more than 800,000 pages of records as of 2000 (all *permanent*). As part of the P-2000 Project, almost all the records are scheduled to be transferred to the College Park National Archives by the end of 2001, and they include the classified subject and correspondence files from the late 1970s and 1980s of the Director and Associate Director of the Office of Science and Technology Policy.

Record Group 220 contains the records of various temporary presidential committees, commissions, and boards from the 1920s to the 1970s, and RG 220 has more than 15 million pages of records at the College Park National Archives. The *finding aids* are good. Records that have been reviewed for declassification and *processed* include:

1. subject files, annual reports, meeting minutes, transcripts of hearings, board decisions, and case-related correspondence of the Subversive Activities Control Board from 1950–1973;
2. subject and correspondence files, and related records of the Commission on Government Security from 1955–1957;
3. subject files, correspondence files, meeting agendas and minutes, and related records of the National Aeronautics and Space Council from 1958–1973;
4. subject and correspondence files, meeting agendas and minutes, and related records of the Commission on the Organization of the Government for the Conduct of Foreign Policy from 1972–1975.

Some regional National Archives have small RG 220 holdings. There are no relevant records in RG 220 at any Federal records center.

## HOOVER PRESIDENTIAL LIBRARY

There are several personal paper collections of interest. One is that of Senator Bourke Hickenlooper, which includes some documents from his tenure as Chairman of the Joint Committee on Atomic Energy. The DOE has reviewed the collection for declassification. Some records were withdrawn, but it is not known where these are now. Another is Lewis Strauss's papers, which include a large number of records from his service as a Commissioner of the Atomic Energy Commission from 1946–1950 and 1953–1958. The DOE has also reviewed this collection for declassification. In this review, about 3,000 pages were withdrawn and these are currently held by the Office of Presidential Libraries at the National Archives in downtown Washington, D.C.[2] In addition, there are several oral history transcripts of possible interest. A complete listing of the personal paper collections and oral history transcripts can be found on the library's homepage at www.hoover.nara.gov.

The library can be contacted in writing at 210 Parkside Drive, West Branch, Iowa 52358, or by phone at 319–643–5301.

## TRUMAN PRESIDENTIAL LIBRARY

The largest collection of records is Harry Truman's papers, and all of it has been reviewed for declassification and *processed*. Subcollections of particular interest include:

1. President's Secretary's Files from 1945–1953;
2. Official File from 1945–1953;
3. Confidential File from 1945–1953;
4. Staff Member and Office Files;
5. Korean War File from 1947–1952;
6. National Security Council Files from 1947–1953;
7. Naval Aide to the President Files from 1945–1953;
8. Psychological Strategy Board Files from 1951–1953.

Summary descriptions of the subcollections are available on the library's homepage at www.trumanlibrary.org. Detailed *finding aids* exist for each subcollection and are available through interlibrary loan.

There are also more than 400 personal paper collections, and among the important ones are the following:

1. Dean Acheson (Assistant Secretary of State from 1941–1945, Under Secretary of State from 1945–1947, and Secretary of State from 1949–1953);
2. Gordon Arneson (Special Assistant to the Under Secretary and Secretary of State from 1948–1954);
3. Clark Clifford (Special Counsel to the President from 1946–1950);
4. Francis Matthews (Secretary of the Navy from 1949–1951);
5. John Ohly (War Department and DOD official from 1940–1968);

6. Frank Pace (Director of the Bureau of the Budget from 1949–1950 and Secretary of the Army from 1950–1953);

7. Sumner Pike (AEC Commissioner from 1946–1951);

8. John Sullivan (Under Secretary of the Navy from 1946–1947 and Secretary of the Navy from 1947–1949);

9. James Webb (Director of the Bureau of the Budget from 1946–1949 and Under Secretary of State from 1949–1952).

The homepage contains a summary description of each collection and indicates whether the collection is available for research. Detailed *finding aids* exist for many of the open collections and are available through interlibrary loan.

There are nearly 500 oral history interviews, and the homepage gives a summary description of each. In addition, some of the interviews can be downloaded from the homepage.

Lastly, there are some important *federal records*. The homepage has a summary description of the holdings in each *record group* and indicates whether they are duplicates or copies of what exists at the College Park National Archives.

The library can be contacted in writing at 500 W. U.S. Highway 24, Independence, MO 64050; by phone at 816–833–1400; by fax at 816–833–4368; or by e-mail at truman.reference@truman.nara.gov.

## EISENHOWER PRESIDENTIAL LIBRARY

The Presidential Papers of Dwight D. Eisenhower (Ann Whitman File) is considered by the library to be the most significant collection. It has been reviewed for declassification and *processed*. There are eighteen subcollections in all, and important ones include the Dulles-Herter Series, International Series, International Meetings Series, and NSC Series. Detailed *finding aids* exist for all the subcollections and are available through interlibrary loan or through the library's homepage at redbud.lbjlib.utexas.edu/eisenhower.

The White House Central Files is divided into five major subcollections. The most important of these are the Confidential File and Official File, both of which have been reviewed for declassification and *processed*. Detailed *finding aids* exist for both subcollections that are available through interlibrary loan.

White House Office is another important collection, and subcollections that have been reviewed for declassification and *processed* include:

1. National Security Council Staff Papers from 1948–1961;

2. Office of the Special Assistant for Disarmament (Harold Stassen) records from 1955–1958;

3. Office of the Special Assistant for National Security Affairs (Robert Cutler, Dilon Anderson, and Gordon Gray) records from 1952–1961;

4. Office of the Special Assistant for Science and Technology (James Killian and George Kistiakowsky) records from 1957–1961;

5. Office of the Staff Secretary (Paul Carrol, Andrew Goodpaster, L. Arthur Minnich, and Christopher Russell) records from 1952–1961;

6. Staff Research Group (Albert Toner and Christopher Russell) records from 1956–1961.

*Finding aids* to the subcollections are available through interlibrary loan.

Among the important personal paper collections that are open are the following:

1. John Foster Dulles (Secretary of State from 1953–1959);

2. Clifford Furnas (Assistant Secretary of Defense [Research & Development] from 1955–1957 and member of the Defense Science Board from 1957–1969);

3. Gordon Gray (Assistant Secretary of Defense [International Security Affairs] from 1955–1957, Director of the Office of Defense Mobilization from 1957–1958, and Special Assistant to the President for National Security Affairs from 1958–1961);

4. General Alfred Gruenther;

5. Christian Herter (Under Secretary of State from 1957–1959 and Secretary of State from 1959–1961);

6. General Lauris Norstad;

7. Donald Quarles (Assistant Secretary of Defense [Research & Development] from 1953–1955, Secretary of the Air Force from 1955–1957, and Deputy Secretary of Defense from 1957–1959).

*Finding aids* to these collections are available through interlibrary loan. A complete list of all the personal paper collections is on the homepage.

The library has more than 500 oral history transcripts. A list of all the transcripts, which also indicates the ones available to the public, is on the homepage. *Finding aids* have also been prepared for the transcripts, and these are available through interlibrary loan. A few of the *finding aids* are also available on the homepage.

The library can be contacted in writing at 200 Southeast Fourth Street, Abilene, KN 67410; by phone at 785-263-4751; or by e-mail at library@eisenhower.nara.gov.

## KENNEDY PRESIDENTIAL LIBRARY

The President's Office Files is one of the most important collections, and it contains the following subcollections:

1. General Correspondence,
2. Special Correspondence,
3. Speech Files,
4. Legislative Files,
5. Press Conferences,
6. Staff Memoranda,
7. Departments and Agencies,
8. Subjects,
9. Countries,
10. Personal Secretary's Files,
11. Special Events Through the Years,
12. White House Signal Agency.

The library's homepage at www.cs.umb.edu/jfklibrary has a good description of each of the subcollections and indicates how much of each has been reviewed for declassification and *processed. Finding aids* to each subcollection can be obtained through interlibrary loan.

The National Security Files is another significant collection, and it contains the following subcollections:

1. Countries,
2. Regional Security,
3. Trips and Conferences,
4. Departments and Agencies,
5. Subjects,
6. Meetings and Memoranda,
7. Chester Clifton,
8. Carl Kaysen,
9. William Brubeck,
10. Ralph Dungan,
11. McGeorge Bundy,
12. Charles Johnson,
13. Robert Komer,

14. Boards and Committees,

15. NSC Administrative Files,

16. indices to NSC Meetings,

17. indices to Standing Group Meetings,

18. indices to ExComm Meetings,

19. indices to Vietnam Meetings,

20. indices to National Security Action Memoranda,

21. indices to Special Group Meetings.


Folder lists for most of the subcollections and all of the indices are on the homepage, and they indicate which portions have been reviewed for declassification and *processed*. Declassified National Security Action Memoranda can be downloaded from the homepage as well.

The White House Staff Files is the largest single collection. Library personnel state, however, that the collection contains very few national security-related materials. *Finding aids* are available through interlibrary loan.

The Presidential Recordings consist of about 248 hours of meetings and 12 hours of phone conversations, and the library has created transcripts and logs for some which are now part of the collection. Much of the material concerns national security matters. A list of all the tapes indicating which have been opened is on the homepage.

There is a number of personal paper collections, and significant ones include the following:


1. George Ball (Under Secretary of State from 1961–1966);

2. Roswell Gilpatric (Deputy Secretary of Defense from 1961–1964);

3. Roger Hilsman (Director of the Bureau of Intelligence and Research from 1961–1963 and Assistant Secretary of State for Far Eastern Affairs from 1963–1964);

4. Jerome Wiesner (Director of the Office of Science and Technology from 1961–1964).


A list of all the personal paper collections indicating which have been opened is on the homepage.

There are more than 1,100 oral history interviews, and the homepage has a complete list that also indicates which are available to researchers.

Lastly, there are some *federal records* of interest. These include the following:

1. files of the Administrator and other high-level officials of the Agency for International Development in RG 286;
2. Arms Control and Disarmament Agency records relating to the Test Ban Treaty and assorted reports and studies on other topics in RG 383;
3. files of the Director and other high-level officials of the Bureau of the Budget in RG 51;
4. files and incoming and outgoing cables of Secretary of Defense McNamara in RG 330;
5. correspondence and subject files of UN Ambassador Adlai Stevenson relating to Cuba and other topics in RG 59;
6. selected subject files of the President's Science Advisory Committee on defense, space, disarmament, and other matters in RG 359.

The library can be contacted in writing at Columbia Point, Boston, MA 02125; by phone at 617–929–4500; by fax at 617–929–4538; or by e-mail at library@kennedy.nara.gov.

## JOHNSON PRESIDENTIAL LIBRARY

Among the significant collections is the White House Central Files Confidential File, which contains records that were not placed in the much larger Subject File because they contained classified information. The collection has been reviewed for declassification and *processed*, and the *finding aid* is available through interlibrary loan.

The National Security File has the working files of McGeorge Bundy and Walt Rostow. It is divided into the following twenty-six subcollections:

1. Country File,
2. Vietnam Country File,
3. Head of State Correspondence File,
4. Special Head of State Correspondence File,
5. International Meetings and Travel File,
6. Speech File,
7. Subject File,
8. Agency File,
9. Committee File,
10. Name File,
11. Intelligence File,
12. Intelligence Briefings,

13. National Intelligence Estimates,

14. Situation Room File,

15. National Security Action Memorandums,

16. National Security Council Meetings File,

17. Files of the Special Committee of the National Security Council,

18. National Security Council Histories,

19. Memos to the President from McGeorge Bundy and Walt Rostow,

20. McGeorge Bundy Files,

21. Walt Rostow Files,

22. Robert Komer Files,

23. Komer-Leonhart File,

24. Gordon Chase File,

25. C.V. Clifton File,

26. Staff File Fragments.

About 40% of the records overall have been reviewed for declassification and *processed*. All the subcollections are briefly described on the library's homepage at www.lbjlib.utexas.edu, and the list indicates for each subcollection whether more or less than 20% thereof is open. Additionally, the *finding aids* for the subcollections are available through interlibrary loan.

Within the Special Files collection, the Meeting Notes File and the Tom Johnson Notes of Meetings File have notes on President Johnson's meetings concerning foreign affairs. Both have been reviewed for declassification and *processed*. A brief description of each is on the homepage, and the *finding aids* are available through interlibrary loan.

The White House Series of Recordings and Transcripts contains recordings and transcripts of telephone conversations between November 22, 1963, through January 1969, and recordings and transcripts of international meetings and Cabinet Room meetings from late November 1967 through 1968. Although originally obtained by the library in 1973 under the condition that they be closed for fifty years, a few were opened in the 1990s under the JFK Assassination Records Collection Act, and the library is proceeding to open the balance in chronological increments. Information about which have been opened and obtaining copies of the tapes, transcripts or *finding aids* is on the homepage.

There are more than 400 personal paper collections, and ones of interest include:

1. Assistant Secretary of Defense Robert Anthony's appointment and subject files from 1967–1969 (closed);

2. Under Secretary of State George Ball's notes on telephone conversations from 1963–1968 (closed);

3. Deputy Assistant Secretary of Defense and Assistant Secretary of State William Bundy's unpublished manuscript on the development of U.S. policy in Vietnam (open);

4. Secretary of Defense Clark Clifford's records on Vietnam, the Pueblo incident, weapons systems, and other matters from 1968–1969 (open);

5. a variety of records from 1963–1969 of James Cross, Military Assistant to the President (closed);

6. a wide range of files and other records from 1960–1969 of Alain Enthoven, Assistant Secretary of Defense (Systems Analysis) (closed);

7. Assistant Secretary of the Air Force for Research & Development Alexander Flax's files on R&D from 1963–1968 (closed);

8. a wide range of records from 1968–1969 of Morton Halperin, Deputy Assistant Secretary of Defense (International Security Affairs) and National Security Council staff member (closed);

9. a wide range of records of Ambassador U. Alexis Johnson from 1963–1985 (closed);

10. a wide range of records from 1964–1968 of Leonard Marks, Director of the United States Information Agency (closed);

11. a variety of materials of Walt Rostow on his government service and work outside the government from 1950–1984 (closed);

12. Secretary of State Dean Rusk's personal appointment books and foreign travel schedules from 1961–1969 (open);

13. chronological files from 1964–1967 of James Webb, Administrator of the National Aeronautics and Space Administration (open);

14. a wide range of records of Gen. William Westmoreland relating to Vietnam and his subsequent service as Army Chief of Staff from 1962–1973 (open).

All the personal paper collections with any significant amount of material are briefly described on the homepage with an indication whether they are open or closed.

The oral history interviews (except special oral history interviews) are listed on the homepage, along with their status and terms of access. Additionally, the transcripts of several can be downloaded from the homepage.

It should be noted that Lyndon Johnson's papers from his service as Congressman, U.S. Senator, and Vice-President are also at the library. The homepage has good summary descriptions of the various records in these collections.

The library can be contacted in writing at 2313 Red River Street, Austin, TX 78705; by phone at 512–916–5137; or by e-mail at library @johnson.nara.gov.

## NIXON PRESIDENTIAL MATERIALS

As discussed earlier, by reason of legislation passed in 1974, the Nixon White House records are located in the Nixon Presidential Materials collection at the College Park National Archives and not in the Nixon Presidential Library in California.

An important collection is the White House Central Files: Subject Files, and relevant subcollections that have been reviewed for declassification and *processed* include:

1. Atomic Energy,
2. Countries,
3. Federal Government—Executive Office of the President,
4. Foreign Affairs,
5. International Organizations,
6. Meetings and Conferences,
7. National Security—Defense,
8. Outer Space,
9. Sciences.

Another significant collection is the National Security Files, and significant subcollections that have been reviewed for declassification and *processed* include:

1. Presidential Daily Briefings,
2. Paris Talks/Meetings,
3. Indo-Pakistani War,
4. Cambodian Operations (1970),
5. Country Files for Europe,
6. ABM/MIRV,
7. SALT,
8. Presidential Press Conferences,
9. Soviet Defector Cases,
10. VIP Visits,
11. Anthony Lake Chronological Files,

12. Henry Kissinger Administrative and Staff Files,

13. Henry Kissinger Trip Files.


A listing of the records open to the public as of December 1995 is on the Nixon Presidential Materials homepage at www.nara.gov/nixon/index.

Information concerning the Nixon Presidential Materials can be obtained by writing the Nixon Presidential Materials Staff, National Archives, 8601 Adelphi Road, College Park, MD 20740-6001; by phone at 301–713–6950; by fax at 301–713–6916; or by e-mail at nixon@arch2.nara.gov.


## FORD PRESIDENTIAL LIBRARY

One important collection is the White House Central Files Subject File. Relevant subcollections include Atomic Energy, Countries, Foreign Affairs, International Organizations, National Security-Defense, and Outer Space. Most of the records in these subcollections, however, have not been reviewed for declassification and *processed*.

The National Security Adviser Files is another significant collection, but only a small number of records are available. Subcollections that have been reviewed for declassification and *processed* include:

1. Memoranda of Conversations (1973–1977),

2. NSC Meeting Minutes,

3. National Security Study Memoranda (NSSM) and National Security Decision Memoranda (NSDM),

4. Presidential Name File,

5. White House Situation Room: Brent Scowcroft's Morning News Summaries.


Additionally, there is a small artificial collection of declassified records from the other subcollections. The Memoranda of Conversations (1973–1977) and NSSM/NSDM records can be viewed on the library's homepage at www.lbjlib.utexas.edu/ford/library.

Relevant personal paper collections include those of William Hyland (Deputy Assistant to the President for National Security Affairs from 1975–1977) and Paul O'Neill (Deputy Director of OMB from 1975–1977). Only the latter is open.

A list of all the *donated historical materials*, open personal paper collections, and oral history interviews is on the homepage.

The library can be contacted in writing at 1000 Beal Avenue, Ann Arbor, MI 48109; by phone at 734–741–2218; or by fax at 734–741–2341.

## CARTER PRESIDENTIAL LIBRARY

An important collection is the White House Central Files Subject File. Important subcollections include Atomic/Nuclear Energy, Countries, Foreign Affairs, International Organizations, Meetings-Conferences, Messages, and National Security-Defense. However, only small portions of these subcollections have been reviewed for declassification and *processed*. The National Security Adviser files are another important collection, and about one-third of it has been reviewed for declassification and *processed*.

Relevant personal paper collections include those of Secretary of Defense Harold Brown (closed), National Security Adviser Zbigniew Brzezinski (mostly open), Deputy Secretary of State Warren Christopher (closed), and Deputy Director and then Director of OMB James McIntyre (open).

Lists of all the *donated historical materials*, personal paper collections, oral history interviews, and *federal records* are available on the library's homepage at carterlibrary.galileo.peachnet.edu/library.

The library can be contacted in writing at 441 Freedom Parkway, Atlanta, GA 30307–1498; by phone at 404–331–3942; by fax at 404–730–2215; or by e-mail at library@carter.nara.gov.

## REAGAN PRESIDENTIAL LIBRARY

The White House Office of Records Management Subject File has a number of relevant subcollections, including Atomic/Nuclear Energy, Countries, Foreign Affairs, International Organizations, Meetings-Conferences, Messages, National Security-Defense, Outer Space, and Sciences. However, very few records in these subcollections have been reviewed for declassification and *processed*.

Relevant personal paper collections include those of Secretary of Energy John Herrington (closed), Deputy Undersecretary for Policy Fred Ikle (closed), Attorney General Edwin Meese, III (closed), Attorney General William French Smith (closed), and Director of the United States Information Agency, Charles Wick (closed).

Lists of *Presidential records*, personal paper collections, oral history interviews, and *federal records* are on the library's homepage at sunsite.unc.edu/lia/president/ReaganLibrary.

The library can be contacted in writing at 40 Presidential Drive, Simi Valley, CA 93065; by phone at 805–522–8444; or by fax at 805–522–9621.

## BUSH PRESIDENTIAL LIBRARY

The library holds the Bush *Presidential records*, Bush and Quayle *Vice-Presidential records*, personal paper collections, oral history interviews, and *federal records.* However, very few of the national security-related records have been reviewed for declassification and *processed.*

The library can be contacted in writing at 1000 George Bush Drive West, College Station Texas 77845; by phone at 409–260–9552; or by fax at 409–260–9557.

## NOTES

1. Letter from Senior Director, Records & Access Management, to author, dated August 6, 1997.

2. Author's conversation with the Office of Presidential Libraries, March 2000.

# Index

**About the Author**

JAMES E. DAVID is with the Division of Space History at the Smithsonian National Air and Space Museum, where he has curatorial and exhibit responsibilities, conducts research and is involved in a wide range of efforts to declassify records.